Local Responses to the English Reformation

Local Responses to the English Reformation

Robert Whiting
Principal Lecturer in History
University College of Ripon and York St John

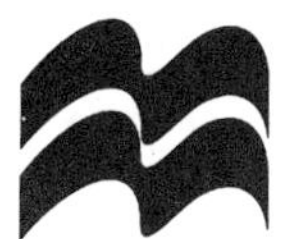

First published in Great Britain 1998 by
MACMILLAN PRESS LTD
Houndmills, Basingstoke, Hampshire RG21 6XS and London
Companies and representatives throughout the world

A catalogue record for this book is available from the British Library.

ISBN 0–333–64244–9 hardcover
ISBN 0–333–64245–7 paperback

First published in the United States of America 1998 by
ST. MARTIN'S PRESS, INC.,
Scholarly and Reference Division,
175 Fifth Avenue, New York, N.Y. 10010

ISBN 0–312–21185–6

Library of Congress Cataloging-in-Publication Data
Whiting, Robert, 1949–
Local responses to the English Reformation / Robert Whiting.
p. cm.
Includes bibliographical references and index.
ISBN 0–312–21185–6 (cloth)
1. Reformation—England. 2. England—Church history—16th century. I. Title.
BR375.W5 1997
274.2'06—dc21 97–31637
CIP

This book is printed on paper suitable for recycling and made from fully managed and sustained forest sources.

10 9 8 7 6 5 4 3 2 1
07 06 05 04 03 02 01 00 99 98

Printed in Hong Kong

For my father and mother

For David and Ruth

For Victoria and Alexandra

And for Rowena

Contents

PREFACE

The aim of this book is to investigate one of the most controversial problems in early modern history: the responses of the English people to the reformation.

While originating in my research on the south-west, it is based also on my examination of a wide range of primary sources relating to all regions of sixteenth-century England, and on the published works of fellow historians such as Margaret Bowker, Susan Brigden, Patrick Collinson, Claire Cross, A.G. Dickens, Eamon Duffy, the late Sir Geoffrey Elton, Christopher Haigh, Ronald Hutton, Alan Kreider, David Loades, Diarmaid MacCulloch, David Palliser, Andrew Pettegree, Bill Shiels and Joyce Youings. To many of these I am indebted for personal communications and advice.

I wish also to express my gratitude to Josephine Evans, Robert Harper and Gillian Turnpenney, for permission to cite their unpublished research; to the staff of the libraries and record offices listed in my bibliography, for their unfailingly courteous assistance; to Bernard Barr and his staff at the York Minster Library, for exertions well beyond the bounds of duty; and to the University College of Ripon and York St John, for granting me a research sabbatical. My greatest debt, for their patience and encouragement, is to my wife Rowena and our daughters Victoria and Alexandra.

In all quotations from primary sources, spelling and punctuation have been modernized and standardized. All dates are new style. Unless otherwise indicated, the dioceses of Bath and Wells, Bristol, Carlisle, Chester, Coventry/Lichfield, Durham, Exeter, Gloucester, Hereford, Oxford, Salisbury, Worcester and York are classified (for purposes of regional analysis) as belonging to the 'north and west', and the dioceses of Canterbury, Chichester, Ely, Lincoln, London, Norwich, Peterborough, Rochester and Winchester as belonging to the 'south and east'.

The counties of Cheshire, Cornwall, Cumberland, Derbyshire, Devon, Dorset, Durham, Gloucestershire, Herefordshire, Lancashire,

Leicestershire, Lincolnshire, Northumberland, Nottinghamshire, Rutland, Shropshire, Somerset, Staffordshire, Warwickshire, Westmorland, Wiltshire, Worcestershire and Yorkshire are classified as belonging to the 'north and west', and the counties of Bedfordshire, Berkshire, Buckinghamshire, Cambridgeshire, Essex, Hampshire, Hertfordshire, Huntingdonshire, Kent, Middlesex, Norfolk, Northamptonshire, Oxfordshire, Suffolk, Surrey and Sussex as belonging to the 'south and east'.

English dioceses (as reorganized in 1541–2)

English counties and major towns

INTRODUCTION

'Of all the miracles and wonders of our time', exclaimed a subject of Henry VIII in 1539, 'I take the change of our sovereign lord's opinion in matters concerning religion to be even the greatest.' Until about 1529 the King had remained almost wholly supportive of traditional piety, making the pilgrimage to Canterbury and earning the title of Defender of the Faith (for his attack on Luther) from the Pope. From 1529, however, the government's attitude perceptibly changed.[1]

The papacy's revenue and jurisdiction were attacked in 1532–3, and its authority repudiated by the Act of Supremacy in 1534. Visitations of the monastic houses were followed by their total dissolution in 1536–40. Secular clerics saw their sanctuary rights and their mortuary and probate fees restricted in 1529, their jurisdictional independence suppressed in 1532, and their monopoly of spiritual knowledge eroded by the provision of vernacular bibles in parish churches from 1538. The crown began to dissolve colleges of priests in 1541, and a statute of 1545 prepared for the disendowment of religious guilds.

A traditional view of the seven sacraments was maintained by the Six Articles of 1539, the 'king's book' of 1543, and the intermittent persecution of dissenters; but uncertainty had been created by the omission of four sacraments from the Ten Articles of 1536. Prayer for the dead was threatened by official restrictions on chantry foundation in 1529 and 1532, by the official suppression of some chantries from 1543, and by a statute empowering the crown to survey and confiscate all chantry property in 1545. Some traditional beliefs concerning intercession were not supported by the 'king's book'. The number of saints' days was drastically reduced in 1536, and the invocation of saints diminished in the officially endorsed Litany and Primer of 1544–5. Pilgrimage, relic veneration and offering to images were all prohibited by the royal injunctions of 1536–8.

The period 1529–39 thus saw crucial components of the traditional religion subjected to an increasingly extensive official assault, which slowed in 1539–47 but did not halt. Its driving forces included not only the King but also his second queen, Anne Boleyn, his Archbishop of Canterbury, Thomas Cranmer, and above all his principal secretary and vicegerent, Thomas Cromwell. It was Cromwell who, for example, issued the injunctions of 1536–8. After his execution in 1540, royal counsellors continued to include anti-traditionalists like the Earl of Hertford.

The assault appears to have been impelled in part by spiritual convictions. Lutheran doctrines were approached (cautiously) in the Ten Articles, and some Protestant preaching was permitted or even encouraged. Protestant tendencies were exhibited by Anne, Cranmer and Cromwell, particularly in the promotion of the English Bible, while the King himself allowed Protestant tutors for his children Edward and Elizabeth. Nevertheless secular considerations were at least as powerful. Henry's rejection of the papacy was triggered by his determination to divorce the infertile Katherine of Aragon and produce a male heir, thus ensuring the dynasty's survival and averting civil war; and his promulgation of the Ten Articles owed much to his need for support from Germany's Lutheran princes. But arguably the strongest motives were not dynastic or diplomatic but financial. To a regime empoverished by inflation, Irish rebellion, and wars against Scotland and France, anti-traditionalist policies offered irresistible gains. These included the first year's revenues from ecclesiastical offices, the donations accumulated at images and shrines, the property of colleges and chantries, and above all the plate, money and land of monastic houses.

That the government failed to move even further in its reforms must be attributed primarily to the theological reservations of the King: his will invoked the saints and required prayer for his soul. Caution may also have been induced by the fear of disorder, especially after the rebellions of 1536. Other restraints, particularly in 1539–47, included the influence exerted on the King by Bishop Gardiner and the Howards, and his need for support against France from the Catholic emperor Charles V.

Under Edward VI, the period 1547–53 saw an intensified assault on traditional religion. Episcopal lands were officially appropriated. The secular clergy was substantially reduced in number, particularly by the chantry dissolutions, and in spiritual status, especially by the legitimization of clerical marriage and the ordinal of 1550. Religious guilds were suppressed. From 1547 the laity was allowed to receive the communion wine, and in 1549 the new prayerbook replaced the Latin mass with a service in the language of the English people; it also omitted actions like the elevation of the host. The replacement of stone altars by wooden tables was ordered in 1550. Even more radical was the prayerbook of 1552, which rejected most vestments, limited singing, and implied a non-miraculous act of remembrance. The inventorying of vestments and plate, which had begun in 1548, culminated in the confiscation of most ritual apparatus in 1553. Orders prohibited processions, holy bread, holy water, palms, ashes and Candlemas candles. An act of 1547 dissolved all chantries and confiscated their endowments. Saints' days were further reduced, and all images were outlawed in 1548.

This programme inevitably owed less to the boy-king than to his adult advisers, particularly the Dukes of Somerset and Northumberland and Archbishop Cranmer. Influence was exerted also by bishops like Nicholas Ridley and immigrant scholars like Martin Bucer. Protestant beliefs were maintained by the official homilies and the Forty-two Articles of 1553, and were expressed by Cranmer, Somerset and the King himself. Northumberland's aspirations, however, were mainly secular, and religious reform throughout the reign was driven as much by politics and economics as by theology. A major motive behind the chantry dissolutions, for example, was the acquisition of their wealth, which Somerset needed to finance his Scottish war. The forces restraining change were less potent, though they included a fear of the disorder that over-rapid alterations might provoke.

Official policies were reversed by Mary's accession in 1553. Papal powers were restored, clerical celibacy enforced, and monasteries and fraternities permitted. The seven sacraments were again approved, together with images, relics, saint-invocations and prayers for the dead. Mass, for example, was imposed by law in December 1553. The heresy laws returned a year later, and burnings in 1555. These policies were formulated primarily by the Queen, though she was influenced by her husband, Philip of Spain, by bishops like Bonner and Gardiner, and by the papal legate Cardinal Pole. Both Mary and her advisers were actuated largely by spiritual zeal – Mary, in particular, had retained her Catholicism through the Henrician and Edwardian upheavals – though other factors, like the bishops' desire to regain their authority, were never wholly absent. At the same time the crown's religious traditionalism was inhibited by its parliaments, which prevented the restoration of church lands, and by its financial problems, which limited its re-endowment of monastic houses.

Reform resumed after Elizabeth's accession in 1558. The Supremacy Act of 1559 proclaimed her supreme governor of the English church. Religious houses and fraternities were dissolved; sacrificial priesthood was denied. Most Catholic rites were modified or suppressed by the Uniformity Act and royal injunctions of 1559, though the new prayerbook's communion wording was more ambiguous than in 1552. Altars were again replaced by tables, and ritual treasures confiscated. Prayers for the dead, saint-invocations, images and relics were once more condemned.

These alterations must be attributed primarily to the Queen and secondarily to her advisers, particularly William Cecil and Archbishop Parker. Protestant convictions were expressed not only by most councillors and bishops but also, albeit less emphatically, by Elizabeth herself. At the same time her anti-Catholicism was in part a political reaction to papal denial of her legitimacy. It was facilitated, moreover, by the support of the House of Commons, and by Spain's reluctance to assist the only credible Catholic claimant to her throne, the half-French Mary Stuart. On the other hand, further reform was restrained by Elizabeth's cautious temperament, the conservatism of many peers, and the continuing fear of internal disorder and foreign intervention.

Of the numerous questions raised by this series of religious revolutions, the most crucial concern its reception by the English people. Did they accept the innovations, or did they resist? According to one view, the reformation attacked practices and institutions that retained the firm support of the population; it therefore provoked extensive opposition and only slowly prevailed. In another interpretation, however, enthusiasm for traditional religion was already in decline; the reformation was therefore generally accepted and rapidly triumphed.[2] Nor is this the only controverted issue. Is it possible, for example, to correlate English responses with variations in geography, social group, gender or age? Was change more readily accepted in the south-east than in the north and west, in towns than in rural communities, among men than among women, and among the young than among their elders? By what motives, moreover, were responses impelled? Were spiritual convictions as powerful as emotional, material or physical drives? And by what influences were attitudes formed, maintained or altered?

Were families, neighbours and teachers, for example, as influential as pictures, sermons and books?

Answers to such questions must be sought in the broadest possible range of sources. Among the most undervalued of these are England's surviving medieval churches. Levels of investment in their fabrics and furnishings offer one index of local attitudes towards parish churches and their rites. An examination of extant sculptures, carvings, screen-paintings, murals and stained glass can reveal the devotional idioms of pre-reformation society, and sometimes the impact of the reformation itself. Additional insights are provided by memorial brasses, particularly those inscribed with dates.[3]

Of the available documentary sources, a number may be classed as unofficial. These include private letters; diaries, like Henry Machyn's; and public petitions, like the rebel 'articles' of 1536. Verse includes both Catholic and anti-Catholic ballads, while drama ranges from mysteries and miracles to the Protestant polemic of John Bale. Tracts and treatises were similarly produced by both sides: Philip Nichols wrote three in 1547–9. Chronicles were written by conservatives like the London Franciscan and Protestants like Exeter's John Hooker, while narratives were composed by both the traditionalist priest Robert Parkyn and the anti-traditionalist minister Thomas Hancock. The most notable study of recent religious history was the *Acts and Monuments* of John Foxe.

Other sources were official in origin. Ambassadorial reports were composed for foreign governments. Documents produced by or for the central organs of English government include statutes, proclamations, state papers, Privy Council proceedings, bills from the courts of Chancery and Star Chamber, and chantry certificates and church inventories compiled for the exchequer. Diocesan records include episcopal registers, visitation returns, ecclesiastical court books, and wills. Of the records produced for urban or parochial institutions, the most important are corporation minutes and (especially) churchwardens' accounts.[4]

The sources vary considerably in thematic scope. The *Acts and Monuments* depicts not only the responses of numerous people to the reformation but also the motives and influences by which they were shaped. Churchwardens' accounts, in contrast, reveal the extent to which (for example) parishes bought bibles in Henry's reign and demolished altars in Edward's; but they seldom show whether such actions were impelled by Protestant belief or by dutiful obedience to the crown. Accounts, moreover, had no reason to record events that did not directly involve church income or expenditure. This explains why image removal by Henrician commissioners, though frequently recorded in other sources, is rarely noted in accounts, and why so few southwestern accounts even mention the region's revolt of 1549. Again, wills indicate attitudes to the saints, as well as levels of investment in monasteries, churches, guilds and prayers for the dead; but motivation is rarely revealed. For example, late-Henrician testators increasingly omitted bequests for intercession, but seldom explained whether their decision was due to Protestant conviction or to fear of an official attack on endowed prayers.

The sources vary also in their geographical and sociological scope. A royal proclamation usually comments on the entire realm, whereas a set of visitation returns concerns a specific diocese, and a set of wardens' accounts a single parish. Some sources relate to both genders and a wide range of age and status groups, while others are restricted. Since wills, for example, were usually drafted in the expectation of approaching death, they represent the older generations more frequently than the young or middle-aged. Since they were made only by people with property to bequeath, they represent the wealthier classes rather than the poor. And since women, apart from widows, were generally barred from owing property, testators were far more often male.

In other ways a source might be less representative than it at first appears. Rebel articles, for example, were composed by leaders rather than the rank-and-file. Churchwardens' accounts could reflect the outlook of the wardens themselves, though, since they were elected by the parish, their religious attitudes must usually have been those prevailing locally. A will, moreover, was generally written out by a cleric or scrivener rather than the testator himself. Nevertheless it is improbable that testators often accepted preambles that contradicted their own views. At Battle, Otley and elsewhere, a single cleric in fact wrote a variety of preambles, both traditional and non-traditional, for his parishioners. The case of Toddington's William Tracey – whose corpse was burned in 1532, because his preamble denied saintly mediation – indeed shows that contemporaries regarded such statements as normally indicative of testators' beliefs.

One factor affecting the reliability of a source is its date. Wardens' accounts were compiled within a year of the events that they record, whereas Foxe's *Acts and Monuments* was written years or even decades after the events it describes. A second consideration is the origin of a source's information. Some writers, like Hooker, used personal experience and observation. Others, like Foxe, consulted earlier records and witnesses. A number, however, including the Greyfriars chronicler, sometimes generalized inaccurately about the national situation from merely local knowledge. A third factor is bias. Legal depositions are often one-sided or overstated, and polemical works were similarly designed to persuade: exaggeration and even misrepresentation are therefore not uncommon.

Part One: Institutions

1

The Papacy

On the eve of its repudiation by Henry VIII, the Pope's headship was still lauded by traditionalists as 'the confession and consent of all the world'. He was depicted, with triple crozier and tiara, in parish churches – at St Neot, glass of 1528 shows him blessing the local saint – while his martyred champion, Thomas Becket, was honoured by murals at Breage, Pickering and elsewhere. Parishes still paid their annual 'Peter's Pence': at Morebath each householder contributed a half-penny, and each cottager a farthing. Papal indulgences were often still valued. In 1530 they were being sold in the south-west by agents of a York guild, and one of the popular errors castigated by a reformer in 1531 was the belief that 'we have redemption through pardons and bulls of Rome'.[1]

On the other hand a minority – including John Household, Robert Rascall and Elizabeth Stamford of London diocese in 1517 – already 'despised the authority of the bishop of Rome'. Household denounced the Pope as a 'strumpet' and 'common bawd', whose pardons had 'drowned in blindness all Christian realms, and that for money'. 'Cruel, devilish blood-supper' was a Londoner's description in 1528. Such outbursts were less frequent in the north and west, though in Devon the Pope's pardons were derided by Walter Langford and John Atwill: Atwill thought them more effective in making money than saving souls.[2]

But the extent of enthusiasm for the papacy is more accurately indicated by reactions to its official suppression. Although a papalist claimed in 1535 that 'three parts of England is against the King', only a small minority rose in the Pope's defence. Even the northern rebels of 1536 sought merely to restore his spiritual headship, 'without any first fruits or pension to him to be paid out of this realm'; and this limited demand – which probably reflects the priorities of Robert Aske and some clerics rather than of the rank-and-file – was absent from the articles of the Lincolnshire rebels. Nor does papalism seem to have motivated the minor disturbances occurring elsewhere in 1536–7. The St Keverne rising was planned as an appeal to the King, while the Exeter rioters explicitly denied opposing his authority.[3]

In most regions even non-violent resistance to the royal supremacy was no more than sporadic. In 1534 it was formally accepted, with little dissidence, by the convocations of southern and northern clergy. The succession oath, with its implicit renunciation of papal authority, was refused by isolated individuals like More and Fisher but dutifully taken by adult males in London, Hampshire, Suffolk, Norwich, Yorkshire and elsewhere. 'You know that we be sworn unto the King's grace', a Londoner reminded a friar in 1536, 'and hath already abjured the Pope.' In Hampshire the oath was sworn 'very obediently' by a large gathering of laymen and clerics, while in one Suffolk parish it was administered by three gentlemen to 92 people. At Ashlower, where the vicar was reluctant to cooperate, he was reported to the commissioners by the parish constable. There are equally few signs of resistance to the explicitly anti-papal oath of supremacy: it was imposed on regular and secular clerics in 1534–5, and on new office-holders from 1536.[4]

A monk of Abingdon, and priests at Barking, Croydon, Exton, Harwich, Kingsbury, Oxhill, Paul's Cray, Stanton Lacy and elsewhere, were slow to erase the Pope's name from their service books. The campaign against Becket, launched in 1538, was also evaded by some: the parson of Gislingham attempted to celebrate his day on 29 December, and a representation of his martyrdom remained in Henley church in 1539. Nevertheless the predominant response to these governmental offensives appears to have been either acquiescence or support. The Pope's name was erased by most monks at Abingdon and by the rural dean at Oxhill, while the recalcitrant clerics at Gislingham, Harwich and Stanton Lacy were reported to the authorities by their own parishioners. At Jacobstowe two men delivered their parson's portis-book to the bishop's chancellor and accused him of failing to remove the Becket service.[5]

The effectiveness of the anti-Becket campaign is demonstrated by his eradication from most extant medieval calendars and service books. Some screen depictions survived, as at Ashton, but many were defaced, as at Burlingham St Andrew. Most parishes, like Breage, used whitewash to obliterate their Becket murals, though at Earl Stonham a painter transformed the archbishop's martyrdom into the death of St Katherine. At Ashford, by replacing an archiepiscopal cross with a wool-comb, the parishioners converted their Becket image into St Blaise. Even dedications were amended. By about 1542 the church at Plympton St Thomas, originally 'so called of Thomas Becket', had been re-dedicated to St Maurice, and by 1545 the name of a chapel in Ashburton church had been changed from St Thomas the martyr to St Thomas the apostle.[6]

The great majority of people seem also to have acquiesced in the destruction of Roman authority. Wardens' accounts throughout England show that the payment of Peter's Pence now ceased. Papal indulgences were no longer purchased, and legal appeals to Rome no longer attempted. John Hooker recorded of 1534 that 'the Pope and his usurped authority was utterly exiled and banished out of this land'. 'All sorts of people', wrote Bishop Gardiner in 1535, 'are agreed upon this point with most steadfast consent, learned and unlearned, both men and women: that no manner of person born and brought up in England hath aught to do with Rome.' Even in the north, according to Archbishop Lee in the same year, 'the people' disliked innovatory preaching but 'otherwise all the King's commandment here obey diligently, as well for the setting forth of his title ... as also of the abolition of the primacy of Rome'. In Cornwall, too, Dr Tregonwell in 1536 discovered 'as much conformity amongst men, and as ready to obey the King's authority, injunctions, and other orders declared to them, as ever I saw any men obey the same.'[7]

In 1532–40 the royal supremacy evoked a number of verbal protests from monks, friars and secular clerics, as well as the nun Elizabeth Barton. The vicar of Muston (for example) foretold the King's overthrow, and the restoration of the true faith by the Pope, while the vicar of Paulet continued to remember the Pope in prayers. Lay protesters were apparently fewer, though emerging from Buckenham Ferry, Herestoft, Leicester, Shelford and elsewhere. 'Rome shall be up again', a husbandman prophesied. Previous kings, asserted a servant, all obeyed the Pope; 'and I pray thee, who gave the King leave to put him down?' That such outbursts were by no means necessarily representative of local opinion is shown by their dutiful reporting to the authorities. With exceptions like John Musard, a

Worcester monk, the informers were most often laymen. When the vicar of Rye declared the perils of papal excommunication, his own parishioners informed against him; he was then examined by the mayor and jurats, imprisoned by Sir Edward Guildford and reported to Cromwell. The abbot of Pershore was accused by a layman, and the abbot of Colchester by two mercers.[8]

By 1537 the government felt confident that 'privy maintainers of [the] papistical faction' were being reduced to 'muttering in corners as they dare'; and by 1540 papalist protest seems almost to have ceased. By the reign's end, even in the south-west, most wardens' accounts had begun to acknowledge the King as 'Defender of the Faith and, on earth, supreme head of the Church of England'. Many of his subjects, moreover, were now vocal in their contempt for papal claims. In 1531 an Exeter schoolmaster had denounced the Pope as the biblically predicted 'antichrist', 'thief', 'hireling', 'boar from the wood' and 'whore of Babylon'. Each national church, he maintained, should be controlled by its prince, 'the supreme governor under God'. In this year a London serving-man called the Pope a 'knave', while in 1533 Rye townsmen dismissed his curses as 'but words'. 'There is no Pope, but [only] a bishop of Rome', a Cambridge ostler assured a papalist visitor in 1534. 'The Roman antichrist' was decried by a Yorkshireman in 1537, and 'the usurped power of Rome' by William Harrison at Pershore in 1538. At Salisbury the under-bailiff John Goodall strove, 'by writing, speaking, and spending his goods, for the extirping of the fucated and usurped authority of the bishop of Rome'.[9]

By Edward's reign even the most militant of religious traditionalists seem usually to have accepted the royal supremacy. In 1548 the Helston rioters required 'all such laws and ordinances touching christian religion as was appointed by our late sovereign lord King Henry VIII'. And although the southwestern rebels of 1549 were sometimes decried (by their enemies) as supporters of 'the authority of the Idol of Rome', in reality they seem never to have demanded its revival. Both at Sampford Courtenay and at Clyst St Mary they indeed required that religion 'remain and tarry in the same state as King Henry VIII left it'. The restoration of papal authority was similarly absent from the articles of the Norfolk rebels.[10]

A virulent anti-papalism was frequently expressed in the Edwardian years. 'Many writers', observed the young layman Philip Nichols, 'have compared the Pope to King Pharaoh of Egypt … .

For, as long as he governed the church, he made us bond-slaves, he and his ministers. Yea, we were so blindly led and so tyrannously handled, and that with such villainy, that I am sure the Israelites were never so shameful intreated of King Pharaoh and his ministers as we have been of this Pharaoh and his shaven generation.' 'The detestation of the Pope is now so confirmed', reported the Venetian Barbaro in 1551, 'that no one, either of the new or old religion, can bear to hear him mentioned.'[11]

How did men and women react to the restoration of his authority in Mary's reign? Some were – or appeared – enthusiastic. In London a crowd knelt to receive his legate's absolution; Stroppiana thought that they 'displayed great joy and piety, begging the cardinal for his blessing'. Some parishes lit bonfires or, like Sheriff Hutton, bought copies of the absolution. On the other hand, papalistic zeal is rare in Catholic literature of this reign; and of 134 sets of wardens' accounts, celebrations of the papal restoration are recorded in only three. A number of people remained openly hostile. In 1555 many Londoners derided the legate's blessing and refused to bow to his processional cross, while at Charing Cross over three hundred reportedly said 'Amen' to a prayer against 'the tyranny of the bishop of Rome'. Antipathy to 'the authority of the apostolic see' was expressed in Northamptonshire (for example) by Thomas and Elizabeth Armstrong and in Cornwall by Sampson Jackman and Agnes Priest: Agnes denounced the Pope as the antichrist, the devil and the whore of Babylon. Foreign ambassadors, both imperial and Venetian, reported that the Pope's name was odious even to religiously conservative Englishmen. Cardinal Pole feared that 'our countrymen' were reluctant to submit again to Rome, on account of 'the old hatred which they had borne so many years to that name'.[12]

Opposition to the final abolition of papal authority by Elizabeth I was minimal or non-existent. During the rebellion of 1569, some men and women were 'reconciled' by Catholic priests; but these were a tiny minority, and limited to the far north. By this date the Pope's removal from English religion had long been accepted by the great majority of the English people.[13]

2

Religious Orders

On the eve of their suppression, signs of a continuing spiritual vigour in the religious orders were by no means wholly absent. They were most conspicuous amongst the Carthusians, especially at Mount Grace, and in the Bridgettine house at Syon. In communities like Woolstrope, too, even the dissolution commissioners would find the monks 'of right good conversation, and living religiously'. On the other hand there is also occasional evidence of drunkenness and sexual incontinence, and substantially more frequent evidence of a preference for individual convenience, material comfort and contact with the outer world. Such declensions from the monastic ideal were reported not only by royal commissioners but also by earlier ecclesiastical visitors, like the Bishop of Lincoln at Peterborough and Ramsey abbeys in 1518. The extant buildings of great houses like Fountains or Rievaulx confirm a pre-reformation trend towards display towers, meat kitchens, divided dormitories, comfortable private chambers and well-appointed abbatial lodgings. In about 1500 a foreigner described England's major monasteries as 'more like baronial palaces than religious houses'.[1]

The number of religious communities had declined from about 1005 in 1350 to 918 in 1500 and 880 in 1534. The approximate number of religious had slumped from 17 600 in 1350 to 9000 in 1400; it recovered to 12 200 in 1500, then fell to 11 600 in 1534. Slump and recovery mirrored demographic trends, but the early sixteenth-century fall occurred during demographic growth: it may imply a waning enthusiasm for the religious life. The late middle ages saw also the virtual disappearance of lay brothers, formerly associated in large numbers with Cistercian houses. Most monasteries, in consequence, now suffered from under-population.[2]

Lay people still visited monasteries to worship in their naves, venerate their shrines, or receive their alms and hospitality. Some also made donations, often for prayer. In 1522, for example, Nicholas Ennis bequeathed tin-workings to the Tywardreath monks, while in 1528 Joan Tackle, seeking 20 years of masses for her soul, entrusted £120 to the abbot of Forde. People resorted also to the friars, for preaching, confession, burial or prayer. One villager, in 1532, travelled 14 miles to confess in an Exeter friary. A Tiverton merchant, in 1529, left money to the Dominicans and Franciscans at Exeter and Plymouth, 'to the intent that the friars there being shall devoutly say and sing four trentals, for my soul and all Christian souls, immediately after my decease'. 'By the merits of your orders', complained a reformer in 1531, 'ye make many brethren and sisters: ye take yearly money of them, ye bury them in your coats'.[3]

On the other hand, patrons no longer financed religious houses on the scale of the twelfth, thirteenth and early fourteenth centuries. Bath is the sole monastic church completely reconstructed in the late fifteenth and early sixteenth centuries. New foundations of abbeys, priories and priory cells had fallen to 13 in 1350–99, six in 1400–49 and nil thereafter. New friaries had dwindled to 13 in 1350–99, one in 1400–49, two in 1450–99 and one since 1500. Of wills from 1520–30, moreover, the percentage containing bequests to monks ranged from a relatively modest 17–18, in the dioceses of Durham, Exeter and York, to 11 in Lincolnshire, eight in Huntingdonshire and nil in Buckinghamshire. The percentage with bequests to friars ranged from 28 in Durham and York dioceses, and 22–3 in Exeter diocese and Lincolnshire, to 16 in Huntingdonshire and nil in Buckinghamshire. At Norwich, where monasteries and friaries were often remembered by lay testators in 1490–1517, donations began to decline in 1518–32.[4]

Relations between the religious and their neighbours were often harmonious. In the 1520s the parishioners of Exeter St Petrock's borrowed vestments from St Nicholas' priory, and the inhabitants of Ashburton and Chagford received gifts for their churches from the abbots of Buckfast and Torre. At Woolstrope, according to the dissolution commissioners, the prior was 'well beloved of all the inhabitants thereunto adjoining'. By 1500–29, however, there were also significant tensions, particularly between the powerful landowning monasteries and the local laity.[5]

Monastic lands and waters were not infrequently disputed. Tavistock abbey had land claimed by a local butcher, and a weir demolished violently by a mob of 300 men. In 1527 its enemies allegedly conspired to attack its precinct and put the abbot 'in jeopardy of his life'. Buckfast abbey was in dispute with its tenants at Staverton and South Brent. Monastic enclosures were vigorously opposed by the townsmen of Peterborough and the inhabitants of Orford, who rioted against Butley priory, and by Thomas Brook, who sued the abbot of Dunkeswell and denounced him as 'cruel and covetous'. Monastic dues were also denied. In 1510, for example, tithe-produce being collected by the prior of Launceston's servant was seized and carried off by Edward Robert; and many testators, like Thomas Hamlyn of Totnes in 1526, admitted that they had 'forgotten' to pay monastic tithes. Mortuaries were withheld from the monks of Dover by the mayor and his officers, and from the abbot of Whalley by the parishioners of Walton-le-Dale. Monastic jurisdiction and privileges provoked complaints at Bodmin, Exeter and St Germans. In Kent these issues caused disputes at Canterbury, Faversham, Fordwich, Lydd, New Romney and Sandwich.[6]

By 1529 the religious were being denounced by pamphleteers like Jerome Barlow and Simon Fish. Fish's *Supplication for the Beggars* dismissed them all as 'holy idle thieves'. Most areas, moreover, including Cornwall, Devon, Lincolnshire and Somerset as well as London, saw a decline in bequests to monks and friars in 1530–5, followed by their dwindling and total cessation in 1536–40. In Cornwall and Devon the percentage of wills with bequests to monks fell from 17 in 1520–9 to 11 in 1530–5 and nil in 1536–9, and that with bequests to friars from 23 to 21 and nine. In London the first percentage dropped from 17 in 1523–5 to eight in 1529–30 and nil in 1534–40, and the second from 43 to 33 and nil.[7]

In their final years the religious houses seem also to have experienced an upsurge of lay hostility. In 1531 men broke into the abbot of Hartland's chamber, causing him 'such fear that he was in danger of his life', while in 1536 locals assaulted the prior of Bodmin's servants, withheld his fish tithes, and invaded his woods and waters. Christopher St German claimed in 1532 that criticism of the religious was also now common, and certainly they were decried in both writing and speech. Abbeys were attacked by London's Nicholas Field (for example) in 1530, and friars by Exeter's Thomas Bennett in 1531. In about 1539 Richard Morison flayed 'merciless monks, false friars and uncharitable canons, and other fools of feigned religion'.[8]

Antagonism was also expressed in litigation and petition. In Devon and Cornwall alone, the years 1529–39 saw anti-monastic suits presented to Chancery, Star Chamber and other central bodies by at least seven individuals and by the communities of Bodmin, Fowey, Plymouth, Torre and Wembury. Their grievances included mortuaries, jurisdiction, and inadequate services in appropriated benefices. Thomas Ashridge, for example, appealed to the recent legislation of the Reformation Parliament, and argued that the prior of Launceston 'ought to have no mortuary, by the statute thereof lately made'. The 'poor neighbours' of the abbot of Torre, in a petition to Star Chamber, not only protested against his supposed threats and oppressions, but also vehemently denounced his 'evil disposition' and his 'vicious and abominable living towards God'.[9]

How were the dissolutions themselves received? The leader of the northern rising of 1536 claimed that they were resented by 'all the whole [north] country'. Certainly the articles of his 'pilgrims', like those of their Lincolnshire counterparts, demanded the restoration of suppressed houses, and about 16 appear to have been temporarily reconstituted by rebel forces. Aske asserted that at York he had organized the monks' return 'because the commons would needs put them in'. Many rebels, nevertheless, showed scant respect for the religious by stealing their horses, threatening to burn down their houses, and even menacing their lives. The pilgrim articles, moreover, specifically sought to limit the entry fines exacted from tenants by their monastic landlords.[10]

In other regions significant resistance to the suppression was conspicuously rare. With few exceptions, notably the abbots of Colchester, Glastonbury and Reading, the religious submitted to the royal will. Serious opposition arose only at Hexham and Norton, where it was rapidly quelled. At Norton, where a large crowd, led by the abbot and some canons, besieged the suppression commissioners in the abbey tower, it was dispersed by a posse under the sheriff of Cheshire. Even the minor disturbance at Exeter was directed against the incidental iconoclasm rather than against the dissolution. In 1539–40, moreover, the suppression of the great houses evoked no rebellion – or even substantial riot – in any region.[11]

Complaints were sometimes voiced. A Leicestershire abbot grumbled that the King 'roots up the churches as the mole roots up the molehills', and the abbot of Colchester questioned the King's authority to suppress his house. Pro-monastic sympathies were occasionally expressed by secular clerics and laymen, including an Oxford chaplain and a Norfolk husbandman. These statements, however, were all relayed to the authorities: the abbot of Colchester, for example, was reported by his servant. They were also countered by expressions of support for dissolution. In 1538, for example, Robert Towson of Cambridge hoped that all monasteries would be suppressed, while Ralph Sheldon argued with the abbot of Pershore and praised the anti-monastic policies of the King. 'Abbeys be nothing esteemed or pitied', reported John Marshall of Nottinghamshire and Lincolnshire in 1539. The commons, he thought, regretted the loss of monastic prayers, but regarded the monks as 'but bellymonds and gluttons of the world, and the most vicious persons'.[12]

If only a minority of Henry VIII's subjects were prepared to oppose his monastic policy, a substantial number were ready to assist. The suppression process was supervised by royal commissioners, usually gentlemen, and often facilitated by urban governors: at Plymouth these included the mayor, the mayor-elect and other leading townsmen. Others cooperated in the identification and conviction of resisters. The abbot of Glastonbury was condemned by an inquest of local men, who (Lord Russell reported) were 'never better willing to serve the king'. 'There were many bills put up against the abbot, by his tenants and others, for wrongs and injuries that he had done them.'[13]

Wealthier laymen proved ready to profit from the dissolution – and to ensure its permanence – by purchasing monastic land. By 1547 some two-thirds had been sold. Buyers came mainly from the gentry, like Yorkshire's Fairfaxes and Malleverers, though yeomen, merchants and clothiers were sometimes represented. By 1543, as Leland discovered, the buildings were already being converted to secular uses. These were primarily residential, as at Barrow Gurney, where a nunnery was 'now made a fair dwelling place by Drewe of Bristol', or at Melwood, where the monastery had become 'a goodly manor place' for Mr Cavendish. At Malmesbury, however, the abbey was now used for production by a clothier named Stumpe – it was 'full of looms to weave cloth in' – while at Gloucester the Franciscan and Dominican friaries had been transformed into a brew house and a draping house. Such conversions were executed by teams of craftsmen and labourers, apparently without reluctance. Lewes priory was demolished by 17 workmen, three carpenters, two smiths, two plumbers and a furnace stoker.[14]

Parochial communities proved no less willing to despoil. In the south-west a window from Barlinch priory was acquired by Morebath, bells from Bodmin priory by Lanivet, and tabernacles, paving stones, desks, organs and a cope from Tavistock abbey by the parish. At Exeter in 1539 the citizens stripped stone from St Nicholas' priory to repair their bridge. Even Yorkshire abbeys like Roche were despoiled by gentlemen, yeomen and other local people. Windows, lead and timber were seized, service books used to fill the holes in wagons, and 'all things of price either spoiled, carped away or defaced to the uttermost'. Many houses were plundered by the local poor. 'A great part' of Bridlington priory's sheep, cattle, corn and household equipment was 'stolen by the poor people' at its suppression in 1537, while at Reading's Franciscan friary in 1538 the 'poor people ... fell to stealing ... in every corner of the house'. In this year it was reported from Warwickshire that 'the poor people, thoroughly in every place, be so greedy upon these houses when they be suppressed that by night and day, not only of the towns but also of the country, they do continually resort as long as any door, window, iron or glass or loose lead remaineth in any of them'.[15]

Pro-monastic sentiment was not wholly eradicated by Henry VIII. In 1549 the southwestern rebels – or at least, their leaders – still hoped to see a restoration of houses for 'devout persons', financed mainly by a confiscation of 'the half part of the abbey lands and chantry lands in every man's possession'. Since, however, this scheme was restricted to 'two places, where two of the chief abbeys was, in every county', it excluded most of the great foundations and all of the small: even the most militant traditionalists no longer envisaged more than a limited revival of religious houses. No such demands were made by the rebels in Norfolk or elsewhere in 1549. Throughout Edward's reign his lay subjects in fact continued to purchase ex-monastic lands – the buyers included some 32 citizens at Exeter alone – and to demolish or convert monastic buildings: at Totnes the townsmen rebuilt their guildhall on the site of the suppressed priory. Memories of the monks were often vehemently hostile: Philip Nichols, for example, dismissed them as a 'rabblement of cloisterers'.[16]

That enthusiasm for the religious life was now rare is confirmed by the events of Mary's reign. Although monks returned to Sheen, Syon and Westminster, friars to Greenwich and Smithfield, and nuns to King's Langley, these six were the only houses of the 880 existing in

1534 to be revived. Against the 11 600 inmates of 1534, the total by 1557 was little more than 100, and even these were usually ageing ex-religious rather than new recruits. All six houses, moreover, were endowed by the crown. With very rare exceptions like the Earl of Pembroke, who considered restoring a friary at Southampton, the Queen's zeal was not shared by her subjects: the gentry proved almost unanimously unwilling to disgorge their ex-monastic lands. Nor did bequests revive. Even in southwestern counties like Cornwall, Devon and Somerset, and in northern counties like Durham, Northumberland and Yorkshire, analyzed wills from this reign contain not one donation to a religious house. Distaste for such institutions continued to be voiced by dissidents like Sampson Jackman at Linkinhorne, and at both Greenwich and Smithfield the friars encountered hostile demonstrations. It is therefore not surprising that in 1559 the final dissolution of the revived houses proceeded quietly and without resistance.[17]

3

The Secular Clergy (1)

Although the secular clergy, unlike the papacy and the religious orders, survived the reformation, its size, wealth, privileges and spiritual status were all significantly reduced. Were these changes accompanied by any discernible alterations in the laity's attitude towards it?

One possible index was laymen's willingness to become priests. In several early sixteenth-century dioceses, particularly in the north, west and midlands, the average number of ordinations per annum remained substantial: approximately 200 in York, for example, and 172 in Lincoln in 1515–20. In the south, however, and particularly in London, recruitment was generally less impressive. The 1520s, moreover, saw signs of a general decline: Lincoln's average fell to 141 in 1522–7.[1]

This trend accelerated in the reformation decades. The Lincoln average slumped to 80 in 1527–35 and only 22 in 1536–46. The Durham figures were 27 in 1531–5, nil in 1536–41 and three in 1542–7, and by 1547 comparable declines had occurred at Exeter, Hereford, Lichfield, London and York. At Chester, Durham, Exeter, Lichfield, Lincoln, York and probably Canterbury, though to a lesser extent in London, Edward's reign saw ordinations either dwindle into insignificance or totally cease. Nor was the Marian recovery more than partial. In 1553–8 the ordinations per annum appear to have averaged about 48 in London, 20 in Chester, five in Durham and two in Exeter. The result – as noted at the beginning of Elizabeth's reign by Archbishop Parker, Sir John Chichester and the Exeter canons – was a serious scarcity of parochial clergy.[2]

A more important index of attitudes was the laity's readiness to provide financial support. Bequests to secular clerics – as gifts, tithe or mortuary payments, or fees for intercession – still featured in 66 per cent of wills from Durham and York dioceses in 1520–33, and in 70 per cent from Exeter diocese in 1520–9. In 1526, for example, the Yorkshireman Nicholas Fitzwilliam not only bequeathed his 'best beast' as a mortuary, 'after the laudable custom of holy church', but also donated 6d for tithes, 6s 8d to his vicar 'to pray for me', and money and a doublet to another priest. In 1520–30, moreover, bequests to the cathedral clergy at Wells and Lincoln were included in over 90 per cent of wills in their dioceses. On the other hand, the willingness of patrons to endow colleges of secular priests or chantry chaplains was in marked decline. The number of new foundations had fallen from 43 in 1350–99 to 29 in 1400–49, 17 in 1450–99 and only five since 1500.[3]

What happened to investment in the reformation decades? In Wells diocese the percentage of testators bequeathing to the cathedral fell to 81 in 1545–9 and 67 in 1550–4, before recovering to 72 in 1555–8. In Lincoln diocese it had slumped to 74, 56 and 54 in Lincolnshire, Buckinghamshire and Huntingdonshire by 1545, and to only 24 and 14 in Huntingdonshire and Lincolnshire by 1550. Even more significant was the percentage of testators donating to priests. In Durham and York dioceses this fell to 55 in 1534–46, 38 in 1547–53, 36 in 1553–8 and 20 in 1558–70. In Exeter diocese the fall was to 56 in 1530–9, 36 in 1540–6, 22 in 1547–9, 26 in 1550–3, 18 in 1553–9 and three in 1560–9. Decline was apparently even faster in London, where the percentage in 1534–46 was only 23. Yarcombe's Richard Lock, who bequeathed 1s 8d to his parish priest in 1550, was becoming markedly less typical than Widworthy's John Deyman, who left nothing to any cleric in 1551.[4]

A third index was the laity's willingness to pay clerical dues. In many pre-reformation parishes these were apparently rendered without complaint. At Lawhitton the parishioners customarily left their butter and cheese tithes in the church, while at Bodmin, in 1526, the inhabitants acknowledged their vicar's right to a tithe of their calves, milk, fruit, vegetables and hay, and to their offerings at All Saints, Christmas, Easter and St Petrock's nativity. On the other hand, frequent evasion is indicated by the provision in many lay wills – like that made by Wolborough's Henry Bartlett in 1526 – for 'tithing and offerings negligently paid'. Tithe avoidance was particularly common in London, as its clergy complained in 1528, while their persecution of Richard Hunne, for refusing a mortuary, provoked public outcry in 1515: Londoners, reported the papal agent, were 'raging against the clergy'. In Kent and Surrey such payments were resisted not only by individuals, as at Milton, Seasalter and Wichling, but also by urban oligarchies and parishes, as at Kingston-upon-Thames and Barfreston. Sussex, in the 1520s, saw a spate of attempts to withhold tithes, offerings and other dues. Ten tithe disputes escalated into legal actions in Norwich diocese in 1524, and another ten in Lichfield diocese in 1525. Though apparently less frequent, conflicts occurred also in remote areas like Lancashire, as at Sefton, and Cornwall, as at Bodmin, St Mawgan-in-Kerrier and St Teath. The Bodmin townsmen challenged their vicar's right to take hearse cloths from corpses and collect tithes of butter and cheese. Some laymen, moreover, were not afraid to pillage priests, as at St Giles-in-the-Wood in 1517.[5]

From 1529 such incidents appear to have substantially increased. The passage of the statute of mortuaries was accompanied by group resistance to death dues, as at Portledge and South Hill, and followed by its exploitation as a weapon against clerical demands. At Dittisham and Harberton, 'since the making of the said statute', parishioners replaced the traditional mortuaries of sheep or oxen with money payments according to their means. At Down St Mary in about 1533 the parson reportedly resented his parishioners 'because he cannot have the best beast in the name of a mortuary, as he before the statute was used to have'. But even the regulated fees encountered opposition. Mortuary disputes in Chester archdeaconry rose from eight in 1500–29 to 13 in 1530 alone, and such payments were still regarded as a burden on 'the common and mean sort' in the north-east midlands in 1539.[6]

Increasing resistance to tithes – including 'denial', 'contradiction', 'molestation' and 'trouble' – is attested by royal proclamations of 1535, 1547 and 1559. A third of London parishes saw tithe conflict in 1521–46. In Norwich diocese the average number of tithe cases per annum rose from 8–10 in 1520–49 to 36 in 1550–9 and 47 in 1560–9. In Winchester diocese the rise was from 3–12 in 1520–49 to 32 in 1560–9. Disputes also increased in the dioceses of Chester and York.[7]

Resistance was mounted not only by individuals – like Richard Richards, who owned land at Bickleigh but 'refuseth to pay the tithe thereof' – but also by groups and whole communities. These were found not only in the south-east, as in London itself and at Hayes, but also in distant counties like Cornwall and Devon, as at Brixham, Crediton, Down St Mary, Helston, Morebath, St Keverne and Sidmouth. At Hayes, in 1530, an alehouse keeper led a mass refusal to pay tithes. At Down St Mary, in about 1533, tithes regarded by the parson as his customary due were denounced by one parishioner as 'exactions'. They were refused by virtually all the parish, which (lamented the priest) contained 'not above five or six honest men and women'. In about 1540 the tithe-refusing mayor and townsmen of Helston were denounced by a priest as 'perverse' and 'froward'. Their refusal, he commented revealingly, was a 'perilous example' to 'the whole country next adjoining'.[8]

Some resisters took legal action, either in Star Chamber, like four London parishes in 1532, or in Chancery, like two Crediton men in 1538–44. Others, like a North Huish farmer in 1569, threatened violence to the tithe collectors. Even more hostile were the Westmorland and Norfolk rebels in 1536 and 1549. The former required 'all the tithes to remain to every man his own, doing therefor according to their duty'. The latter wanted clerics' income restricted to a money payment, to avoid the 'trouble and suit between them and their poor parishioners which they daily do proceed and attempt'.[9]

Offerings were sometimes reduced, as at Lamerton in 1551. 'Some of the parish', it was reported, 'was glad thereof, and contented to pay but a little'. When restoration was attempted in 1555, one man refused to contribute and another told the vicar: 'I trust and if it be not my duty, you will pay me back again!' The payment of 'chrisoms' to vicars also ended, as at Hatherleigh in about 1564 and Crediton in 1565.[10]

In Norfolk the 1549 rebels sought to prevent clerics from acquiring more land, and to reduce the rents paid to them by their tenants. Even in the south-west priests now frequently experienced the withholding of their rents, the purloining of their dues, and the plundering of their houses, lands, goods and personal possessions. At St Stephen's-by-Saltash, for example, the vicarage was forcibly entered, damaged and pillaged by the vicar's enemies, while at Bridestow several laymen seized corn from the parson's barn and livestock from his glebe.[11]

A fourth index was respect for the authority of clerics and church courts. On the eve of the reformation their excommunications could still evoke a 'terrible fear', and even their suspensions were usually sufficient to induce submission. Throughout the reformation decades, moreover, men and women continued frequently to submit to the penalties imposed by church courts, and even to cooperate with them as plaintiffs or witnesses. Nor did these years see the eradication of deference to clerics. In the 'Catholic' rebellions of 1536, 1549 and 1569, laymen largely followed the leadership of priests. In 1568 a Plympton St Mary man could still assert that because his vicar was ordained, 'we must all obey him'.[12]

On the other hand, clerical authority was certainly sometimes resented before the reformation. John Colet, in 1510, complained that people were 'sore vexed' by the corrupt activities of church courts. Common lawyers strove to restrict their jurisdiction, and in Canterbury and London dioceses, from about 1500, the volume of litigation within them apparently declined. There is some evidence of indifference or contempt. In Canterbury diocese a quarter of defendants ignored summonses to the archdeacon's court, and in 1511 one Kentishman proclaimed that he 'setteth not a straw by the suspension of the commissary or official'.[13]

Resistance to clerics appears to have risen significantly in the reformation decades. Their spiritual authority was increasingly challenged by laymen, like Philip Nichols, and even laywomen, like Agnes Priest. 'Thou art an unlearned person, and a woman', an astonished bishop told Agnes; 'wilt thou meddle with such high matters, which all the doctors of the world cannot define?' At the same time their commands were increasingly disobeyed. A Kenton man, for example, 'defied' his vicar; a North Huish man ignored his parson's rebukes, remained seated in his presence, and insultingly called him 'thou'; and a disobedient parishioner of Dean Prior, 'in scorn and derision', laughed in his vicar's face.[14]

Particularly unpopular were attempts to discipline the erring laity. Even in Devon a number of laymen refused penances, derided excommunications, or sued (in Chancery and Star Chamber) the priests who excommunicated them. The sources suggest also a substantial erosion of respect for church courts. In 1536 a statute complained that many people had 'attempted in late time past to disobey, condemn and despise the process, laws and decrees of the ecclesiastical courts of this realm, in more temerous and large manner than before this time hath been seen'. Evidence from several dioceses, including Chichester and Norwich, indicates a marked increase in disobedience from the 1530s. Summonses were evaded by many offenders; and when, in Mary's reign, a Shute man was summoned for committing fornication, he responded by giving the summoner 'one blow with his fist'. The traditional sanctions were also losing power. A Kenton adulterer dismissed public penance as 'but a sheet matter'. A Tiverton man, in about 1562, ignored his excommunication for evil living and flatly disobeyed his vicar's command to leave church. 'So little reverence he gave to the spiritual laws', lamented the vicar, who warned that if punishment were not imposed 'it were in vain for us in Tiverton to declare and excommunicate any. The people are so stout, and careth so little what they do and how evil they live, when they will laugh out the matter and say, "It is but a money matter". So little they regard it.' Of 225 offenders suspended or excommunicated in Gloucester diocese in 1569–70, 81 per cent seem never even to have sought their restoration to the communion of the church.[15]

4

The Secular Clergy (2)

A fifth index of lay people's attitudes is provided by their spoken or written expressions of opinion. Respect for the clergy and its sacred functions was not infrequently voiced both before and during the reformation decades. In 1535–6, for example, Axminster's Thomas Crabbe asserted that every man 'must needs have a priest at his coming into the world, and a priest at his departing'. His neighbour Margery Hoare was similarly respectful of the episcopal office: 'for', she explained, 'the bishop was anointed with holy oil'.[1]

Even before the reformation, nevertheless, some lay people decried the clerical estate. At Kennington, in 1511, Richard Ricard was 'so infest against priests that he is ever talking of them, and ready to say the worst against them and their order'. In London diocese the clergy were dismissed as 'antichrists' and 'whore mongers' by dissidents in 1517, while a Londoner declared in 1520 that 'all the priests should be slain'. Similar scorn was expressed by a London writer, Simon Fish, in 1528. Denigration of the priesthood was apparently less common in the north and west, though in 1505–6 a Devonian both criticized its greed and denied its exclusive authority to absolve. Complaint was more frequently directed against its individual members, and often included charges of financial or sexual impropriety. At Michaelstow in about 1510, for example, Richard Broad accused a priest of smuggling women into his lodgings at night, dressed in male clothing for disguise. Parishioners were also sometimes prepared to inform the authorities of the actual or supposed inadequacies of their spiritual guides. Some 25 cases of sexual misbehaviour by clerics were reported from Lincoln diocese in 1514–21, and 11 from Winchester archdeaconry in 1527–8.[2]

Complaints appear to have multiplied in the reformation decades. 'There is no good priest', many laymen were reportedly saying in 1532; 'all priests be naughty [i.e. wicked]'. 'Priests', announced an Axminster shoemaker in 1535–6, were 'all naught'. He added that 'priests did put Christ to death', and that 'the blessing of a bishop was as good as the blessing of his old horse'. In 1536 a Cumberland man reportedly exclaimed that it would be better if all the priests' heads were cut off. 'It is best that we cut off a great many priests' heads', agreed a school master at West Malling in 1537. In 1541 a group of Exeter people entertained each other by 'jesting upon priests': they swapped stories about the clerical propensity to 'live incontinently with men's wives'. In 1545 Henry VIII himself lamented the fashion for laymen to 'rail on bishops' and 'speak slanderously of priests'. The trend continued into Edward's reign – when Philip Nichols, for instance, dismissed priests as 'caterpillars, which do all for lucre' – and was not suppressed in Mary's. 'I would all priests were hanged!', declared Sampson Jackman at Linkinhorne. At Colchester, according to an alarmed cleric, priests were 'hemmed at in the open streets and called "knaves"'. In London a cat was dressed in priest's clothing and hanged on a gallows, and a dog's head was shorn 'like a priest's', while at Bedford, 'in mockery of the priestly order', a baby's head was similarly tonsured. 'As yet these malicious mockers cease not in many places, when they can spy a priest, to play the like part', lamented John Christopherson.[3]

Complaints against individual priests seem also to have risen. The charges included covetousness and extortion, as at Awliscombe, drunkenness, as at St Michael Penkevil, swearing, as at Ilsington, and hawking or hunting, as at Glasney and Sheepwash. But the most frequent accusation was sexual misconduct. Sometimes it was the cleric's alleged concubine at whom the charge was flung. 'Thou art a whore and a priest whore', a Winkleigh woman was told in 1561, 'for a priest had to doing with thee at home, in the midst of thine own floor'. More often, however, the cleric himself was directly denounced.[4]

In 1541, for example, a Yealmpton man composed a ballad about his parson's sex life, sang it in the village street, and even taught it to the young people. 'Now it is a common song', reported a witness, 'and sung abroad in the country'. In 1542 the constable of St Breock 'did speak against the misliving and unchastity of one Sir Matthew Poldon, priest': 'the which priest', he declared, 'ordered his life and living contrary to the laws of almighty God'. In 1544–7 the parson of

Uplyme was accused by several parishioners of sexual laxity, and denounced in the street 'before a great multitude', while at both Exeter and Paul censorious laymen secured the indictment of priests for sexual incontinence. At Paul the vicar's relationships with local wives were 'the common fame and report ... in all the said parish'. Such accusations remained frequent under Edward, Mary and Elizabeth. Edward Ward, for example, warned his companions that the vicar of Dawlish would 'jape your wives and maidens, all them that be in your parish'. The accused priests were often crudely reviled – as 'vicious', 'whore monger' and 'knave' at Alvington, 'knave' and 'whore master' at St Austell, and 'vagabond' at Whitchurch. At Spreyton it was in church, at service time, that the vicar was called a 'whore monger and bawdy priest', while at Sheepwash the vicar was in the pulpit when he heard himself denounced as a 'naughty knave', 'rascal knave' and 'varlet knave' for his sexual misdemeanours.[5]

That such accusations were inspired by malice as well as moral indignation is suggested by the denials and slander suits that they frequently evoked. At Paul in about 1546, for example, the vicar regarded his accusers as 'malicious' and 'evil disposed': he produced witnesses to his good character and was acquitted. At Honiton Clyst in 1568, an unmarried woman was pressurized by several local people into falsely naming a cleric as the father of her child.[6]

Slanders against priests were more likely to be recorded than statements in their favour. The latter undoubtedly continued: in 1558, for instance, it was reported that the vicar of Hatherleigh was regarded throughout his parish as an honest man. The evidence nevertheless indicates that the level of anticlerical complaint increased significantly in the reformation decades.[7]

A sixth index was the physical violence employed against priests. Before the reformation this seems to have been relatively infrequent, though clerics were assaulted at Kennington in 1511 and St Teath in 1527. That it subsequently increased is indicated by a royal proclamation of 1547 and confirmed by local evidence. One priest, at St Cleer, was threatened by 'misruled persons' and put 'in dread of his life'. Another, at Launceston, was terrorized by some 20 men, who declared their determination to 'have a limb or an arm of him'. Both were reportedly beaten. Others were imprisoned, as at Awliscombe, or enstocked, as at Duloe and Silverton; one, in Somerset, was kidnapped, bound and held to ransom. According to convocation in 1532, clerics in London and elsewhere were injured and thrown into gutters, 'in the open street at midday'. London apprentices and servants beat priests in 1543.

Priests were attacked with fists, as at Paignton and Silverton, sticks, as at Colebrooke and Exminster, stones, as at Burrington, and even knives, swords or hatchets, as at Morebath, Wardley and Westminster. The assault at Westminster occurred as the priest said mass. That on the vicar of Morebath was provoked by his attempt to collect tithe, and those on the vicars of Colebrooke and Exminster by their attempts to discipline parishioners. 'What hast thou, priest, to do withal?', the vicar of Exminster was asked by Thomas Langmead, before being thrashed by the furious layman. Nor were killings unknown. One priest, collecting a mortuary in 1529, was reportedly almost buried alive by his own parishioners; and many were hanged by laymen for their supposedly treasonable utterances during the Henrician reformation, or for their involvement in the rebellions of 1536–69. In 1549 the most enthusiastic priest-killer was Lord Russell's servant Bernard Duffield, who mockingly dressed one victim in his mass vestments, with a holy water bucket, sacring bell and other ritual apparatus around him, and then hanged him in chains from his own church tower.[8]

Finally, attitudes were indicated also by contemporary observations. A number of pre-reformation observers reported the existence of anticlerical sentiment among the English people. 'The laymen be more bolder against the church than ever they were', complained Bishop Nix in about 1505. Antagonism to the clergy was similarly lamented by Archbishop Warham in 1510. 'In this time also', agreed the Dean of St Paul's, John Colet, in the same year, 'we [clerics] perceive contradiction of the lay people.' Clerical worldliness, he feared, had made the laity 'contrary unto us'. In 1528 a Syon monk, Richard Whitford, thought that a characteristic of his times was 'priesthood disdained'. In the same year the Archbishop of Canterbury observed that if the bishops had shown more enthusiasm for reform, 'the dignity of the church had not been so cold, and almost extinct in men's hearts'.

Such comments multiplied in the subsequent years. 'Nearly all the people here hate the priests', reported the imperial ambassador after the assembly of the Reformation Parliament in 1529. 'Now of late', asserted Christopher St German in 1532, 'the great multitude of all the lay people have found default as well at priests as religious.' Clerics were reportedly concluding that 'laymen love not priests'. In

1533 Sir Thomas More, though accusing St German of exaggeration, admitted the existence of the laity's 'grudge' against the clerical estate. 'Well nigh every man goeth about to oppress us poor men of the King's clergy', complained the Bishop of Salisbury in 1537. 'The whole order of priesthood ... is so run into contempt', observed Cuthbert Scott in 1544, 'that it is now nothing else but a laughing stock for the people.' In Edward's reign, recalled Dr Watson, 'the priests [were] had in derision'. In Mary's reign a Cornish vicar bemoaned the 'disturbance' experienced by priests in 'the unquiet time which lately hath grown'. 'The priests complain that we laymen love them not, nor have them in honour', it was reported from Norfolk in 1556. Cardinal Pole, in 1557, lamented that the English had, 'above all other nations that I know, dishonoured the ministers of the church and priesthood itself'.[9]

Contemporaries both clerical and lay, and both traditional and non-traditional, thus agreed on the reality of English anticlericalism before and during the official reformation. It should be noted, however, that their experience was more often of the south-east than of the north or west.

The evidence would suggest that while the pre-reformation relationship between priest and people was characterized more often by cooperation, or at least coexistence, than by open conflict, it nevertheless contained a number of actual and potential tensions. If the image of a nation irrevocably alienated from its priests is overdrawn, the opposite image – of a people still humbly submissive to its spiritual guides – is similarly open to objection. The evidence suggests also a continuing and apparently accelerating erosion of respect for clerics after 1529. Although some sources inevitably stress the discords rather than the harmonies, and although respect for the clergy had certainly not been eliminated by 1570, it therefore appears probable that attitudes towards this traditional religious institution experienced a significant modification in the reformation decades.

5

Parish Churches, Chapels (1)

The inhabitants of a pre-reformation parish might worship in a parochial chapel, or in the private chapel of a local gentleman. But the structure that accommodated the most important religious activities of the parochial community was invariably its church.[1]

Usually, though not always, it stood near the geographical centre of the parish. Its walls were generally of local stone, and its roofs of timber. Its most spacious component, the nave, housed the parishioners: here, during services, they stood, knelt or sat. The nave might also contain altars, as marks on rood screens indicate, as well as the images before which people prayed and the graves in which they were finally interred. But the building's focal point was always the chancel at its eastern end. Reserved to the clergy, it contained the high altar at which the central rite of traditional religion was performed. A rood screen divided it from the nave, though screen windows afforded parishioners a distant view. Its south wall contained a piscina, or basin for ritual ablutions, and sedilia, or seats for the priest and his assistants. Sometimes its north wall had a recessed sepulchre for the Easter celebrations.

Nave and chancel were usually supplemented by additional components. Transepts extended north and south from the main axis; aisles ran along both sides of nave and chancel; and chapels, enclosed by screens, projected from the plan or were contained within it. Surviving piscinae show that these areas often accommodated subsidiary altars, particularly for masses on behalf of guilds or individuals, though they might also boast venerated images or even shrines. South-west of the nave was usually a porch. This accommodated legal and commercial transactions as well as parts of processions, baptisms and marriages, for which purposes it was frequently fitted with stone seats; often it contained a stoup for holy water. It sometimes had an upper chamber, for storage, schooling or a priest's lodging.

Most churches possessed a substantial tower, usually west of the nave though sometimes elsewhere. It functioned as landmark, communal status symbol and amplification system for the ritually important bells. Finally, the entire building was encircled by a churchyard, with hedge or wall and lich-gate entrance. This accommodated not only burials and processions but also fairs, markets, revels and ales, for which reason a separate church house was often erected within it or nearby.

In many pre-reformation parishes such buildings continued to be constructed and furnished at substantial expense. Costs included not only the price of stone, timber and glass, and of their carriage from quarry, wood and workshop to the site, but also the wages of skilled masons, carpenters and glaziers and unskilled labourers. Although sizeable donations were sometimes received from wealthy ecclesiastics, like the prior of Montacute at Awliscombe, or from aristocratic families, like the Beauforts at Bovey Tracey, the principal benefactors were more often local gentlemen – like the Tames at Fairford, where they lie in a chancel chapel, or the Trecarrels at Launceston, rebuilt in 1511–24, where their arms are prominently displayed. Merchants and clothiers might also invest. The ornamented porch, south aisle and south chapel of about 1517 at Tiverton, and the fan-vaulted south aisle of 1526 at Cullompton, were financed by the wool merchants John Greenway and John Lane: the Lane aisle is decorated with sheep shears, ships and other emblems of the donor's trade. Smaller contributions came from less prosperous levels of the social hierarchy. At Golant, rebuilt in about 1509, the inscribed names of donors include five local fraternities. At Probus the magnificent tower was erected in 1520–3 by the parishioners themselves: they not only employed masons and labourers, but also transported the stone in their carts. Three windows at St Neot, dated 1523, 1528 and 1529, were donated by the local wives, young men and young women: 20 wives are portrayed, and 20 young women.[2]

That late medieval investment in church furnishings was often considerable is visibly demonstrated by the extant pulpits, benches, screens and glass. Devon's rood screens, for example, of which over 100 survive, were painted, gilded and enriched with fan vaults and carved cornices. A fifteenth- or early sixteenth-century origin is indicated by stylistic features, and dates are sometimes provided by heraldry, as on the Holne pulpit of 1504–19, or inscriptions, as on the St Neot glass of 1523–9. Since, however, such precision is usually impossible, it is difficult to assess whether investment remained as frequent in 1520–9 as in 1500–9 or 1480–9. More adequately attested are the dates of fabrics. The evidences include not only arms and inscriptions but also references in wills, wardens' accounts, episcopal registers and other documents. The four-staged and pinnacled tower at Chulmleigh, for example, is dated approximately by the will of William Coxhead, who bequeathed £20 to its construction in 1528.[3]

A survey of such sources from eight English counties has identified some 250 parish churches and chapels with dateable evidence of major construction in 1490–1569. In four counties of the north and west, namely Cheshire, Devon, Lancashire and Yorkshire, the number of churches and chapels experiencing such construction rose from 48 in 1490–1509 to 58 in 1510–29. In Devon, for example, the structures wholly or partly erected in 1520–9 alone included churches at Sandford and Thornbury, towers at Chulmleigh, Tiverton and Ugborough, porches at Awliscombe and Axminster, and aisles or chapels at Axminster, Cruwys Morchard, Cullompton, Honiton, Kentisbeare, Littleham, Marldon, Ottery St Mary and Tiverton. In four counties of the south and east, namely Kent, Middlesex, Norfolk and Suffolk, the figure in the first period was markedly higher, primarily because of their greater wealth. In the second period, however, it began to diminish: a total of 84 in 1490–1509 fell to 71 in 1510–29. The statistics may therefore indicate the beginnings of a downturn in churchbuilding zeal. There are also some signs of local indifference. In 1520–3 the reconstruction of Probus church was deliberately obstructed by a local gentleman, Nicholas Carminow, and in 1526 some parishioners of Great Dunmow refused to contribute to the building of a tower: the structure eventually raised was relatively unimpressive.[4]

For some parishioners, participation in the church extended beyond its construction and furnishing to its maintenance and supervision. A leading role was usually played by a small lay council, which, as at Halberton, was 'elect and chosen by all the parishioners', and entrusted with 'the rule, keeping and whole governance of the church goods'. Similarly elected were the two or more churchwardens. Mainly substantial farmers, tradesmen or craftsmen, these important officials received the church's revenues, maintained its fabric and furnishings, safeguarded its ritual apparatus, bought replacements and additions, and annually presented detailed accounts of their stewardship to their fellow parishioners. Urban corporations might also perform a supervisory function: at Dartmouth, the mayoral oath included a pledge to maintain divine service in St Saviour's church.[5]

The laity was vital also in the financial sustenance of parish churches. Incomes showed considerable variation: in 1529, Exeter Holy Trinity's £9 19s 7d contrasted with Ashburton's £61 14s 4d. For most, nevertheless, one major source of revenue was rent, paid by the tenants of lands and properties donated by previous generations. Similarly lucrative were church ales. Plymouth's was held in the churchyard at the feast of Corpus Christi, 'for the honour of God and for the increasing of the benefits of the church of St Andrew'. Some ales were associated with revels, in which parishioners dressed as Robin Hood and his men. Revenue was further supplemented by contributions from parish guilds, by annual collections like 'wax silver' and 'housling money', and by fees for pew hire, burial, intercession and a range of other services. Also important were gifts. In 1526, for example, Arksey's Nicholas Fitzwilliam donated 6s 8d to his own parish church, 3s 4d to Sprotbrough church and 2s each to nine other churches in the neighbourhood. In 1520–30 the percentage of testators bequeathing to parish churches ranged from 86–97 in Buckinghamshire, Huntingdonshire and Norwich, and 76 in Lincolnshire, to 65 in Somerset and 49–53 in Durham, Exeter and York dioceses.[6]

The picture, however, should not be overdrawn. By 1530 a substantial number of parishes had allowed their churches and chapels to fall into ruin. Most were in major cities like Canterbury, Lincoln, Norwich, Winchester and York, though some were in smaller towns like Ilchester and Sherborne. Other churches, moreover, suffered from neglect. Often the appropriator of the parish was at fault; sometimes, the parishioners themselves. In 260 Kent churches in 1511–12, defects were found in 32 per cent of chancels, 18 per cent of churchyards, 7 per cent of naves and 4 per cent of towers. In Sussex some 71 cases of disrepair were reported in 1520, at which date one Cornish church was 'in marvellous great ruin and decay, insomuch that God's divine service there conveniently could not be done'. Churches might also be deprived of income. At Ashburton in 1519–20 the Forde family disputed properties with the church, while at Exeter in 1518–29 the mayor and bailiffs acquired property from St Kerrian's by dubious means – thus allegedly ensuring 'the great decay of the said church for evermore'. Nor was robbery unknown, as is attested by the heavy locks on doors, chests and cupboards in pre-reformation churches. Churches were plundered at Tavistock, for example, in 1504–19, and at Blackawton, Powderham and Rattery in 1517–20. Sometimes they were desecrated by violence – as at Dartmouth in 1506, Ashburton in 1526 and St Teath in 1527 – and on occasion they evoked disdain. John Clarke of Claufield, in 1521, declared that 'it was as good to be buried in the field as in the church or churchyard'. James Algar, hearing in 1530 that a church had been robbed, 'said openly it made no great force, for the church hath enough already'.[7]

6

Parish Churches, Chapels (2)

Investment in churches did not cease in 1530. Pulpits and benches were still bought: the bench-ends at Dowland and Lewannick, for example, are dated by inscriptions to 1546. The continuing erection of screens is indicated by renaissance motifs, and occasionally by inscribed or documented dates: those at East Allington, Modbury and Throwleigh are from 1544–7. Apart, however, from some possibly Marian structures, as at Lustleigh, few screens are attributable to after 1547. Expenditure on stained glass also plunged. In the St Neot windows, the latest of the inscribed dates is 1529.[1]

Some church building continued after 1530. In Devon the structures datable to 1530–49 include the church at Woodland, aisles at Instow, Mortehoe and Tawstock, and towers at Cullompton and Exeter Allhallows. At Instow an inscription attests the construction of the north aisle by Richard Waterman and his wife in 1547. Nevertheless in the four analyzed counties of the north and west, the number of parish churches and chapels with major construction now fell substantially – from 58 in 1510–29 to 36 in 1530–49. In the four counties of the south and east the decline was even steeper. A total of 71 in 1510–29 dropped to only 29 in 1530–49.[2]

Construction projects were now sometimes abandoned. At Launceston, where most of the church had been impressively rebuilt in 1511–24, the outmoded fourteenth-century tower was allowed to remain. At Kea a rebuilding planned in 1532 was subsequently dropped, and at Cury an aisle planned in 1543 seems never to have been built. At Fremington a new tower was projected in 1545, when John Thomas left 20s for it; but the antiquated pre-perpendicular structure remains to this day. By 1538 an Oxford conservative was already nostalgic for the days when 'good men were wont to build and maintain churches'. Now, he lamented, 'they be more ready to pluck them down'. After mid-century the decline was even more dramatic. In 1550–69 the number of buildings with major new construction fell to a mere 12 in the north and west, and 10 in the south and east. Devon, for example, saw only the raising of the tower at Bradford in 1550 and the rebuilding of St Budeaux church in 1563.[3]

The waning of constructional activity was accompanied by a serious deterioration of financial health. Analysis of 32 southwestern parishes with accounts reveals that the average annual income per church in 1535–41 was £12 in rural areas and £20 in towns. The rural average remained at £12 in 1541–7, but fell to £6 in 1547–50 and only £4 in 1550–3. Even these totals were artificially boosted by the sale of ritual apparatus, which at Woodbury, for example, earned over £13 in 1550–1 alone. Some churches, like Morebath, now fell into debt. The level then rose to £8 in 1553–6 and £14 in 1556–9 and 1559–65. Since, however, the purchasing power of English money approximately halved in 1540–70, the failure of church incomes to double implies a substantial long-term fall in their real value. Decline was even steeper in the towns, where the average income fell to £18 in 1541–7, £12 in 1547–50, and £11 in 1550–3. The Edwardian figures were again inflated by sales, which earned over £63 for Exeter St Petrock's in 1550–1. Thereafter even the apparent recovery was only partial: the average rose to £13 in 1553–6, £16 in 1556–9 and £18 in 1559–65.[4]

One major factor in this downward trend was a fall in rents. Land or buildings that had maintained 'superstition' were frequently confiscated by the chantry commissioners: for example, property that had financed antiphons at Exeter St Petrock's was sold by the government in 1549. But there are signs also of an increasing willingness in local people to withhold or even expropriate the rents due to their churches. Southwestern cases are recorded at Ashburton, Bradstone, Broadclyst, Kentisbeare, Marystow, Pelynt and St Giles-in-the-Wood under Henry VIII, at Callington and North Lew under Edward and Mary, and at Coldridge, Exeter and Littlehempston under Elizabeth. A rent devoted to the maintenance of Callington church was withheld by Anthony Will in four successive years, while lands belonging to Marystow church were allegedly seized by five men.[5]

A second important factor was the disappearance of religious guilds, whose contributions to church income had often been substantial. Frequently dissolved in the last decade of Henry's reign, these organizations were comprehensively suppressed under Edward and only rarely revived under Mary. At Stratton and elsewhere this factor was the main cause of the church's financial decline. Other traditional revenues were beginning to weaken. The profitable Robin Hood revels apparently ended at Stratton in about 1540, and the ales themselves ceased at Ashburton, Morebath, Woodbury and elsewhere in Edward's reign. Of 17 English parishes with recorded ales, 12 ended them after 1549. Ales generally returned in Mary's reign and often survived into Elizabeth's. Sometimes, however, they were not restored, as at Boxford, or were neglected, as at St Gennys. Robin Hood festivities failed to reappear at Stratton, and had ended at Antony, Braunton and Chudleigh by 1565.[6]

Traditional collections were suppressed. Wax silver, for instance, and the gatherings at hocktide and on Plough Monday, generally ended under Edward, returned temporarily under Mary, and ceased permanently after 1559. Church rates were disrupted and sometimes resisted. At Aveton Giffard the parishioners had customarily contributed wheat, barley and oats to the maintenance of their church. Under Edward, however, they paid only money, 'as they could agree'; and even under Mary at least one parishioner refused to contribute. Others refused rates at Kenton in 1557 – when one offender admitted that he 'gave no penny to the church these three years, towards the reparation of the church' – and at Fremington in 1565.[7]

A final and particularly significant factor was the reduction of gifts. Accounts show that these often continued through Henry's reign. At Woodbury Richard Westcott bequeathed a ewe and lamb, and Mother Trapnell a ewe, in 1538–9, while at Morebath in 1542 parishioners donated both money and labour to repair their church house. After 1547, however, the accounts record either a substantial diminution of gifts, as at Holy Trinity, St John's Bow and St Petrock's in Exeter, or a virtual cessation, as at Ashburton, Exeter St Mary Steps, Morebath and Woodbury. Morebath, after 1548, saw 'no gift given to the church, but all from the church'. 'By time of King Edward VI', lamented its vicar, 'the church ever decayed'. Donations generally resumed under Mary – at Morebath the vicar noted 'how gently (for the most part) men have paid of their own devotion' – and continued into Elizabeth's reign.[8] Analysis of wills, however, suggests that by 1570 the level of voluntary contributions had been in decline for some three decades.

By the last years of Henry's reign, the percentage of testators bequeathing to parish churches had already started to fall – to 70 in Lincolnshire, 62–4 in Buckinghamshire and Huntingdonshire, 49 in Durham and York dioceses, and 43–6 in Exeter diocese, London and Somerset. Edward's reign saw accelerating decline, the figure falling to 45 in Somerset but plunging to 19 in Exeter diocese, 17 in Durham and York dioceses, and ten in Huntingdonshire and Lincolnshire. Mary's reign witnessed temporary revival, to 68 in Somerset but to a less impressive 48 in Exeter diocese and 36 in the dioceses of Durham and York. Decline resumed after Elizabeth's accession, the percentage slumping to 29 in Exeter diocese in 1560–9 and 11 in Durham and York dioceses in 1558–70. John Cosowarth of Colan, who bestowed £1 13s 4d on six churches in 1568, was now much less typical than Robert Eliot of Morchard Bishop, who gave nothing in 1565.[9]

An apparently increasing number of people proved willing to exploit the churches for private gain. Money detention, fraud and outright robbery occurred not only in the south-east, as in London and at Long Melford, but also in the south-west, as at Antony, Ashbury, Broadhembury, Halberton, Rewe, St Michael Penkevil, Spreyton, Stoke Gabriel and Week St Mary. At Long Melford the church was 'despoiled' by thieves who broke open its chest in 1532. John Ellis and others stole £37 from Broadhembury church in 1549, and as many as 24 parishioners detained money from Antony church in 1558. In 1557 Cardinal Pole lamented that many of London's parish churches had been 'in like manner spoiled as the monasteries were'.[10]

By 1557 a chapel at St Austell lacked both roof and glass, 'by reason whereof divine service cannot conveniently be celebrated in the choir'. Chapels formerly associated with saint cults or images were allowed to decay, as at St Endellion and Tredrizzick, or sold, as at St Day in 1568. But neglect was also the increasingly common fate of parish churches. This continued under Henry VIII – as at Nymet Tracey, where both chancel and churchyard were 'greatly in ruin and decay' by 1544–7 – and became widespread after 1547. It provoked an unprecedented number of complaints in Hampshire and Norfolk in 1550–1, and is abundantly attested by the visitation records of Mary's reign. Defects in fabric were reported from about one-third of churches in Bath and Wells diocese, from more than one-half in Lincoln diocese, and from almost two-thirds in the diocese of Canterbury.[11]

Only a minority of Marian parishes, like Prescot, made serious efforts to repair the damage. At Ewerby, in 1556, a gentleman still detained lead stripped from the chancel roof, while at North Lew the church still faced 'utter decay and ruin' in 1556–8. In Canterbury diocese the proportion of neglected churches had been reduced only to one-half by 1557. In this year Pole complained that London's parish churches had been 'suffered to fall down of themselves many', and warned Londoners that their continuing neglect would encourage the populace to 'wax brutish and wild'. The regime was similarly worried by the 'waste, decays and ruins of churches ... within this realm'. Nor did the situation improve after Elizabeth's accession. Fabric defects were discovered in 21 of the 56 Wiltshire parishes visited in 1565. In five deaneries of Norwich archdeaconry, between 1538–9 and 1569–70, defective church fabrics had increased from nil to nine, defective chancels or rectories from six to 23, and defective churchyards from three to 20. 'It is a sin and shame', lamented the Book of Homilies in 1562, 'to see so many churches so ruinous and so foully decayed in almost every corner. ... Suffer them not to be defiled with rain and weather, with dung of doves and owls, stares and choughs, and other filthiness, as it is foul and lamentable in many places in this country.'[12]

Disrepair was due not only to neglect but also – and increasingly – to deliberate destruction. By about 1542 a chapel at Barnstaple, once dedicated to Becket, had been 'profaned', while at King's Sutton, where a chapel of St Rumwold had stood 'of late', this was now 'defaced and taken down'. In 1548 four London chapels were 'pulled down'. Several York chapels were stripped under Edward and only partly restored under Mary. The repair of Ouse bridge chapel, though ordered by the council in 1554, was apparently not accomplished until 1556, while in 1555 it was agreed that the 'late chapel' on Foss bridge should become a storehouse.[13]

In parish churches, guild or chantry chapels were sometimes attacked. In 1541–2 the dissolution of St Mary's guild at Stratton was followed by the 'drawing down of Our Lady chapel', while in 1549, after the suppression of the important St George guild at Lostwithiel, its chapel in the church was 'defaced' on the mayor's orders. Chancel screens might also be defaced or destroyed, as at Exeter St John's Bow under Edward or at Bures under Elizabeth. Porches were sometimes mutilated by the 'taking down of the holy water stone', as at St John's Bow and Woodbury in 1559–61, and glass windows were frequently damaged or removed, as at St Breock in 1565. Anti-Catholic parishioners hurled stones at the windows of Hadleigh church in 1553.[14]

Some churches were extensively damaged or destroyed. In 1548 London's Strand church was 'pulled down, to make the Protector Duke of Somerset's place larger'. At Exeter, during anti-rebel operations in 1549, the mayor and aldermen 'pulled down and defaced' the towers of St Edmund's and St Sidwell's. At York in the same year, after the mayor and aldermen had received parliament's permission to 'put down the churches which they shall think superfluous', four were sold: the buyers were two gentlemen and two aldermen. In 1552 'the late church of St Helen's' was sold to a citizen, on condition that he build a house on its forefront 'or else deface and pull down the said church and walls'. Lesser men were equally eager for spoils: the lead of several churches was stripped and used by parishioners in 1551. In October 1553 the church at Halberton was vandalized by a mob of husbandmen, labourers and other local men, 'bent utterly to deface and abolish the honour of God'. They removed the pews and seats, pulled down the chancel screen, attacked the walls, stole glass and iron from the windows, and even tried to dig up the foundations. Similarly hostile laymen reportedly attempted to burn down a Suffolk church in 1554. Nor was such damage more than partly repaired in Mary's reign. In 1555 the York council noted that 'the late church and churchyard of St Peter the Little do now stand desolate', and Exeter's mayor and aldermen were rebuked by the regime for failing to repair the demolished church towers.[15]

The reformation decades may also have witnessed a deterioration of lay behaviour within the consecrated precincts. Acts of irreverence included the male wearing of headgear, the deliberate disruption of services, and the perambulation of churches in service time. A Kenton man, in addition, blithely allowed his livestock to wander into his parish church. Even more suggestive was the upsurge of 'quarrels, riots, frays and blood sheddings', which, according to a proclamation of 1552, 'doth daily more and more increase'. This phenomenon was most conspicuous in London and the south-east: in five Norfolk deaneries, cases of church disturbance rose from six in 1538–9 to 16 in 1569–70. But even the south-west saw a number of churches and chapels defiled by threatening language or abuse. At St Cleer in 1534 a group of men stormed into the church, 'even to the high altar', and issued threats. Actual violence, moreover, erupted not infrequently in churchyards and even in the sacred buildings. In about 1540 a man was 'violently and riotously' ejected from Launceston church by an angry crowd. In 1548 a Stoke Climsland man was dragged from his pew and threatened with death, while a dagger was drawn during a 'brawl' in North Huish church in 1569.[16]

Finally, overt contempt for churches was occasionally voiced. At Axminster, in 1535–6, Philip Gammon announced that he 'would never go to the church for devotion, or holiness of the place'. He added that 'he had as lies to be buried in a dung heap as in any church'. At Canterbury, in about 1543, Margaret Toftes expressed a desire to burn down her parish church and the 'idols' within it, while at Blunham, in 1556, Thomas Troughton declared flatly that 'the bells of the church be the devil's trumpets'. Such blatant hostility remained uncommon, but the evidence suggests that support for the sacred buildings declined substantially in the reformation years.[17]

7

Guilds

In its most elaborate form, as exemplified by the Boston fraternity of Our Lady, the religious guild in pre-reformation England was a wealthy corporation with priests, choristers and other employees. Much more commonly it was an association of neighbours with a relatively modest 'store' of goods and money, and few or no paid staff. Often it was financially dependent on gifts, fees for its services, and the sale of commodities like wool or ale.[1]

Some were monopolized by specific occupations or élites. Shoemakers constituted the Holy Trinity fraternity at Helston in 1517, while members of the civic oligarchy were expected to join the St George fraternity at Exeter by 1531. Others, like Morebath's Young Women and Young Men, recruited from particular age or gender groups. Most were in theory open to the parish, though often the poor were excluded by entry fees and other costs.[2]

Each guild was supervised by its own elected wardens. The office was filled by women as well as men, Leve Dolbeare controlling the wives' fraternity at Ashburton in 1525–6. Sometimes its responsibilities were refused, as at Stratton (by Thomas Priest) in 1519. Among the activities organized by such wardens were the worship of God, the honouring of saints and the veneration of sacred images. Most guilds were dedicated to God, Christ or a saint – whether an international celebrity, like Mary, or a local figure, like Ia, Meriasek or Winwaloe. The Camborne guild of St Ia maintained an image of its patron saint, while Stratton's High Cross guild bought wax, tapers and candles for the rood and painted Lent cloths for other images. The prime function of a guild, nevertheless, was usually intercession. Many arranged the burial of their departed members, sometimes with tapers, knells and processional crosses. Many, moreover, maintained bede rolls, listing their dead for the purpose of prayer. Most years in 1512–30 saw Stratton people buy places for their family or friends on the High Cross roll, which the vicar would recite. In 1527 Alison Pudner paid 6s 8d 'for her husband's grave, and to set him upon the bede roll'. An early sixteenth-century roll from North Petherwin begins with an exhortation to pray for the deceased brothers and sisters of St Michael's guild, then lists their names.[3]

Fraternities also hired priests to say intercessory masses at altars in the parish church. Ashburton church had chapels associated with the guilds of Sts John, Katherine, Margaret, Mary, Nicholas and Thomas, while masses were said in Helston church for the Holy Trinity guild's departed. At Stratton the High Cross guild not only maintained a chantry priest but also paid the vicar to perform obits and a 'bede man' to announce them with a bell. Even in small communities like North Petherwin, guilds arranged *diriges* and masses on behalf of their dead.[4]

Guild activities could be elaborate. Each year an armoured St George rode in parade to Lostwithiel church, where he heard a *dirige* in St George's chapel. The members of St George's guild then retired to enjoy their annual feast, and next day attended a requiem mass on their brethren's behalf. Such practices explain the fraternities' often extensive collections of ritual apparatus. Stratton's High Cross guild owned vestments, altar cloths and chalices; it paid for the blessing of five altar cloths in 1512, and of two chalices in 1518.[5]

The pre-reformation popularity of such organizations is suggested by the numbers in which they were maintained. London boasted some 81, and Norwich 21. Southwestern totals ranged from approximately 16 at Ashburton to 11–12 at Antony, Camborne, Chagford, North Petherwin and Winkleigh, nine at Stratton and 5–7 at Broadhempston, Morebath and South Tawton. Those at North Petherwin were dedicated to the Trinity, Our Lady, Allhallows and Sts Christopher, George, John, Luke, Michael, Nicholas, Patern and Thomas. Most guilds continued to recruit members, and some, like St Mary's at West Tarring, were new-formed in the 1520s. Others, however, were less thriving. In the Exeter churches they were relatively few. At Lincoln in 1519 Our Lady's guild was reportedly 'fallen in decay and almost desolate', while at Norwich in 1527 St Luke's guild was 'almost fully decayed'.[6]

In Cornwall and Devon, 57 per cent of testators bequeathed to religious guilds in 1520–9. In 1520 a Bovey Tracey man donated 3s

4d to every local 'store', while in 1526 a South Molton merchant ordered an annual *dirige* and mass from his High Cross guild, gave 1s each to seven fraternities, and left money, cloth and timber to build a 'chantry house' for the Trinity guild. Wills nevertheless suggest that in other regions, particularly the south-east, support was markedly less extensive. In 1520–30 the bequest percentage was only 14–15 in Durham and York dioceses and in Lincolnshire, ten in Huntingdonshire and two in Buckinghamshire. In Somerset it fell from 24 in 1520–4 to 16 in 1525–9, while in Norwich the percentage of donations to religious and craft guilds dropped from 22 in 1490–1517 to 14 in 1518–32.[7]

What happened to such groups in the reformation decades? The evidence indicates, firstly, that the late Henrician years saw their frequent dissolution. Often this was apparently in response to the campaign against images and the uncertainty concerning intercessions. Even in the south-west, guilds began to disappear from churchwardens' accounts. Several vanished at Ashburton, for example, after 1537, and at Camborne after 1540. Payments to guild priests sometimes ended, as at Exeter St John's Bow in 1536, and the accounts kept by or for guild wardens often ceased. Those of the Launceston guild of the Blessed Virgin ended after 1537; those of the Morebath guilds of Sts Antony, Mary, Sidwell and Sunday, after 1539; and those of the North Petherwin guild of St George – which had organized *diriges*, masses and a bede roll – after 1543. When the Woodbury guild of Our Lady ceased to operate in 1543, its beads, altar frontals and other goods were transferred to the church. Analysis of the southwestern accounts suggests that the average number of religious guilds maintained by each parish was beginning to decline. In rural communities it fell from six in 1535–41 to five in 1541–7; in towns, more steeply, from five to three. [8]

Although at Uffculme, for instance, the fraternity of Our Lady was bequeathed a chalice, mass book, bell, cruets and vestments by John Brown in 1535, in most places the level of donations was also beginning to fall. By the reign's last years, the percentage of wills with bequests to guilds had slipped to 28 in Exeter diocese, 13 in Somerset, ten in Lincolnshire, eight in Durham and York dioceses, four in London, two in Huntingdonshire and nil in Buckinghamshire. There were signs, moreover, of increasing willingness to exploit them. At York, in about 1533, funds belonging to the guilds of St Christopher and St George were embezzled by their masters. At Zeal Monachorum a parishioner defrauded two guilds in 1534. In 1538–44 laymen attempted to expropriate land from St Katherine's guild at Holsworthy and the Jesus guild at South Petherwin, while in 1544 over £16 in money and rings was stolen from the Yealmpton guild of Our Lady – resulting in the cessation of the 'good and godly purposes', presumably intercessions, for which they had been donated. At Antony a number of parishioners detained money from eight stores, while at Godmanchester the bailiffs burned deeds relating to two guilds and diverted their income to the town. In addition a number of guilds, including those dedicated to Corpus Christi at Coventry and the Holy Trinity at Sleaford, saw recruitment slump in the 1530s. Guild wardenships were refused at Chagford, Crediton and Morebath, and the Cullompton guild of St John was paralyzed by internal disputes.[9]

How did local communities react to the Edwardian orders for the suppression of their guilds? At Ashburton in 1548 some 20 parishioners attempted to resist the confiscation of lands and market tolls from St Lawrence's guild. The more usual reaction, however, was again compliance. Accounts throughout England show that by 1550 the dissolution was almost complete. At Modbury the High Cross, Our Lady and Young Men's guilds compiled their last accounts in 1546–7. By 1549 only three survived at Antony, and one at Camborne and Stratton: all soon ended. At Woodbury the fraternity *diriges* ceased in 1548, and sheep once owned by St Margaret's store were sold in 1549–50. In the rural parishes of the south-west, the average number of guilds fell to two in 1547–50 and 0.4 in 1550–3; in the urban parishes, to two and 0.1.[10]

The few survivors were invariably shorn of their intercessory and image-supportive functions. At North Petherwin, for example, St Christopher's guild had regularly organized a *dirige*, mass, and bede roll recitation. It remained in existence throughout the reign, but after 1548 these activities were conspicuously absent from its accounts. Bequests to guilds, moreover, plunged in 1547–9, then ceased: not one appears in the analyzed wills of 1550–3 from Huntingdonshire, Lincolnshire, Somerset, or the dioceses of Durham, Exeter and York. This Edwardian devastation of the guilds may help to explain the aisle deletion still evident in many parish churches.[11]

Some guilds revived in Mary's reign, albeit slowly. Morebath waited until 1556 before seeing the 'beginning of the Young Men wardens again, that stayed eight year [i.e. ceased in 1548–56] and had no wardens'. Yet only one-third of the southwestern parishes appear to have reconstituted as many as two, three or four of their traditional groups: Coldridge, with its Hogners, Grooms, Whitsun wardens and St Antony's wardens, was unusually well provided. In another third, one only was recorded; and in the final third, none. In 1553–9, therefore, the average number of guilds was no more than two in the rural parishes and one in the urban. Throughout the realm, moreover, accounts confirm that only a small minority of fraternities were ever restored.[12]

Nor did the restored groups necessarily resume their traditional functions. St Brannoc's guild at Braunton might buy provisions 'against St Brannoc's obit for the brothers and sisters', and hire a priest to say mass, but this was far from typical: guild intercessions were recorded in less than one-quarter of the southwestern parishes in 1553–9. Many groups were now little more than fund-raising agencies of their parish churches. At North Petherwin the guild of St Christopher failed to revive the *diriges*, masses and bede roll recitations that it had organized until 1548, while at Stratton the obits and bede roll readings formerly sponsored by the High Cross guild seem never to have been restored. Equally significant was the failure of Marian guilds to attract donations. In Exeter diocese the proportion of testators remembering them was 2 per cent; in Durham and York dioceses, and in Somerset, it was nil.[13]

It is therefore unsurprising that responses to the Elizabethan assault on guilds were predominantly acquiescent. Many, like the Hogners' and St Antony's at Coldridge, were dissolved in 1559–60; others, like St Christopher's at North Petherwin or Our Lady's at Chudleigh, vanished in the subsequent decade. In both urban and rural parishes the number of religious guilds in 1559–65 averaged only one, and even this had often ended by 1570. The few survivors, moreover, had been almost wholly stripped of their specifically Catholic functions. At Chagford they seem merely to have raised money for the church. At Braunton, St Brannoc's and another guild still dispensed food and drink to the poor on 'brotherhood day', but no longer arranged the traditional intercessions. The North Petherwin guild of St Christopher survived in a similarly emasculated state until its suppression in 1566. In 1560–9 such groups were sometimes financially exploited, as at Ashbury, and in most areas –

including even the dioceses of Durham, Exeter and York – proved unable to attract a single bequest.[14]

The suppression of guilds entailed the damaging of parish church finances, the loss of social services, and the end of activities like image veneration and prayer for the dead. In three decades, and against only limited resistance, another important component of traditional religion had been destroyed.

Part Two: Practices

8

RITES (1)

Of the various rites performed by pre-reformation priests, several marked the stages of human life. Baptism was administered after birth; confirmation, in childhood; marriage, in maturity. Death was preceded by extreme unction and followed by obsequies. Some observances, however, were annual: they included Easter vigils, Corpus Christi processions, and the distribution of candles, ashes and palms on Candlemas day, Ash Wednesday and Palm Sunday. Others were more frequent. One was confession, from which ensued absolution. The most important was mass, which transformed bread and wine into Jesus' body and blood; it was performed in language incomprehensible to lay spectators, and in an area separated from them by a screen.

Pre-reformation people continued to express faith in such rites. 'Without baptism', proclaims an inscription of about 1522 on the Goodmanham font, 'no soul may be saved.' Communion bread was known widely as 'Our Lord's body', and the communicant as one who 'receiveth his Maker'. Painters, glaziers and sculptors – like those who produced East Anglia's fonts – still reverently depicted the seven sacraments of traditional religion.[1]

Sometimes, however, and especially in Lincoln and London dioceses, they were already challenged. Speakers 'against the sacrament of the altar' included two men and a woman of London diocese in 1517 and Richard Collins of Ging in 1521. Collins protested that it was 'not very God, but a certain figurative thing of Christ in bread', and that 'the priest hath no power to consecrate the body of Christ'. Others, like Long Witham's John French, asserted that 'priests had not power to absolve from sins'. Such views were rarer in the north and west, though in 1505–6 a Devon man declared that a servant had as much ability as a priest to hear confessions and absolve. The popularity of tales about people who disbelieved in transubstantiation suggests, moreover, that doubts were not uncommon. The story of St Gregory's vision appeared in both literature and art, as on a Paignton screen of about 1526.[2]

Attitudes towards rites are indicated not only by oral, written and artistic expressions but also by levels of participation. Most people still sought immediate baptism for their children, as at Wembury in about 1535, and arranged traditional funerals for themselves, as at Honiton in 1528. Many, like Ashburton's John Rich in 1517–18, still submitted to confession, penance and absolution. Processions were often well supported, as at Long Melford on Palm Sundays. Attendance at mass seems generally to have been high – on both Sundays and weekdays, according to a foreign visitor in about 1500.[3]

At Dartmouth in 1501, on the other hand, John Chevilstone preferred playing games to attending mass. A man absented himself from services at River in 1511; a woman abandoned church-going in Rutland in 1518; and many people watched bear-baiting instead of attending evensong at Beverley in 1520. Nor were attenders always reverent. One, at Woodchurch in 1511, 'jangleth and talketh in the church ..., and letteth others to say their devotions'. Others, like Helen Heyer in London diocese, refused to be confessed by priests.[4]

Attitudes may also be gauged by levels of expenditure. In about 1500 an Italian was impressed by the crucifixes, candlesticks, censers, patens, cups and other treasures to be seen in England's parish churches. These were accompanied by a rich variety of vestments, like the cassock, cope, surplice and stole shown on a brass of about 1520 at St Just in Roseland. By 1529 Long Melford possessed over 152 cloth items, such as altar cloths, sepulchre cloths and banners, as well as 44 vestments and copes. There were 50 metal items – like crosses, paxes for congregational kissing, and pyxes for the sacrament – and 13 chalices, together with 46 mass books and other pieces of liturgical literature. More typically, Exeter St Mary Major had some 20 vestments and copes, five chalices, numerous vessels, cloths, frontals and candlesticks, and a variety of books.[5]

Such equipment was often of relatively recent purchase. The accounts for 1500–30 reveal persistent expenditure on plate, vestments, cloths, books and other apparatus. Parishioners' gifts are recorded in both accounts and wills: in 1524, for example, Christopher Stephen bequeathed a missal to Highbray church. The extant equipment from this period includes lecterns for service books, like Bigbury's of 1504–19; fonts, like Goodmanham's of about 1522; and chalices and patens, like Morval's paten of 1528–9.[6]

Expenditure was sometimes high. Inhabitants of Golant contributed £10 towards Tywardreath's bells in about 1508, while copes and vestments cost some £39 at Ashburton in 1528–9 and £27 at South Tawton in 1531–2. More often it was less spectacular. In 1520–1, for example, Ashburton's spending included 10s for mending vestments, 5s 6d for an altar cloth and 4s 9d for service books. It is also evident that many early sixteenth-century parishes retained ageing apparatus instead of buying new. Some individuals were not afraid to steal: at Bratton, two men seized a chalice, mass book and vestments in 1500–15.[7]

Support for the traditional rites remained substantial; but enthusiasm was not ubiquitous, and hostility not unknown. How successfully did they withstand the Henrician Reformation?

A considerable number of people continued to speak or write in their defence, as at Axminster in 1535–6. On the other hand, conservatives lamented in 1536 that mockery of the Catholic rites was now 'commonly preached, thought and spoken'. Although this phenomenon was most conspicuous in the south-east – a Suffolk traditionalist, in 1534, bemoaned the rise of 'many false opinions and schisms against the sacraments of the church' – it was discernible also elsewhere. Infant baptism, for example, was decried by Axminster's Philip Gammon, and the font abused as a 'stinking tarn' by Dewsbury's William Bull. Many men (it was said in 1536) now dismissed holy water as 'more savourer to make sauce with', and a Canterbury woman announced that her daughter 'could piss as good holy water as the priest could make any'. Penance was challenged by several people at Rye. Confession was denied in London and at Axminster, Colchester, Dewsbury and Topcliffe. By 1542, according to the Yorkshireman Richard Flint, 'there was a saying in the country that a man might lift up his heart and confess himself to God almighty, and needed not to be confessed at a priest'.[8]

But it was the sacrament of the altar that attracted the most denunciation. 'Is it anything else but a piece of bread', many people were reportedly asking by 1536, 'or a little pretty piece round Robin?' It was attacked by a number of dissidents in London diocese – one grocer called it 'the baken god' – as well as at Mendlesham, Rye, Salisbury and elsewhere. Rye townsmen allegedly derided the mass as 'of a juggler's making', and church services as 'of no more effect than the bleating of a cow to her calf'.[9]

Accounts and wills show that many parishes and individuals continued to invest in altars, fonts, chalices, vestments, books, organs, bells and other ritual apparatus. A late Henrician date for furnishings like the East Down font and the Swimbridge font cover is suggested by their early renaissance motifs. By 1540, nevertheless, high expenditure was becoming more rare. Vestments cost only £12 at Exeter St Petrock's in 1540–1, £7 at Antony and Stratton in 1545–6 and £6 at Morebath in 1546–7. Sometimes, as at Silverton, donations towards apparatus were retracted.[10]

Parochial collections of equipment were in fact often beginning to diminish. At Long Melford, by 1541, cloth items had fallen in number to about 84, copes and vestments to 42, metal items to 35, chalices to nine and service books to 40. Some losses were due to sale. In 1543–6, chalices and other treasures were sold for over £41 at Plymouth, some £16 at Dartmouth and over £6 at Stratton. Other losses were due to fraud or theft. In 1534 a thief stole a chalice from Morebath church. In about 1545, at Davidstow, the constable persuaded the parishioners to sell their best chalice, then retained the proceeds for himself. He similarly removed bells from local chapels. In about 1546, 'of their devilish minds against God and Our Blessed Lady', Christopher Sampford and John Warren stole vestments, chalices, ornaments and service books – together worth over £40 – from the church at Halberton.[11]

Observances not yet targeted by the regime remained regular features of parochial life. Vigils, for example, were still mounted at Easter, hosts paraded at Corpus Christi, and Catholic baptisms, masses and funerals unceasingly performed. But there is evidence also of non-participation. By 1541 a substantial number of Londoners avoided confession, communion or church services, or acted irreverently at the consecration. At Colchester St Giles', in 1540–2, more than half the adults reportedly absented themselves from services on Sundays and holy days. At Pluckley, in 1543, a majority of the parishioners no longer received holy bread. Even the south-west saw some obstruction of the mass, refusal to contribute holy bread, and alleged absence from services or confession. In Cornwall the host was 'irreverently handled'.[12]

How did men and women react to the Edwardian onslaught against traditional rites? There were attempts at non-violent resistance. Some gentlemen attended mass in the French ambassador's residence or at Princess Mary's court, while at Oakham a priest attracted people to his private Latin services. Latimer would recall that Edward's reign had seen 'mass mongers in corners'. Of large scale Catholic recusancy, however, there is no sign. Even less extensive was physical resistance, with exceptions like the 'tumultuous assembly' in one Cornish hundred in 1547.[13]

In 1549 the Cornish and Devonian rebels demanded traditional baptism and confirmation as well as holy bread, holy water, palms, ashes and 'all other ancient old ceremonies used heretofore by our mother the holy church'. Mass was to be celebrated, in Latin, 'as it hath been in times past'. Consecrated bread was to be displayed for worship, and received by the laity (without wine) at Easter alone. The rebels revived the Latin mass at Sampford Courtenay and elsewhere, and reportedly marched behind the reserved sacrament. Nevertheless it is certain that their motives were by no means exclusively religious; that even within the south-west their recruitment was relatively limited, and opposition substantial; and that the English people as a whole showed little inclination to rise in defence of the ancient rites. Outside the two counties, observed John Hooker, the new service was 'with all obedience received in every place'. The riots in Buckinghamshire, Hampshire, Oxfordshire and Yorkshire were small-scale and only partly inspired by religion. Catholic rites were not supported by the Norfolk rebels, and even the north failed to rise on their behalf.[14]

Most local communities in fact proved acquiescent in the official assault. In 1548, a conservative later recalled, 'all godly ceremonies and good uses were taken out of the church within this realm'. Wardens' accounts throughout England attest the disappearance of ashes, palms, Candlemas candles, paschal candles, font hallowings, Easter vigils, and Rogationtide, Corpus Christi and other processions. In London, 'all going abroad of processions' was 'put down'; in Yorkshire, 'no procession was made about the fields'. Funerals with knells, crosses and tapers generally ended. In 1549, moreover, 'the holy mass was utterly deposed throughout all this realm of England'.[15]

The accounts for 1547–9 show also that most parishes obediently compiled inventories, sent representatives before the commissioners, and even began to deliver treasures into confiscation. Woodbury's surrendered goods included three copes and ten vestments. Morebath was untypical in distributing vestments, copes, banners and a chalice to sympathetic individuals. Even the more comprehensive seizures of 1550–3 appear to have encountered little opposition. 1553 saw plate, vestments and copes 'taken out of all the churches of London and about'. In Suffolk the commissioners removed most of the remaining plate from Long Melford and elsewhere. 'In the execution of this commission', reported their Devon counterparts, 'we have found the people very quiet and conformable.' Even Morebath surrendered two copes, two tunicles, a paten and a pax.[16]

Some bells were removed, or retained only by the payment of fines. Extensive compliance with the decree against service books is indicated by frequent Marian expenditure on replacements. Woodbury's Latin books were despatched to Exeter, 'according to the commandment', while Long Melford's were 'scattered abroad, and delivered to certain light persons': many were 'spoiled and mangled'. Morebath was again unusual in entrusting its mass book to a parishioner. Fonts, chrismatories and Easter sepulchres were damaged or neglected: many would need repair in Mary's reign. Pyxes, for suspending hosts over altars, were in 1548 'pulled down in divers places through the realm'. Even in Yorkshire they were 'despitefully cast away, as things most abominable'.[17]

The parochial collections of apparatus were devastated not only by official confiscations, but also by an unprecedented spate of sales and thefts. Of 90 parishes with Edwardian accounts, sales occurred in at least 69. Woodbury sold goods in 1547, 1547–8, 1548–9, 1550–1 and 1552–3. Those in 1547 alone included sacrament canopies, sepulchre cloths and albs as well as a surplice, altar cloth, pax and pyx. Banners, candlesticks, altar cloths and other goods were 'sold away without commission' at Morebath, and plate worth over £200 was sold by eight of the Exeter churches.[18]

Thefts multiplied – not only in the south-east, where Wennington church (for example) was pillaged three times, but also in the south-west, where at least 22 churches were attacked. Woodbury was robbed of chalices, cruets, housling towels, altar cloths and sepulchre cloths as well as a cross, pax, censer, ship and pall, and 'a fine white canopy cloth to hang over the sacrament'. Torrington's losses, valued at £200, reportedly ensured the 'utter empoverishing' of its church: they included chalices, a cross, and a monstrance to carry the sacrament in processions. Exeter St Sidwell's, which lost all its vestments and a large quantity of plate, was 'spoiled of all things moveable'.[19]

Even more significant was local cooperation in the attack on altars. The deposition of such structures in churches almost everywhere is recorded by the Edwardian accounts and confirmed by Marian expenditure on their re-erection. In several places it preceded the opening of the official campaign in April 1550. By November the council was confident that it had been executed in most parishes, and by December it was comprehensively enforced. Even in the north, recalled Robert Parkyn, 'all altars of stone was taken away'. The accounts show that although compliance was usually more rapid in London, Essex and Kent than in Devon, Worcestershire and Yorkshire, by the end of 1551 it was virtually complete. The four Lancashire parishes that retained altars in 1552 were therefore far from typical. [20]

Often the deposed structures were sold. Woodbury paid for 'the taking down of the altars', rewarded a man for 'carrying out of the rubble of the altars', and then sold 'stones of the altars' and '3 broad stones that lay upon the altars'. Although some were bought by religious conservatives, like Richard Troughton in Lincolnshire, many were treated with scant respect. At Dartmouth the altar stones were thrown into the churchyard, and their frontals into a vault, while two coffers were filled with the broken fragments of the reredos. At Halberton, impelled by his 'cankered mind toward God's service', Christopher Sampford 'did spoil and take away the high altar, and laid the altar stone, sanctified, in his kitchen; where he keepeth the same to convey his kitchen and filthy waters upon'. Other altars were used to cover tombs, as at Ulcombe, pave roads, as at Smarden, or build chimneys, as at Sutton Vallence.[21]

Finally, hostility to the rites was now frequently voiced. Philip Nichols, for example, denounced mass, confession, palms, ashes, and holy bread and water: these were 'fondly [i.e. foolishly] instituted, and much more fondly used among the people'. Mass, in particular, was widely attacked. London heard 'much speaking against the sacrament of the altar': 'some called it Jack-of-the-box, with divers other shameful names.' In the south-west, the rebels complained that 'many' were speaking against transubstantiation, 'with many other abused terms'. Even in Yorkshire, to Parkyn's dismay, the host was 'villainously despised': people were 'uttering such words thereby as it did abhor true christian ears for to hear'.[22]

9

RITES (2)

The first year of Mary's reign saw the re-erection of high altars by most parishes with accounts. Some preceded the order of December 1553; others followed it. Woodbury's provided three days' work for a mason and appentice. On the other hand, high altars were still absent or defective in 36 of the 226 Bath and Wells churches in 1554, and in 47 of the 243 Kent churches in 1557. Goudhurst, for example, was ordered to 'enquire where the high altar stone was bestowed'. Many parishes, including Woodbury, restored secondary altars in 1553–4. Elsewhere, however, the process was delayed or never happened. Secondary altars had not been adequately restored in several Devon churches by 1555, or in 90 of the 243 Kent churches by 1557. At Goudhurst an altar stone still lay abandoned in the church. Of 134 parishes with Marian accounts, only four appear to have rebuilt more than two such structures.[1]

The accounts for 1553–9 record innumerable payments for vestments, cloths, canopies, banners, crosses, chalices, pyxes, censers, sepulchres, bells, books and other apparatus. The chalice at Braddock is a rare survival. By pre-reformation standards, however, the investment was seldom impressive. More typical than the £23 devoted to Woodbury's bells were the £6 spent on a vestment at Exeter St John's Bow, the £4 on a cope at Coldridge, or even the £1 10s on a cope and vestments at Molland. Easingwold, in 1553–6, mended a sepulchre and organ, and bought surplices, service books, bell wheels, a vestment, a sacrament covering and a holy water can; but the total expenditure was only around £8.[2]

Equipment was sometimes donated by groups, like the Morebath wives, or individuals, like Exeter's William Hurst. Such gifts, however, occur only once in the southwestern wills; and their general insufficiency is confirmed by the resort of most parishes to capital depletion or compulsory rates. Compulsion was sometimes resisted, the inhabitants of Raskelf (for example) refusing to finance the restocking of their mother church at Easingwold. Often, moreover, the equipment used in Mary's reign was not a new purchase but a pre-Edwardian survival. Some had been retrieved from confiscation. Service books, for example, had been restored to Woodbury; plate, including a cross, chalice and holy water bucket, to Camborne; and vestments to Ashburton, Dartmouth, South Tawton and Woodbury. Some had been taken out of local storage, as at Long Melford, or returned by local purchasers, as at Oxford – though sometimes this required payment, as at Ludlow, or legal action, as at Luton.[3]

Nevertheless much of the confiscated, sold or stolen apparatus was not recovered. Norwich diocese saw seven suits concerning goods detention in 1555, and Winchester diocese nine in 1556. Goods were still detained by Exeter's mayor and aldermen in 1555, and by several inhabitants of Lincoln diocese in 1556: a gentleman of Coston had vestments, and a Westbury man a silver chalice. In 1557 the authorities were still seeking 'the restitution of the church goods within Colchester and the hundreds thereabout, to the use of God's service'. Nor did theft cease. Vestments and altar cloths, and even 'the pyx with the sacrament', were stolen by a thief who broke into Morebath church in 1554.[4]

Only very seldom, therefore, were the extensive pre-reformation collections of equipment ever matched in Mary's reign. Even the officially required minimum had not been attained in 23 per cent of Lancashire churches and chapels by 1554, or in 9 per cent by 1557. Deficiencies were discovered in 20 per cent of Salisbury diocese churches in 1556, and pyxes for displaying hosts were absent from 9 per cent of Somerset churches in 1557–8. Chalices were missing in 24 of the 243 Kent churches in 1557; so were patens in 35, altar candlesticks in 43, holy water stoups in 45, pyxes for host display in 45, pyxes for the communion of the sick in 53, altar crosses in 60 and service books in 61. There were no lights before the sacrament in 96, and cloth items like vestments and altar hangings had not been adequately restored in as many as 223. Font covers, processional crosses, paxes and sepulchres were similarly often missing or defective. While some churches met most of the official requirements, a considerable number remained seriously depleted.[5]

Robert Parkyn rejoiced that Mary's reign saw the return of 'all old ceremonies laudably used beforetime in holy church'. Certainly it witnessed the revival of the traditional sacraments, particularly mass, and of many processions, like that for London's mayor, aldermen and craft guilds. Also restored were Catholic funerals, Candlemas candles, Palm Sunday palms and Easter vigils. The speed of restoration varied. Some parishes – or their priests – revived mass swiftly after Mary's accession; more waited until her August proclamation. By September, at least in Yorkshire, churches without mass were reportedly 'very few'. The return of other practices seems usually to have followed official orders, like those requiring palms and ashes in December and processions in the following March.[6]

A substantial number of people appear to have welcomed the revival. Catholics claimed that in Yorkshire, and even in some London parishes, mass was restored 'not by commandment but of the people's devotion'. The prime movers were sometimes laymen, like Hadleigh's John Clarke and Poole's Thomas White. York city council revived processions on St George's day and at Corpus Christi, 'according to the old usage', while the inhabitants of Hatherland persuaded their parson to restore masses, processions and other observances in their chapel. In Cornwall John Combe thanked God that, after four years, he had again heard mass and received holy bread and water, and Agnes Priest's husband and children were so 'addicted to the superstitious sect of popery' that they forced her to participate in the restored rites.[7]

Many, however, were less enthusiastic. Sometimes, as at Ipswich and Kingsnorth, baptism and confirmation were neglected. Confession was avoided in London, Devon, Lincoln diocese and elsewhere. Processions were missed by some 100 Londoners in 1554, and those ordered by their bishop in 1556 were (to a conservative's dismay) 'but little looked upon'. In 1557 processions had still not been revived by the people of Goudhurst, and were being evaded by the mayor and aldermen of Bristol. At Axminster Thomas Perry absented himself for nine months, and Roger Gill for twelve. Menheniot's Twelve Men obstructed the distribution of holy water to local households and of communion to the sick – a rite rejected also by Martin Alley and his wife.[8]

Nor were all eager for the mass. By January 1554 it had still not been restored in some 30 London churches. At Halberton the lessee refused to restart masses in a chapel, and at North Lew the revived service was obstructed by a layman's withholding of rent. Communion was avoided by many people, particularly in London, Kent and Suffolk, and a considerable number absented themselves from services. In 1554 some 190 Londoners were charged with absences, while objectors at Colchester 'and thereabouts' dissuaded others from attending. At Much Bentley, it was reported in 1557, three dissidents not only avoided services but also 'daily allure many other away from the same'. In Kent, this year, some 45 people were accused of non-attendance, and Wye butchers opened their shops to customers in service time. Southwestern absentees included Boyton's Agnes Priest, who persistently 'made excuses not to go to the popish church', and Upottery's Joan Sweetland, who 'never came to her parish church'.[9]

Significant numbers still dared to speak against the rites. Confession and absolution were denounced – in London, for instance, by John Leafe – while holy bread and water were derided. Processions were mocked by Brampton's Laurence Burnby. The mass, above all, evoked protests from 'such as was of heretical opinions'. A Cornish woman reviled 'that foul idol which, with your mass, you make a god'. At Beverley, it was charged, an alehouse keeper 'doth not only himself rail against the holy and blessed sacrament of the altar, but also hath many and sundry other evil disposed persons resorting to his house, that in like manner rail against the same most holy sacrament'. In London, in 1554, some 90 people were accused of speaking against the sacrament, while at Colchester, in 1557, it was 'blasphemed and railed upon in every alehouse and tavern'. Similar abuse was hurled by pamphlets, ballads and rhymes, as in Norfolk in September 1553.[10]

Some dissidents refused to kiss the pax, as at Ipswich, or walked around the church at sacring time, as at Bradninch. Others used gestures like turning from the altar: 40 people were so charged in London in 1554. One Londoner halted a procession by wresting the sacrament from the priest; another mockingly presented a pudding to a prebendary as he processed. Consecrated hosts were stolen at Halifax and Hull. Protest might also be violent, particularly in 1553–4. London saw 'tumults over the mass', reportedly compelling Bishop Gardiner to deploy a guard of 200 men. At Hadleigh the rebuilt altar was pulled down by local men, and mass had to be said under armed guard. At Poole, too, the altar was demolished, forcing Catholics to hold masses in a private house.[11]

Powderham's William Thorning evaded punishment for three years before being charged with absence from communion and confession. Seven Marden parishioners avoided communion for three years, while an Ipswich shoemaker 'received but twice these 17 years'. Such cases suggest that less persistent offenders often went uncharged, and therefore unrecorded. Certainly in several towns the presentments for religious offences omitted a number of their known dissenters. One Ipswich priest reportedly accepted bribes to erase names from his register of non-communicants. It therefore seems probable that Marian presentments constitute only the visible tip of a considerably larger non-Catholic iceberg.[12]

What happened to the rites after Elizabeth's accession? In London some people attended mass at the French ambassador's house in 1560, and others had mass 'and other superstitious ceremonies' performed in their homes in 1567. Clandestine services occurred also in the houses of some peers and gentlemen, including several in Herefordshire in 1564. On the other hand, public support for the old rites was now relatively rare. One exception was provided by Thomas Stephens, who still spoke in favour of holy bread and water at Alphington in 1567 – though his zeal was not shared by the five neighbours who informed against him. Even rarer were attempts to defend the rites by force. In 1559, and for the next ten years, the campaign against them encountered no opposition remotely comparable to 1549: even local riots were unknown. Only in 1569, and then only in parts of the north-east, did rebels revive the mass in parish churches. At Sedgefield, for example, a holy water stoup was re-erected, and an abandoned altar stone hauled back to the church. Such objects were again demolished after the rebellion's collapse.[13]

That most early Elizabethans were markedly less enthusiastic about the rites is confirmed by their reactions to the official assault. Some, especially around London, indeed anticipated the government's decrees. In 1559 the abbot of Westminster bewailed the people's readiness to 'run before laws': he lamented their 'spoiling of churches', 'pulling down of altars', and 'most blasphemous treading of sacraments under their feet, and hanging up the knave of clubs in the place thereof'. Outside London, some communities like Rye also removed altars before the official prohibition of the old liturgy in April 1559. In that month John Jewel rejoiced that in many places the mass had 'of itself fallen to the ground, without any laws for its discontinuance'. In most parishes, moreover, the subsequent campaign appears to have encountered either acquiescence or cooperation. In the south-west, for example, the royal commissioners reached Exeter in September, and promptly 'forbade any more masses or popish services to be used'. The southwestern accounts for 1559–60 duly record not only an end to expenditure on Catholic apparatus but also a virtually total cessation of prohibited rites. In this and other regions, Candlemas candles, Easter vigils, Catholic funerals and other traditional practices now disappeared. Processions 'after the old fashion' were seen in some places in 1559, then ceased.[14]

Parishes again submitted to the inspection, confiscation and destruction of their ritual equipment. Copes, altar cloths, crosses, censers and books, 'with much other gear', were publicly burned in London in August 1559. That autumn Exeter St Mary Major saw the melting down of candlesticks, a censer and a cross, and the removal of a pax, canopy, oil box, holy water bucket and small bells. At Crediton a sepulchre and paschal candle were 'cut in pieces', a tabernacle, censer and four candlesticks 'broken', and two holy water pots and a cross 'broken in pieces'. The damage inflicted on vestments is exemplified by the St Mary Arches cope, from which a figure of Christ has been ripped.[15]

Large scale selling also recommenced. By late 1559 Long Melford's once magnificent collection had been reduced to eight items of cloth, seven of metal, and three vestments; there were no chalices or service books. Exeter St Mary Major sold cloths from its altars and sepulchre in about 1559, and copes, vestments, cloths, chalices, bells and plate shortly after 1567. Copes, vestments, cloths, a canopy and a chalice were sold at Ashburton in 1568–70. Service books also disappeared. St Breock lost a psalter, processional and manual in 1560, and a mass book, portis, processional and manual before 1565. 'Old papistical books in the Latin tongue' were destroyed at Aysgarth in 1567. Morebath was again untypical, entrusting a chasuble, altar cloth, banner and mass book to sympathetic individuals.[16]

In 1566 over 143 Lincolnshire churches were subjected to official scrutiny, in order to discover all 'superstitious' objects in useable condition. Vestments were found in only 36, plate or other equipment in 29, service books in four and Easter sepulchres in two. A number of objects had been removed under Edward and never restored under Mary, but most had been destroyed, defaced, sold, stolen or otherwise lost since 1559. Of the dated losses of vestments, some 43 per cent occurred in 1559–62 and 57 per cent in 1563–6. For equipment the percentages were 51 and 49, for Easter sepulchres 59 and 41, and for service books 76 and 24. At Witham, in 1559, the Latin books were burned, and vestments sold and defaced, while censers, candlesticks, bells, a cross and a chrismatory were sold to a Stamford pewterer, and a holy water stone was 'put to profane use'. The devastation at Kelby, though mostly delayed to 1566, proved equally comprehensive – 'so that there now remaineth no trash nor trumpery of popish peltry in our said church of Kelby'.

Some vestments were converted into surplices, pulpit covers or communion table cloths. Others were turned to sacrilegious uses, including clothes at Denton and Horbling, bed hangings at Dowsby and cushions at Haconby. Service books were transformed into spice containers at Horbling, and Easter sepulchres into a communion table at Castle Bytham, a bier for corpses at Stallingborough, a clothes press at Denton and even a chicken coop at Durrington.[17]

The widespread effectiveness of the campaign against ritual equipment is confirmed by other visitation records, like those from Canterbury and Norwich dioceses in 1569. Some remained in churches in 1570, but even this seems usually to have disappeared in the subsequent decade. And although some parishes allegedly retained items in order to be 'ready to set up the mass again', slowness to sell probably owed less to enthusiasm for the old rites than to uncertainty about the future of the Elizabethan settlement. Chalice retention, moreover, was due largely to a reluctance to spend money on communion cups. What is certain is that the confiscations and sales of these years, together with the Edwardian devastations, were primarily responsible for the present scarcity of pre-reformation plate, cloth and books in English churches.[18]

Altars were subjected to similar assaults. Although in Shropshire they reportedly still stood in 'the most part of churches' in October 1560, accounts and other records show that in the majority of English parishes – some two-thirds – they were obediently removed in 1559. At Exeter, for example, it was in this autumn that the royal commissioners 'did deface all the altars and monuments of idolatry'. Woodbury sent its wardens to appear before them; then three men pulled down the high altar and St Margaret's altar and carried out the stones. Destruction continued in the subsequent years, as at York in 1561, Thame in 1564 and Chudleigh in 1568, though sometimes the structures demolished were already defaced. Surviving altars were recorded in only two of 140 parishes in Essex in 1565, eight of 143 in Lincolnshire in 1566, and none of 169 in Kent in 1569. Of the Lincolnshire cases of dated destruction, 53 per cent had occurred in 1559–62 and 47 per cent in 1563–6. Only exceptionally, as at Morebath, do altars appear to have remained in position in 1570. Local compliance with the early Elizabethan campaign, and with its Edwardian predecessor, will chiefly explain the rarity of undamaged medieval altars in churches today. Survivors, like those excavated at Carlton-in-Lindrick and Royston, have usually been retrieved from pavements, churchyards or elsewhere.[19]

The violence of altar destruction is demonstrated by the fractures on restored examples, as at Holy Trinity Goodramgate in York. And although portions were sometimes acquired by traditionalists – like Roger Martyn, who retained a 'decayed' reredos from Long Melford's Jesus altar – in many cases the demolished structures were treated with contempt. In Lincolnshire, by 1566, they had been not only broken and defaced but also converted to menial uses. They were turned into grave covers and pavements in several parishes, a road at Bradley, a fence at Durrington, stairs at Somerby, a stile at Thurlby, stepping stones at Habrough, a bridge at Bitchfield, a well at Scotter, a cistern at Langtoft, a sink at Croxby, and a fire hearth at Boothby Pagnell. At Kelby two altar stones were 'defaced and laid in highways, and serveth as bridges for sheep and cattle to go on'.[20]

10

INTERCESSION

In pre-reformation England, prayer for the dead was believed to hasten their passage through the purifying fires of purgatory and into the eternal joys of heaven.

It began even before burial. At Down St Mary the parson visited corpses in their homes, to 'say *dirige* and other prayers with the neighbours of the dead man, for the souls of all such corpses'. Such intercession continued at the funeral and often long thereafter. Congregations were asked to pray 'for all the souls [that] bideth the mercy of God in the bitter pains of purgatory: that God, of his mercy, the sooner deliver them through your devoted prayers'. 'Of your charity, pray for them that this font made', urges an inscription of about 1522 at Goodmanham. 'Pray for the soul of Joan Burton', pleads a Carshalton brass of 1524, '... on whose soul, Jesu have mercy'. Some people, like Branscombe's John Hugh in 1521, paid a priest to 'pray for my soul'. More, like Dartmouth's Alice Philip in 1529–30, paid a church or a guild to add themselves or others to its bede roll. Most parishes still paid their priest annually 'for the bede roll of all the benefactors of the said church, naming them from the pulpit and praying for them'.[1]

Intercession was considered particularly effectual when incorporated in a mass. Some testators, like Exeter's John Bridgeman, entrusted this to friars; others, like Widecombe's Gilbert Rugge, to monks. More endowed parish priests, chantry priests or guild chaplains. In 1524 William Sellick arranged thirty masses for his soul in Tiverton church, together with five masses known as 'the ladder to heaven', and John Simon instructed his wife to pay a priest £20 for four years of masses in Exeter St Petrock's – 'for the wealth of my soul and hers, and for such friends as she and I be bound to pray for'. Some founded perpetual chantries, 'for the souls of the founders and all christian souls'. In 1526 a chantry was established in Badsworth church by John Courtney, Brian Palmes, Agnes Rockchurn and Katherine Ursewick, while in 1529 priests were endowed to pray and sing masses for the founders' souls in the chapels recently erected by John Greenway at Tiverton and John Lane at Cullompton.[2]

Lincolnshire, Wiltshire and Yorkshire had together seen some 97 new chantries founded in 1350–99. This total fell to 60 in 1400–49, but then recovered to 75 in 1450–99 and 81 in 1500–48. In Essex, Kent and Warwickshire, however, the total in 1350–99 had been a modest 32; and thereafter it dropped to 23 in 1400–49, 18 in 1450–99 and only ten in 1500–48. Since the south-east and midlands were wealthier than the north and west, the statistics appear to indicate not a shortage of financial resources but a waning of enthusiasm for intercessions.[3]

With some exceptions, this regional variation is confirmed by wills. In 1520–30 the percentage with bequests to intercession ranged from 79 in Lancashire, and 70–2 in Durham, Exeter and York dioceses, to 60 in Huntingdonshire, 44–9 in Somerset and only 22–6 in Buckinghamshire and Lincolnshire. In London, between 1479–86 and 1529–30, the percentage bequeathing to anniversaries for souls remained a modest 21, while that bequeathing to chantries fell from 43 to 20. In addition, an analysis of ten counties suggests a fall in the percentage value of charitable bequests directed to prayers for the dead – from 37 in 1491–1500 to 24 in 1521–30.[4]

The pre-reformation years saw also the suppression of some chantries, by patrons, feoffees or the founders' descendants. In Kent this was discovered in 1511 at Herne, Ivychurch and Waldershare: at Waldershare, a son withheld money from the priest hired to sing for his father's soul. Intercession, moreover, was sometimes overtly decried. 'Many men', declared Simon Fish in 1528, now believed 'that there is no purgatory, but that it is a thing invented by the covetousness of the spiritualty'. In Buckinghamshire, in 1530, William Wingrave denied the existence of purgatory and ridiculed the idea that masses could deliver souls. Even in Devon, bede rolls were denounced by John Atwill in 1505–6 – he thought them more effective in enriching clerics than in saving souls – and intercessions were dismissed by Otto Corbin in 1515. 'When ye see my soul hang on the hedge', he mocked, 'cast ye stones thereto!'[5]

Throughout the Henrician Reformation parishes continued to organize prayers and masses for their dead. Woodbury still rang knells for its parishioners, like Richard Westcott in 1538–9; paid the parish priest to celebrate its 'brethren *diriges*'; and bought bread and wine for its 'soul priest', 'to sing withal'. Individuals, moreover, continued to invest. In 1536 Joan Bidwell of Shobrooke arranged her registration on a local bede roll, 'to be continually prayed for, for ever'. She also ordered a trental and required a priest 'to sing and pray for my soul, my friends' souls, and for all the souls departed, abiding the mercy of God'. In 1540 Robert Hone of Ottery St Mary required masses for his soul, 'after the old customable usage', and registration on fraternity rolls at Cullompton and South Molton, 'there to be prayed for amongst the brothers'.[6]

Yet there were also signs of change. In Lancashire, the percentage of wills with bequests to intercession rose to 90 in 1530–9 but fell to 60 in the following decade. In Durham and York dioceses it fell to 51 in 1534–46; in Exeter diocese, to 51 in 1530–9 and 33 in 1540–6; in Huntingdonshire, to 42 in 1535 and 18 in 1545; in Somerset, to 28 in 1535–9 and 11 in 1540–4. In Buckinghamshire and Lincolnshire the percentage rose, but only to 32 and 28 in 1545. It was 54 for East Sussex in 1530–46, and only 20 for London in 1534–46. Some testators, it is true, expected their executors to arrange prayer; but this practice was long established, and seems not to have increased dramatically in these years. It is also true that some had prayer provided by surviving relatives, but this does not prove that they believed in intercession: even Edward VI would have prayer arranged for his soul by his half-sister.[7]

Other types of evidence, moreover, confirm a reduction of investment in intercession. Bede roll registrations, for example, were recorded in every account of Stratton's High Cross guild in 1530–9, but totalled only four in 1540–6. The founding of chantries was also in decline. In Essex, Wiltshire and Yorkshire, the number of new foundations dwindled from 28 in 1520–9 to eight in 1530–9 and only one in 1540–8. The cessation was faster in Essex, where none were founded in 1530–48, than in Yorkshire, where seven were founded in 1530–9 and one in 1540–8.[8]

The late Henrician years saw also a markedly increasing willingness among laymen – in the north, west and south-west as well as the south-east – to expropriate the endowments of existing chantries and privately suppress them. This trend began in 1530–5, at Dursley,

Scarborough, Stockerston, Thornbury and elsewhere, but accelerated noticeably from 1536: the chantry commissioners discovered at least four recent cases in Essex, four in Sussex, six in Wiltshire, seven in Yorkshire and 13 in Somerset. In Cornwall and Devon, commissioners' reports and other sources show that the period 1530–47 saw chantry property claimed or expropriated in at least 18 parishes.

Sometimes the offenders were local gentlemen. A chantry founded at Halifax in 1515, 'to the intent to pray for the soul of the founder and to do divine service in the said church', was terminated by Sir Edmund Ackroyd's appropriation of its lands in about 1539. At Canterbury, Colchester, Lincoln and York the culprits were urban governors. At York in 1536 the city council obtained a private act to suppress a number of obits and seven chantries. At Looe, in about 1544, land donated to maintain obits was used by the townsmen to finance the repair of their bridge. Not infrequently the culprits were lesser men, acting as individuals or in concert. Revenues that had maintained intercessions in two Exeter churches were appropriated in 1533–8 by Richard Drewe. At Badsworth, in about 1543, funds that had maintained a chantry were diverted by the inhabitants to the repair of their church. At Davidstow, in about 1545, the parishioners sold oxen which had been hired out to finance a chantry priest. The constable, who had persuaded them to do so, then kept the proceeds for himself.[9]

Finally, open denials of intercession appear to have increased. 'Masses for souls in feigned purgatory' were decried at Exeter in 1531, and purgatorial beliefs challenged in London diocese in 1531–2. In 1537 a Rye townsman declared that he would rather 'have a dog to sing for him than a priest'. In 1540 a butcher of Barwick-in-Elmet reportedly attacked the saying of *diriges* for the dead, 'for it could not prevail'.[10]

How, then, did people react to the Edwardian assault on intercessions? In 1549 the southwestern rebels required 'every preacher in his sermon, and every priest at his mass', to 'pray specially by name for the souls in purgatory, as our forefathers did'. Such demands, however, were not made by the Norfolk rebels; and the evidence indicates that in most regions the official orders were generally obeyed. In 1548, with apparently little resistance, London saw 'all the chantries put down', and intercessions of all types vanished from wardens' accounts throughout the realm. Even the southwestern accounts show that bede roll recitations usually ended in 1548, and that prayers and masses for the dead had everywhere ceased by 1549. At Woodbury the last payments for 'brethren *diriges*' occurred in 1547–8, while at Morebath the last *dirige* was performed in 1548–9. And although a number of communities, including Lancaster, attempted to evade the confiscation of their former chantry lands, most seem to have submitted quietly to the destructive proceedings of the royal commissioners. Morebath sent its Three Men and wardens to Tiverton in 1547, 'to make an answer for chantry ground', while three chalices belonging to a chantry at Liskeard were dutifully surrendered to the commissioners in 1548.[11]

Individuals were similarly submissive to the government assault. At Stratton, after a final spate in 1547, names ceased to be added to the bede roll in 1548. Bath and Wells, Chichester, Durham, Exeter, Lincoln, York and other dioceses saw bequests to intercession slump in 1547–9 and almost wholly cease thereafter. Among the last was the shilling left to a priest, in return for his prayers, by Hemyock's John Southwood in March 1549. More typical now was the Yarcombe husbandman Richard Lock, who left nothing for prayers in 1550. Testators who bequeathed to the poor may sometimes have hoped for their prayers in return, but only a small minority of Edwardian wills reveal such expectation. An increasing number of people in fact proved openly derisive of purgatory and intercession. Philip Nichols, for example, declared purgatory to be a lie, and denounced 'matins mumblers and mass mongers, with *diriges* and trentals, with such superstitious prayers'. Prayers and masses for the dead, he proclaimed, had been invented by priests, to increase their wealth and maintain their ascendancy over 'simple consciences here, in this world'.[12]

Could such practices revive in Mary's reign? The southwestern accounts show that whereas the percentage of communities recording expenditure on intercessions had stood at 94 in 1535–41, and had dropped to nil in 1550–3, it recovered to no more than 48 in 1553–9. One of the more traditionalist parishes was Morebath, which re-started general *diriges*, on behalf of all benefactors, in 1553–4 – though even here the once popular masses for individual souls seem not to have been revived. In several parishes the restoration was delayed to 1556 or even later. The percentage of communities recording bede roll recitations had stood at 81 in 1535–41; after falling to nil in 1550–3, it rose to a mere eight in 1553–9. It therefore appears probable that most parishes failed to restore this once ubiquitous form of prayer. In England as a whole the revival was even less impressive. Of 134 parishes with Marian accounts, prayers or masses for particular souls were recorded in only 24 per cent.[13]

Individuals were correspondingly reluctant to invest. The Marian accounts of Stratton's High Cross guild record not a single registration on its bede roll. The percentage of wills requesting prayers or masses for the dead exceeded 40 in Lancashire, but totalled only 28 in Durham and York dioceses, 21 in East Sussex, 18 in Exeter diocese and eight in Somerset. Richard Friend of Ermington, who endowed a priest 'to sing for my soul and all my friends', was thus markedly less representative than William Stretch of Brampford Speke, who arranged no prayer or mass. And with only a few exceptions, like that established at Terling by Sir Robert Rochester, the number of chantries founded in this reign was insignificant. In ten English counties, in fact, the proportion of charitable money directed to prayers for the dead in 1551–60 was a mere 2 per cent. Nor was the expression of disbelief in such practices ever effectively suppressed. In Kent, for example, John Archer and William Foster refused to pray for souls in purgatory. Three Gloucestershire men mocked purgatory as the Pope's cattle pound, while a Cornishwoman denied its existence and dismissed prayers for souls as 'foolish inventions'.[14]

In 1559 such practices again collapsed. By 1560, in every southwestern parish with accounts, prayers and masses for the dead appear to have ceased. Morebath's general *diriges*, for example, ended after 1558, and Dartington's bede roll readings after 1559. Testators sometimes still wanted their property employed 'for the wealth of my soul and all Christian souls', like a Bradninch man in 1560, or requested commemorative knells, like a Broadhembury husbandman in 1567. Some, especially in Lancashire, still hoped for prayer; but in most dioceses, including Durham, Exeter and York, these were no more than a tiny minority. In the ten counties, the proportion of charitable money directed to intercessions in 1561–70 was less than 0.1 per cent.[15]

Even in remote York, the mayor and aldermen had to inform Sir Martin Bowes in 1561 that, 'by reason of alterations', they had been unable to organize the intercessions arranged by him in Mary's reign. 'Since the late change', and 'not offending any law', the planned *dirige* and mass had been replaced by the Protestant evening prayer and communion service. But even this modification proved unacceptable, forcing Bowes to concede that 'so much thereof as may be thought superstitious' should be converted into preaching or poor relief. Elsewhere, as a proclamation complained in 1560, hostility to prayers for the dead expressed itself in an upsurge of violent attacks on church memorials.[16]

11

Prayers, Fasts, Feasts

Prayer offered the pre-reformation laity a means of personal contact with the powers of heaven. Individuals employed it at home or in church. Fraternities recited prayers on behalf of their brethren, as at Helston in 1517. The inmates of almshouses interceded for their benefactors, as at Cullompton from 1523. The poor prayed at the funerals of the rich, in return for food or money: John Greenway provided both at Tiverton in 1529.[1]

Aids to prayer included primers, fasts and feasts. Primers provided the layman with words to recite and images to contemplate. Fasts, on specific days and especially in Lent, compelled him to abstain from animal products and meat: they were intended to sharpen his spiritual appetite. Feasts gave him some forty days per annum of special observances and freedom from work.[2]

Prayer might be addressed directly to God or Christ. It tended to focus on Christ's suffering and wounds, which featured often in woodcuts and on bench-ends. Frequently, however, it was channelled through the Virgin Mary or some other saint. In about 1500 a foreigner noted that English women habitually carried rosaries. A string of beads with six *Pater Nosters* and 53 *Ave Marias* was inventoried at Crediton in 1524, and such objects appear often on early Tudor brasses and memorials. Commemorative inscriptions asked spectators for both *Pater Nosters* and *Aves,* and many bells were dedicated to saints and engraved with invocations. In Canterbury, Durham, York and other dioceses, over 90 per cent of testators still bequeathed their souls not only to God or Christ but also to Mary or the saints. Brixham's Gregory Colvercock, for instance, commended himself in 1523 'to almighty God, my maker and redeemer; and to the most blessed virgin, Our Lady St Mary, his mother; and to all the holy company of heaven'.[3]

Feasts tended similarly to focus on the saints. At Halberton, where the church was dedicated to Our Lady, the inhabitants participated in services and revels on the day of her assumption and the following Sunday. Braunton organized feasts on Easter Monday to commemorate St Brannoc. In Exeter diocese the commemoration of saints included the public reading of their 'legends'.[4]

Although art often showed the Trinity, as on the Kenn screen, or Christ, especially as a suffering man, these were outnumbered by the saints. Mary's pre-eminence is demonstrated by innumerable depictions of her childhood, salutation, motherhood, sorrow, assumption and celestial coronation: she is sometimes enthroned beside God himself. Examples include Tiverton sculpture of 1517 and St Neot glass of 1523. Next came the apostles, martyrs and other celebrities – Christopher, for example, appears in many murals – then national figures like Thomas Becket or Henry VI. Local legends are typified by St Sidwell, a virgin shown with the scythe of her martyrdom on Devon screens. Some art, like St Neot's, showed donors before saints, with inscriptions – like '*S. Johannes, ora pro nobis*' – asking for their intercession.[5]

Support for the traditional prayers, fasts and feasts was extensive but never universal. Dissidents like London's Nicholas Field declared that 'they needed not to fast so many fasting days', and that 'God almighty biddeth us work as well one day as another, saving the Sunday'. Eight men and women of London diocese broke fasts in 1527. The increasing pre-reformation emphasis on the host and the feast of Corpus Christi might indicate a rise in devotion to Jesus at the expense of traditional saints. Certainly a number of wills invoked no saints, and some men and women – including three in London diocese in 1517 – spoke openly against them. 'It booteth no man to pray to Our Lady', agreed a Lincoln diocese fuller in 1521, 'nor to any saint or angel in heaven.'[6]

How were these practices affected by the reformation? Until 1547 the traditional forms of prayer were often still recited. In 1540 an Ottery St Mary man donated 1d to everyone at his burial in return for prayers, and 1s to his godchildren 'to say a *Pater Noster*, *Ave* and creed, praying for my soul'. Such prayer, however, was already being reduced by the dissolution of almshouses and guilds – as at Cullompton, where Trotte's almshouse ended in about 1544. In

Edward's reign it was devastated by the suppression of chantry foundations, and requests for it disappeared from wills. Under Mary only a small minority of testators paid others for their prayers, and such bequests almost wholly ended in 1559. Praying from Latin primers, especially at home, proved somewhat harder to suppress: it was reported from Hereford in 1564.[7]

From 1537 the laws on fasting were relaxed by royal proclamations. Conservatives tore down the announcements at Salisbury in 1537, and a baker swore never to eat eggs in Lent at Windsor in 1538. Fasts, nevertheless, were neglected in London in 1531, denounced as 'nothing in value for [the] health of man's soul' at Axminster in 1535–6, ignored at Ticehurst in 1538, dismissed as popish tradition at Windsor in the same year, and deliberately broken by a number of people at Oxford and elsewhere in 1539. In 1538 a conservative complained that fast-breaking was now so common that the price of eggs had soared. It continued in Edward's reign – when 'flesh and other kind of prohibited sustenance' were 'eaten everywhere upon days forbidden, without remorse of conscience' – and proved difficult to stop in Mary's. Devonian offenders included a Swimbridge man who announced 'that he would not fast ... but that the curate should fast [for him]'. Twelve people were accused of fast-breaking in Lincoln diocese in 1556. 'Prayer and fasting is not regarded', it was reported from Colchester in 1557. The popularity of 'open flesh-eating ... in Lent and days prohibited' was lamented by Abbot Feckenham in 1559.[8]

From 1536, when a proclamation ordered their drastic reduction, feast days were also subjected to official attack. In some parts of the north – including Kirkby Stephen, where anger was provoked by the priest's failure to announce St Luke's day – this policy contributed to the pilgrimage of grace. In other regions, however, reactions were generally more subdued. Although one participant in the Walsingham conspiracy wanted abrogated days restored, the only demonstration planned in their defence was at St Keverne, where two fishermen hoped to persuade the King 'that they might have their holy days'. They were reported, arrested and apparently hanged.[9]

Passive resistance occurred in Canterbury diocese, which in 1537 was 'very obstinately given to observe ... the holy days lately abrogated', and in Exeter archdeaconry, where in 1539 many craftsmen, husbandmen and labourers still ended work at noon on holy days.

Fishermen here would not put to sea on saints' days, while blacksmiths and hay carriers refused to work on St Eligius' day: 'some shoesmiths', it was said, 'be so fondly and superstitiously set to worship St Loye's day that [they] in that day will not shoe any man's horse'. After the instigation of a campaign by the bishop of Exeter and the Council of the West, however, such practices appear to have declined; and by 1549 not even the southwestern rebels would advocate their restoration. Laymen elsewhere were often quicker to comply. At Bishop's Stortford, where clerics kept Holy Rood day, they were opposed by parishioners who went to work. At Rye, where the vicar kept prohibited days, he was supported by the mayor and jurats but withstood by townsmen of lesser rank: their charges landed him in gaol. In Nottinghamshire and Lincolnshire, in 1539, the poor remained reluctant to work on abrogated days, but the more substantial were already doing so. Even days still officially considered holy were worked by some Londoners in 1541.[10]

The trend continued under Edward. Although some London parishes still observed Corpus Christi day in 1549, 'many kept none, but did work openly'. By 1550 'Corpus Christi was not kept holy day', and St Barnabas' day 'was kept no holy day through all London'. At the assumption of Our Lady, 'some kept holy day, and some none'. By 1552 this feast, too, had been suppressed, together with Mary's conception, Mary's nativity, St George's day and St Nicholas' day. At Morebath, where the church was dedicated to St George, 'cleansing of the churchyard against St George tide' ended after 1547.[11]

Several observances returned under Mary. Some Londoners, nevertheless, refused to observe Corpus Christi, and a number of Kent people – including wood setters from Cranbrook and butchers from Maidstone and Wye – continued work on holy days. Elizabeth's accession renewed the assault. Parishes ceased to buy lights for their patronal day – at Woodbury, St Swithun's was last celebrated in 1558 – and by 1561, even in York, Corpus Christi was 'not now celebrated and kept holy day as was accustomed'. Hereafter the abrogated days seem only to have been kept by private groups or individuals, like Hereford's Thomas Havard in 1564. The public reading of legends had also been suppressed. An Elizabethan Catholic would lament that much saint literature had been destroyed by 'the violence of hostility', and many saints had been forgotten.[12]

The use of rosaries, especially in private, was apparently less quick to disappear. Users included Thomas Havard's wife and maidens at

Hereford in 1564, and some women and old people of Sussex in 1569. On the other hand, the rosary was denounced by a Warwickshire parson in 1537 and a Devon gentleman in 1549. Under Mary it was rejected by individuals in Cornwall and Devon and seven parishes in Kent. From Dover St James' it was reported that 'there be not four (besides women) in the parish that wear beads'. By the 1560s such objects were seldom shown on brasses or memorials. 'Lady' bells, which had announced the hours for saying *Aves*, were also attacked: Ashburton's had to be mended in 1553–4.[13]

Behind many of these changes lay a decline of confidence in saints. 'We ought to worship God only', declared Exeter's Thomas Bennett, 'and no saints'; and at his death, in 1532, he refused to invoke any. In London diocese this year Margaret Bowgas refused to recite the *Ave Maria*, and John Medwell 'thought he should not put his trust in any saint'. Philip Gammon, at Axminster in 1535–6, proclaimed that he would never pray to Mary. He also denied her virginity, assumption and coronation, maintaining that her conception of Jesus was by 'actual deed of man', that she was 'buried as any other woman was, and lieth in the ground', and that she was 'no better than a queen that was painted upon the cards'. 'There be some women do say they be as good as Our Lady', it was reported from Bristol in 1536. 'If Our Lady were here in earth', an inhabitant of Rye allegedly declared in 1537, 'I would no more fear to meddle with her than with a common whore.' Prayer to Mary was denounced as 'naught' by an Essex man in 1538, and prayer to saints denied by Londoners in 1541. Anti-saint ballads were composed and sung by southeastern dissidents like William Hunt and William Gray. Contempt for the saints and their 'false, feigned lives and miracles' continued to be expressed by lay people in the subsequent decades: they included Philip Nichols in Edward's reign, and William Foster, Alice Potkins and Agnes Priest in Mary's.[14]

Until 1547 testators often continued to commend themselves to Mary and the saints. In 1545 Musbury's Tristram Hooper bequeathed his soul to 'Almighty God, the Father, the Son and the Holy Ghost; and holy virgin Mary, mother of God our saviour Jesus Christ; with all the blessed company of heaven, to pray for me'. In York the percentage of wills with such commendations fell only from 98 in 1501–37 to 96 in 1538–46. In Durham and York dioceses, however, it dropped from 93 in 1520–33 to 80 in 1534–46; in

Canterbury diocese, from 95 in 1532–4 to 80 in 1535–40 and 63 in 1541–6; and in London, from 85 in 1530–9 to 67 in 1539–47. Edward's reign, moreover, saw it decline to 64 in York, 62 in Durham and York dioceses, about 52 in Northamptonshire, 24 in both Hull and London and only 16 in Canterbury diocese.

Under Mary it revived to 88 in York and 74 in Durham and York dioceses, but only 43 in London, 31 in Canterbury diocese and 24 in Hull. Decline resumed after Elizabeth's accession. In York the percentage fell to 83 in 1558–60, then 24 in 1561–70. In Northamptonshire it dropped to 60 in 1558–61, then 13 in 1562–5. Durham and York dioceses saw a fall to 24 in 1558–70; Canterbury diocese, to 14 in 1559–60; Hull, to six in 1558–68. By the 1560s, moreover, saint invocations were almost always omitted from inscriptions on memorials, bells and glass.[15]

The decline of traditional preambles under Edward and Elizabeth was evidently in part a prudent response to the changes in official policy. On the other hand, such preambles seem seldom to have been penalized by the Edwardian and Elizabethan regimes: there was no Catholic William Tracey. The decline under Henry, moreover, occurred without official pressure. Although the Ten Articles and the 'king's book' discouraged prayer to particular saints, both allowed invocation of the saints in general. It is also significant that even the return of official approval in Mary's reign proved insufficient to restore traditional preambles to their pre-reformation level. It therefore seems probable that the long term change in will formulae reflects in part a gradual erosion of confidence in the 'holy company of heaven'.[16]

12

IMAGES (1)

Contact between the pre-reformation laity and the powers of heaven was further facilitated by their three-dimensional images in alabaster, stone or wood. These stood not only in cathedrals and monasteries but also in parish churches and chapels, usually in pier niches, over altars or on rood lofts. Although the Trinity might be shown, as at Long Melford, a solitary Jesus was more frequent. In most churches the dominant image was the crucified saviour above the chancel screen. Several retain a beam for this rood, or a painted ceilure to enhance it. More frequent still were saints. At Ashburton in 1530 these included Mary, the apostles Andrew and John, and the internationally celebrated Christopher, Erasmus, George and Roche, as well as the nationally revered Thomas Becket and Henry VI and the local Nectan of Hartland. Such figures were painted, gilded and clothed, sometimes with mantles, beads and rings, and furnished with identifying emblems.[1]

The early sixteenth century saw a number of rood lofts erected for image display. Cornwall and Devon funded or built at least eight in 1520–9 alone. That raised at Ashburton in 1522–6 cost over £43, and £36 was bequeathed by William Sellick 'to the making of the rood loft' at Tiverton in 1524. Images, too, were still bought and decorated. In 1528–38 Morebath purchased a rood with Mary and John, and new figures of Our Lady's nativity and George, as well as painting, gilding or ornamenting its Jesus, Lady of Pity, Eligius and Sidwell. George cost some £10, Our Lady's nativity £9, and the rood group £8. Much was financed by gifts, those to Our Lady's nativity ranging from Joan Rumbelow's 19s to Joan Trychay's 4d. More typical, however, was Ashburton, which in 1520–30 erected George and Becket and painted or ornamented Jesus, Erasmus, John and Roche. Some individuals and communities were less enthusiastic. Many early sixteenth-century churches retained old lofts, and three people refused to finance the construction of a new loft at Tywardreath in 1508. Expenditure on images was also often unimpressive, not only in London and Canterbury but also in southwestern communities like Exeter, Chagford and South Tawton.[2]

God or the saints might be invoked by the burning of candles before their images. Lights were maintained not only by parishes – for which purpose they annually collected 'wax silver' – but also by fraternities and individuals. At Morebath in 1528, for example, a man donated bees to finance lights before Jesus and Sidwell. An alternative to a light was an offering in money or in kind. In 1528 a Honiton woman bequeathed a silver cross to Our Lady and All Saints, her best blue girdle to Our Lady, and her red girdle to Our Lady at Awliscombe. Such offerings were sometimes accompanied by pilgrimage. 'They come by flocks out of the west country to many images', complained Latimer in Gloucestershire in about 1533. At Chittlehampton, where her elaborate niche remains, St Urith still drew some £50 from pilgrims every year. At Looe a St George attracted 'great resort of all the country thereabout', while at Pilton in 1530–3 the offerings to Our Lady were some £12 per annum. New pilgrimages were occasionally established, as at Canterbury (to a Mary) in 1525.[3]

On the other hand, the gifts displayed around images had often been inherited from previous generations. At Rewe, it was said in 1538, they had been 'set up of long time past'. At Camborne, where a St Ia was maintained by her guild, only 1d was donated 'for offering to the saint's foot' in 1534–5. At Iddesleigh, where a guild maintained a Mary, no more than 1d was received 'from the gift of pilgrims' in either 1536 or 1537. At Boxley priory the rood had attracted devotion 'in time past'. By 1538, however, it had decayed into 'old wire' and 'old rotten sticks', and had ceased to draw large offerings: none were recorded in the priory evaluation of 1535. Only a minority of people, moreover, still bequeathed to images. Even in the dioceses of Durham, Exeter and York they totalled less than 25 per cent.

Some men and women, in addition, were already openly hostile to the cults. Alice Cooper, in London diocese, refused to pray to a St Lawrence, and protested that 'none ought to go on pilgrimage to any image ... but only to almighty God'. Pilgrimages, she thought, were 'nothing worth, saving to make the priests rich'. James Brewster declared that image offerings should be given to the poor, while Nicholas Field considered prayer to images futile and pilgrims cursed. Others derided the rood as 'block almighty', and images as 'carpenters' chips', 'stocks and stones' or 'dead things'. Images were burned by dissidents at Rickmansworth in 1522.[4]

Support for images appears to have declined further in 1530–9. At Awliscombe, John Searle reneged on his promise to finance the painting of a rood ceilure. At St Austell, John Cockmathew's feoffees refused to provide the image lights that he had endowed: instead they converted the endowment 'to their own uses'. Thieves stole offerings to Our Lady at Long Melford and St Sidwell's silver shoe at Morebath. Crucifixes were mocked or denounced at Cambridge, Chelmsford and Farnham: 'the devil blind that rood that cannot see at noonday except he have candles set before him!', exclaimed a man at Cambridge. Images were decried in London and at Axminster, Rye, St Osyth and elsewhere: 'idols and mammets', Rye townsmen called them. There were outbursts of unauthorized destruction, especially in 1531–2. At Dovercourt a pilgrimage rood was burned by four men, while Coggeshall, Great Horksleigh, Ipswich, Stoke park and Sudbury saw saints and wayside crosses violently pulled down. Even at remote Hawkshead, St George's sword was broken over his head.[5]

But more significant were local reactions to the official assault. Although local people had sometimes offered to monastic images, like Michael on St Michael's Mount, few tried to resist their destruction by the King's commissioners in or after 1536. Nor was there extensive opposition to the parochial campaign initiated by the 1536 injunctions. The despatch of a commission to the Bishop of Exeter and two local gentlemen was followed by the apparently unopposed removal of Pilton's pilgrim-attracting figures of Our Lady in 1537. 'By reason whereof', it was reported, 'the resort of the King's liege people ceased, and is clearly extinct.' Offerings to St Ia at Camborne ended after 1535, and to Our Lady at Iddesleigh after 1537 – by which date, at Worcester, Our Lady had been stripped of her clothes and jewels.[6]

A more comprehensive attack was launched by the injunctions of 1538. Wardens' accounts show that lights before saints were almost everywhere quenched. At Henley the 'old fashion' of lighting had ended by 1539, though light-supports remained, and Morebath's six lights had all vanished by 1541. Despite some delays, especially in Chester diocese, offerings and ornaments were also usually removed. Among objects delivered to the anti-traditionalist mayor of Plymouth in 1539–40 were a cross from St Saviour's hand, clothes from the Virgin and Child, a crown from Our Lady and tapers that had lit St Clare, together with 'offering pence' and other gifts. At Long Melford the treasures accumulated by Our Lady before 1529 – principally coats and girdles, and offerings in the form of beads, jewels, silver and gold – had totally disappeared from the inventories by 1541. Offering beads, and a gold collar for St Nicholas, were sold at Cambridge in 1541, and silver shoes for a rood figure at North Elmham in 1542.[7]

Images sometimes remained in churches after the suppression of their cult, and were 'yet lurking in some places' in 1547. The great majority, however, were deposed. 'Images that were used for common pilgrimages ... were taken down', recorded Wriothesley, '... that the people should use no more idolatry to them.' Philip Nichols would recall that Henry VIII had 'commanded, and caused, such images in all places to be plucked down'. 'The Azotic Dagon falls down everywhere in this country', reported John Hoker in 1538. 'Pilgrimage saints go down apace', agreed John Hussey in the same year. Mary figures were deposed at Caversham, Coventry, Doncaster, Ipswich, Southwark, Walsingham and elsewhere. There were public burnings in London, and frequent acts of destruction in Kent. A Canterbury rood had its arms and legs broken, and a Lenham Lady of Pity was smashed to pieces. The Midlands saw the fall of venerated figures like St Anne of Buxton and St Modwenna of Burton-on-Trent. Even Exeter diocese felt the impact of royal orders 'for defacing and pulling down of all such idols and images as whereunto any offerings and pilgrimages had been made'. Commissioners like Dr Heynes operated 'throughout this diocese', not only in Exeter but also in distant villages. St Mawe-in-the-Sand's St Saviour was 'defaced and pulled down', and Chittlehampton's St Urith deposed – causing an end to pilgrim gifts and a dramatic slump in vicarage income. The Archbishop of York similarly ordered his clergy to remove all venerated images, 'and suffer them no more to be set up'.[8]

By about 1540 the impact of these campaigns was visible throughout the realm. At Sonning, for instance, Leland saw a chapel 'whither, of late time, resorted in pilgrimage many folks'. At Cleeve he found a chapel where offerings to Our Lady had evidently ceased, and an inn which had 'a-late' been used by pilgrims. In Cheshire he noted an apparently suppressed 'pilgrimage of Our Lady of Hilbre', and at Liskeard a chapel of Our Lady, 'where was wont to be great pilgrimage'.[9]

In parts of the south-west the iconoclasts were 'marvellous hated and maligned at'. At Worcester in 1537 the despoiling of Our Lady was resented by a servant, while at Walsingham in 1538 a woman claimed that the deposed Mary was still producing miracles. 'The said image', it was reported, 'is not yet out of some of their heads.' Resistance, however, was conspicuously rare. One man attempted to stop the priest and churchwardens from defacing images at North Mongeham; another tried to re-erect a deposed figure at Milton. Craftsmen destroying monastic images at Exeter in 1536 were attacked by several women, and bills were posted in the protesters' defence. The campaign, however, was dutifully supported by the Exeter authorities, who arrested them. It was also executed eagerly by the craftsmen, who boasted 'that they would pull down the crucifix ... with all the saints there, naming them to be "idols"'.[10]

People elsewhere proved ready to cooperate. In 1538 a Cornish friar indeed complained that 'men were too busy pulling down images without special commandment of the prince'. He was brusquely assured by William Dynham that those destroyed were 'such as idolatry was committed unto'. At Rewe, in response to the injunctions, four parishioners removed mantles, coins, rings, girdles, beads and other treasures formerly 'offered there to certain images'. A Christ image at Salisbury was removed by a servant of the Bishop's under-bailiff. At Thwaite the image prickets were destroyed by John Augustine and the parson, while at Canterbury the attack on images was actively assisted by layfolk like the Toftes. The deposed rood of Boxley was first mocked by the Maidstone townspeople – 'some laughing heartily, some almost as madly as Ajax' – and later torn to pieces by a London crowd. The miraculous rood of St Margaret Patten's was 'broken all in pieces, with the house he stood in', by parishioners and 'lewd persons'.[11]

Images untainted by pilgrimage or offering remained permissible throughout the reign, but even these were losing their appeal. Although rood lights were sometimes still endowed, as at Ottery St Mary in 1540, bequests to saint images appear to have everywhere ended by this date. Wardens' accounts throughout England record the construction of only one new image in 1538–47. Expenditure now was usually limited to cloths for the Lenten veiling, or minor repairs like the painting of Woodbury's rood (for 1s 8d) in 1545–6.[12]

In 1531 Stratton had ordered furnishings worth £200: they included a rood loft, a rood with Mary and John, and figures of St Armil and Mary's visitation. The work was apparently curtailed in 1539, when only about £75 had been spent. Major expenditure on the Ashburton loft similarly ended with its painting in 1538–9. Among the few lofts erected after 1538 were those at Atherington, Cranbrook and Eye, and at Atherington the craftsmen's work cost no more than £14 7s 7d.[13]

13

IMAGES (2)

Support for images had thus been in decline for several years before their comprehensive proscription by the Edwardian regime. The new campaign aroused controversies – 'almost in every place is contention for images', thought Cranmer – but again seems to have encountered only sporadic resistance. It apparently triggered the Helston riot of 1548, and provoked the southwestern rebels to require 'images to be set up again in every church' in 1549 – though except at Stratton, where the rood was re-erected, deposed figures seem not to have been restored. Resistance in other regions, as at High Wycombe and St Neots, was only small scale, and image restoration was absent from the programme of the Norfolk rebels.[1]

By 1549 rood lightings, rood bequests and wax silver collections had everywhere ceased, and images were almost everywhere deposed. Sometimes, as in London and Portsmouth, deposition preceded the official decree. In parts of the south-east it was virtually completed in 1547, when the Greyfriars chronicler recorded 'all images pulled down'. In Yorkshire and the south-west it was comprehensively executed in 1548. Only occasionally, as at Ashburton, was its completion delayed to 1549–50. Its victims included all roods and many outdoor crosses, which even in Yorkshire were 'despitefully' thrown down. Saints also disappeared from public view. Two apostles and a mounted George were 'carried out of the church' at Exeter St Lawrence, while Mary, John and a George tableau were removed from Morebath church. In 17 of 91 parishes with accounts, the rood loft was also mutilated or demolished. St Breock's, for example, was 'drawn down, by commandment'.[2]

Sometimes the deposed figures were placed in storage, or, as at Morebath, entrusted to parishioners for safekeeping. Nevertheless sales and expropriations resulted in the loss of many lofts, crosses, saints, tabernacles, cloths and lights. St Breock sold its loft for a derisory £1 6s 8d. Crediton and Morebath sold gold from their images. Woodbury's sales included part of the churchyard cross, St Margaret's tabernacle, a rood cloth, and eleven bowls that 'did stand upon the rood loft, to set tapers on'. In Norwich archdeaconry not one parish appears to have retained images or tabernacles by 1549.[3]

Although some deposed objects were carefully preserved, others were treated with contempt. At Portsmouth Christ and the saints were 'most contemptuously pulled down and spitefully handled'. Here, Gardiner feared, the 'multitude' was 'persuaded in the opinion of destruction of images'. At Halberton Christopher Sampford removed not only the rood, Mary and John, and the rood loft, but also a great stone image of Our Lady's assumption: 'and hath laid the same image in his oven ..., and doth bake his bread upon the back of the same image'. At Whitchurch William Gooding bought St George's tabernacle and used it 'contemptuously' to seal his 'purlieus'. Figures in Exeter cathedral lost their noses, and St Peter's face at South Tawton was apparently mutilated. At Ashburton the images and tabernacles were burned by the parish, while at Leeds a Mary was burned by Christopher Jackson. That such destruction was frequent is confirmed by Marian repairs and replacements. Images were also widely denounced: Philip Nichols was typical in decrying them as 'abominable idols'.[4]

Could they regain their charisma in Mary's reign? Rood lofts, with roods, Marys and Johns, were obligatory by 1555, and patron saints by 1556. Surviving roods were sometimes quickly re-erected. Woodbury, in 1553–4, paid small amounts for 'setting up of the rood' and 'dressing of the rood with Mary and John'. Chagford, on the other hand, failed to act before 1555. Accounts in fact suggest that only about 45 per cent of churches erected roods before the 1555 decree. Most then conformed, though in 1557 adequate rood figures were still missing from 9 per cent in Canterbury diocese and 11 per cent in Bath and Wells.[5]

Saint restoration could be even slower. Not until 1554–5 did Morebath's parishioners, 'like good Catholic men', return images to their church; not until 1555–6 did South Tawton spend 4s on repairing its saints; not until 1556–7 was the patron, Brannoc, re-erected at Braunton; and not until 1557–8 was George restored at Braunton, and Andrew, the patron, at Ashburton. At Chagford the images were not repaired and reinstated before early 1559, and in some parishes the saints may never have returned. Even the obligatory patron saints were absent or defective in some 25 per cent of Kent churches in 1557. Accounts suggest that only about 35 per cent of parishes restored non-rood images before the order of 1556. Loft repairs were delayed until 1555–6 at Morebath and 1557–8 at Kilmington. Lofts had not been restored in 15 Kent parishes by 1557, nor in at least six Lincolnshire parishes by 1558. At Witham, where the loft had been sold to Mr Harrington in Edward's reign, it was never restored or replaced.[6]

Even in the south-west only two new lofts were recorded in accounts or wills. At Exeter St Petrock's the craftsman's part payment was only £10, to which parishioners contributed only £5 9s 8d, while at St Breock the loft constructed by Christopher William cost no more than £16. With few exceptions, like the £7 at London's St Mary-at-Hill, expenditure on roods was also modest. Only £2 3s 4d was spent at Crediton, some £2 at Ashburton, £1 14s 4d at Tavistock, £1 13s 4d at South Tawton, £1 6s 8d at Harwich, £1 5s 0d at Exeter Holy Trinity, 16s 8d at Easingwold, 15s at Coldridge, 13s 4d at Yatton, 12s at Antony and 6s 8d at Exeter St Mary Steps. Some were mere makeshifts – a painted cloth, as at Harwich, or a canvas, as at Ludham. Coldridge bought its rood in 1553–4, but purchase was delayed to 1554–5 at Antony, Crediton and South Tawton, 1555–6 at Ashburton, Exeter Holy Trinity, Harwich, St Mary-at-Hill and Tavistock, and 1556–7 at Braunton, Exeter St Mary Steps and Yatton. Rood ornamentation and illumination were also inexpensive: Antony spent 10s on painting, and Stratton 2s 6d on tapers. Many parishes revived wax silver, but some did not; and 22 per cent of Kent churches lacked rood lights in 1557.[7]

Of 134 parishes with accounts, only one burned lights before images other than on altars or lofts. Only a minority, moreover, bought figures other than the compulsory rood group and patron. New saints were purchased in at most two of the 21 southwestern parishes with accounts, Coldridge acquiring a 'tablement and two images' for £1 10s and Woodbury a St Swithun for 13s. At Stratton, 3s 4d was spent on repainting St Andrew, and 4s on 'gold for the tabernacle' at Braunton, though Morebath never replaced the gold stripped from its images in Edward's reign. St Mary-at-Hill was unusual in spending £4 on saints. Some images, like the Trinity at St Day and Our Lady at Camborne, may have attracted offerings. But there is no evidence, even in local wills, of gifts to once venerated figures at Chittlehampton, Pilton, Sidbury and elsewhere. Nor does the Mary cult at Long Melford appear to have revived. Sixty southwestern wills contain only three bequests to rood lights and one to saints: an Ermington man left 6s 8d for a new Peter and Paul. Donations to images appear in only 4 per cent of wills from Durham and York dioceses, and in only five of the 134 sets of accounts.[8]

Nor did attacks upon them cease. Especially in the south-east, people were prosecuted for 'holding against ... images set up and worshipped in the church'. In London roods were publicly mocked, and kneeling before them refused, while a re-erected Becket was mutilated and beheaded. 'Creeping the cross' was refused by a Kentish woman, and had not been revived in several Kent parishes by 1557. The south-west also witnessed irreverent outbursts. Near Silverton a stolen cross was hanged with pictures of Mary and John, to resemble a gallows bearing thieves. A Kenton man refused to creep the cross, and three Swimbridge people disdained their rood: one declared that it 'looked like the knave that made it'. All images were condemned by Agnes Priest as 'stocks and stones', 'idols', even 'whores'.[9]

The official assault was renewed in 1559. Accounts show that it was followed by a virtually total cessation of image illumination and, in most parishes, another wave of deposition. In 1559–60 even the south-west saw roods and saints removed at Exeter and in most towns and villages. The Chagford wardens, after meeting the commissioners at Exeter, paid for 'taking down of the images', while their Dartington counterparts, after conference with the commissioners at Totnes, arranged the 'taking down of all the images and tabernacles'. At the same time images were being removed by royal visitors in the north. Although the process was sometimes more extended – to 1562 in one York parish, and 1563–4 in some Lancashire churches – the deposition of imagery under Elizabeth was generally quicker than its erection under Mary. By 1569 not one of 169 Kent parishes retained an image, and empty niches throughout England confirm the extent of compliance with the official campaign. Physical resistance was almost non-existent.[10]

Some deposed figures were 'reserved and conveyed away', as in Shropshire in 1560, or 'hidden up', as in Sussex as late as 1569. Saints have been discovered in church walls or floors at Flawford, Long Melford, Stamford and elsewhere. Many, however, were sold, together with their Lent cloths and accoutrements. Exeter St Petrock's sold two stone images for 6d in 1562–3. Even more were defaced and destroyed. 1559 saw some popular iconoclasm: Abbot Feckenham complained of 'cutting of the faces and legs of the crucifix and image of Christ'. It saw also public burnings, not only in London – where 'all the roods and Marys and Johns' were thus destroyed – but also in distant counties like Devon and Lincolnshire. When the commissioners reached Exeter in 1559, they 'defaced and pulled down and burned all images and monuments of idolatry'. 'They which in Queen Mary's days were accounted to be most forward in erecting them up, and in maintaining of them, were now made the instruments to make the fire and to burn them.' Similar holocausts occurred at Ashburton, Barnstaple, Crediton and Woodbury. The images 'defaced' and 'burned' at Crediton included the rood, Mary and John, Sts George, Katherine and Margaret, and three angels. At Woodbury the wardens paid men 'for taking down of the images and for burning of them'.[11]

An investigation of 143 Lincolnshire parishes in 1566 found only one with undefaced rood figures, and none with undefaced saints. 74 per cent of the dated cases of rood destruction had occurred in 1559–62, and only 26 per cent in 1563–6. For saint destruction the percentages were 76 and 24. Witham, where rood, Mary and John were burned by the wardens in 1559, was thus more typical than Kelby, where they were not 'defaced and burned in the presence of the parishioners' until 1566. Further north, though more slowly, the sacred figures were similarly destroyed. The York High Commission ordered burnings in some 14 parishes in 1562–5, and the Archbishop's officers took action against 17 in 1567. At Aysgarth, where nine parishioners were found concealing images, they were ordered to do public penance and burn the offending objects. At Welwick, where a John was discovered, the wardens subsequently reported that all images were now defaced and burned. Only a small minority of English images – like those burned at Masham in 1571 – appear to have survived the 1560s.[12]

Many rood lofts would not be totally destroyed until the 1570s, or occasionally later. These, however, had long lost their religious significance by being denuded of their images. In some parishes of the north, moreover, and in most of the Midlands, south-west and south-east, they had already been substantially reduced. In several, particularly in London and East Anglia, this action preceded the 1561 decree; elsewhere it followed the official lead. Resistance, as at Uttoxeter, was again rare. In 1561–2 the south-west saw the partial or total destruction of lofts in parishes like Chudleigh, Exeter St Petrock's, Morebath, North Molton, St Breock, Tavistock and Woodbury. At Woodbury the wardens provided drink for 'the workmen which pulled down the rood loft this year', while at St Breock the wood carver Christopher William demolished the loft which he himself had raised in Mary's reign. Some Cornwood people wanted to see the Queen's broad seal before proceeding with the demolition; but it was apparently executed after their reporting to the Bishop's chancellor by other local men. The same fate probably befell the Rockbeare loft when, in August 1562, a yeoman informed the consistory court that it was 'not down'. Lofts at Ashburton, Coldridge, Dartington, Exeter St Mary Steps, Kilmington, South Tawton and Stratton were similarly reduced in 1563–5. At Stratton the ceiling and beam were demolished in 1564, and men were paid for 'taking down of the rood loft' in 1565. Visitation records indicate that lofts had been reduced in all but three of 140 parishes in Essex by 1565, in all but one of 143 in Lincolnshire by 1566, and in all of 169 in Kent by 1569.[13]

The dismantled structures were ejected from their churches and frequently sold. St Breock sold 'a piece of timber that was in the rood loft' in 1565, while Stratton arranged the sale of its loft in 1570: it fetched £5 6s 8d. The Lincolnshire lofts had been comprehensively mutilated by 1566: at Kelby, for example, the purchaser Thomas Green had 'defaced and broken it in pieces'. Sometimes they were converted to secular uses, as windows, doors and chests at Ulceby, gates at Belton, seats at Barroughby, a bed at Osbornby, bed ceilings at Haconby, a weaver's loom at Horbling, and even a bridge for sheep at Boothby Pagnell. With fragmentary exceptions, particularly at Atherington, Flamborough and Hubberholme, rood lofts no longer survive in English churches.[14]

14

Wells, Relics, Shrines

An even more tangible contact with the powers of heaven was offered by their material remains. Saints, particularly in Cornwall, were connected with trees, as at St Breward, and chairs, as at Germoe. Wells were associated with saints' lives or martyrdoms, as at St Columb Major. Personal possessions included Thomas of Lancaster's hood at Pontefract, Neot's horn at Bodmin and Henry VI's sword and spurs on St Michael's Mount. Christ's crown of thorns was preserved in part at Bodmin, and his cross at Grade, St Buryan and elsewhere. A 'relic of the pillar that Our Saviour Christ was bound to' survived at Long Melford in 1529.[1]

The most sacred relics were corporal. Christ's blood was shown at Hailes. Some saints lay in secular cathedrals, like Hugh at Lincoln and Lacey at Exeter; others in monasteries, like Becket at Canterbury, Cuthbert at Durham, and many lesser figures like Bodmin's Petrock. More remained in parish churches and chapels. In the south-west these included Brannoc at Braunton, Endellion at St Endellion, Ia at St Ives, Meubred at Cardinham, Piran at Perranzabuloe, Sidwell at Exeter and Urith at Chittlehampton. Tavistock owned hair from St Katherine, Mary Magdalene and Our Lady.[2]

In cathedrals and monasteries the main shrine stood east of the high altar, possibly in a separate chapel. It was often sizeable and enriched with silver, gold and jewels. Parish shrines were usually more modest. They might stand in or off the chancel, as at Chittlehampton, or in an aisle or transept, as at Whitchurch Canonicorum. Smaller relics were preserved in altars, reredoses, caskets, monstrances, paxes and crosses: Crediton had a cross 'with a crucifix in the midst, for relics', in 1524.[3]

Many such objects still attracted veneration. At Durham, on certain festivals, Cuthbert's shrine was uncovered, bells rang, and devotees approached to pray. At Perranzabuloe the relics of Piran were on occasions 'carried up and down in the country', while at East Newlyn four parishes assembled annually to display the crosses and relics of their patron saints. Some people still made offerings. Piran's head and image received 1s 4d from John Mowla in 1503, 6d from John Ennis in 1510 and 4d from Marion Lelley in 1525. Pilgrims visited wells like St Madern's at Madron and St Nun's at Altarnun. Our Lady's shrine at Walsingham, which boasted a phial of her milk, drew devotees from throughout the realm. The relic collection on St Michael's Mount was 'greatly haunted ... by far travelling', and St Richard's tomb at Chichester would be denounced in 1538 for maintaining superstition 'long heretofore and yet at this day'. The more adventurous visited foreign centres. At Crediton in 1524 'a staff and a scrip of St James' were possibly souvenirs from Compostella, while at Truro in 1537 some 50 people would sail on a 'Pope-holy pilgrimage' to Brittany.[4]

On the other hand, Becket's last miracle at Canterbury had apparently occurred in 1474, and the last in the collection of Henry VI's miracles at Windsor in 1500. It may also be significant that whereas several new cults had arisen in the fifteenth century, none seem to have been created in the early sixteenth. Most surviving reliquaries similarly pre-date 1500, and the York shrine of about 1470 was among the last to be erected. By 1520–9, moreover, even in the dioceses of Durham, Exeter and York, only a small minority of testators donated to shrines or paid deputies to visit them in pilgrimage.[5]

At Walsingham the offerings in 1535 exceeded £260. At Canterbury, however, the average annual offerings to Becket's and other shrines had plunged from £370 in 1390–1439 to only £27 in 1440–89 and £14 in 1490–1538. At Durham the comparable figure for Cuthbert's shrine had fallen from £31 in 1370–1419 to £20 in 1420–69 and £9 in 1470–1519. The income of another Durham shrine had dwindled from £5 in 1456 to less than a shilling. Gifts to St Hugh at Lincoln had also dropped significantly by the early sixteenth century, while those to Thomas Cantilupe at Hereford had fallen so low that chapel lights could not be bought: only 15 rings would be found here in 1538. At Exeter, where 'great pilgrimages' had followed Bishop Lacey's death in 1455, annual offerings seem to have averaged only £7 13s 4d by 1528. Even at Hailes, by 1535, offerings to Christ's blood were worth only £10.[6]

These statistics suggest that many cults, including several of the traditionally most important, were already in decline. For several generations, moreover, relics had been subject to criticism and abuse. By the early sixteenth century their opponents included occasional clerics like John Colet, who expressed disdain for the Canterbury relics in 1514, and a number of lay dissidents, like the man who denounced both Becket and the offerings made to him in 1523.[7]

The official assault began with the Henrician Reformation. Some wells were attacked. St Anne's wells at Buxton were locked and sealed, 'that none shall enter to wash them [selves]', and the veneration of a saint-associated well at Droitwich seems to have been similarly suppressed. But it was relics and shrines that were targeted by the monastic visitations, the subsequent dissolutions, and the royal injunctions of 1536–8. In 1536 the northern rebels already complained of 'the violating of relics by the suppressors'. Their victims included Christ's blood at Hailes and Apollonia's jaw-bone on St Michael's Mount. Bury St Edmunds was stripped of Becket's knife and boots, Edmund's nails, Laurence's coals and 'pieces of the holy cross able to make a whole cross of'. Monastic shrines were demolished at Bury St Edmunds, Canterbury, Chester, Durham, Oxford, Reading, St Albans, Westminster, Winchester and elsewhere. The campaign was equally effective in cathedrals. Shrines, relics and reliquaries were destroyed at Chichester, Exeter, Hereford, Lichfield, Lincoln and York. At Lincoln, in 1540, 2621 ounces of gold, 4285 ounces of silver and numerous pearls and precious stones were plundered from the recently demolished shrines of John of Dalderby and St Hugh. At Exeter, by 1542, Lacey's tomb had been 'defaced': an indent shows where his brass was ripped away.[8]

Parish churches and chapels also proved submissive. Accounts show that throughout England they obediently delivered relics for destruction. A box of relics was inventoried at Dartmouth until 1536–7, a piece of the crown of thorns at Bodmin in 1539, and a portion of Christ's cross, with hair from St Katherine, Mary Magdalene and Our Lady, at Tavistock in the same year; thereafter all vanished. Long Melford's piece of Christ's whipping post had been delivered to William Mayor by 1541, and by 1547 had disappeared. A 'little monstre or relic of St Nicholas' oil' was sold by Great

St Mary's at Cambridge in 1541. North Elmham, in 1542, sold silver from 'the cross that the relics were in'. At Chittlehampton the veneration of St Urith's tomb appears to have ended in 1539, while at St Endellion, the resting place of another female saint, 'her tomb was defaced in King Henry VIII's time'. Even the remote Scillies saw the Elidius cult suppressed: 'in times past at her sepulchre was great superstition', noted Leland in about 1542. [9]

According to Wriothesley, 1538 saw 'all shrines of saints taken down throughout England'. Some destruction, however, occurred earlier, as at Bridlington in 1537. Some was later: in about 1542 it was reported that Petrock's shrine 'yet standeth' at Bodmin, and that Germoc's tomb 'is yet seen' at Germoe. In 1541, however, the King complained that shrines 'do yet remain in sundry places of our realm', and ordered bishops to ensure their immediate demolition. Undefaced structures like Etheldreda's at Ely were destroyed in response to this command. By this date, moreover, offerings everywhere had been halted, and conveyed, with shrine ornaments, to the royal treasury. The gold and jewels from Becket's shrine filled two coffers, and the offerings twenty-six carts. At Durham the confiscated treasures included $1578\frac{1}{2}$ ounces of precious metal and innumerable jewels.[10]

The shrines themselves were invariably smashed. St Richard's at Chichester was to be 'razed and defaced, even to the very ground'. Fragments of St Frideswide's at Oxford – including a mutilated nun's head which probably represented her – were built into a mid-Tudor well. Parts of St William's at York were built into the walls of local houses. The sacred bones were usually burned and scattered, as at Canterbury, or reburied, as at Durham, Westminster and York. Some were walled up: skulls have been recovered at Probus, and bone-containing reliquaries at Brixworth, Folkestone and Whitchurch Canonicorum. The Whitchurch reliquary is inscribed with St Wyte's name and bears the marks of violent damage. Only occasionally, as at Lichfield, Oxford and Perranzabuloe, do sacred objects appear to have been saved from destruction or enmurement. At Lichfield, some of Chad's relics were acquired by two traditionalist noblewomen.[11]

In 1536 the northern rebels resented relic violation, and some marched behind the miracle-working banner of St Cuthbert. In most regions, however, protest was normally limited to individuals. Pilgrimage to Becket and Henry VI was verbally defended by a

Canterbury friar and a Windsor priest, and 'this new law against pilgrimage and such like' was denounced by a Norwich townsman. Even rarer was physical resistance. In most monasteries, cathedrals and parish churches the once revered objects were attacked without effective local opposition.[12]

The assault was organized by bishops, like Shaxton at Salisbury, clerics, like Dr Leighton at Canterbury, and gentlemen, like Sir William Goring at Chichester. In several cases they were actively supported by local people. At Winchester, in 1538, St Swithun's shrine was destroyed by the commissioners with the aid of senior clerics, the mayor, eight or nine aldermen and 'as good appearance of honest personages besides'. Nor were labourers unwilling to assist. The spoil from Becket's shrine was removed on the shoulders of eight men. At Durham the shrines of Cuthbert and Bede were demolished by five workmen, and Cuthbert's tomb was smashed open by a goldsmith with a great hammer.[13]

Some contemporaries openly welcomed the destruction. In 1537 Yorkshire's Wilfrid Holme rejoiced at the exposure of saints' relics, and mocked their 'girdles invented', 'fair hairs dyed', and 'chalk oiled, for the milk of Our Lady'. In about 1542 John Leland deprecated the 'superstition' formerly engendered by the cults. They continued to be condemned in Edward's reign, when Philip Nichols, for example, decried all pilgrimages as 'abuses'. The Norfolk insurgents never sought their restoration; nor did even the southwestern rebels.[14]

John Jewel would subsequently claim that 'the darkness of the Marian times' had seen the re-emergence 'in all places' of relics of Jesus and the saints. The local evidence suggests that this was largely hyperbole. Frideswide's relics were again revered at Oxford, and Piran's paraded at Perranzabuloe, but few other pre-reformation objects appear to have been restored. Even at East Newlyn, where local assemblies revived, it is not clear that relics were displayed. Most of the known medieval relics – like those inventoried at Dartmouth until 1536–7, and at Tavistock in 1539 – failed to reappear in their parish accounts. At Long Melford, similarly, Jesus' whipping post was absent from the inventory of 1559.[15]

In 1557 Westminster saw St Edward's shrine repaired and his relics disinterred. 'It was a goodly sight to have seen it', rejoiced Henry Machyn. Canterbury, however, witnessed no attempt to restore the shrine of Thomas Becket. Wills, accounts and other sources furnish little evidence of efforts to resurrect the former shrines in cathedrals like Exeter, Lincoln and York, or in parish churches like Braunton, Chittlehampton and St Endellion. At Braunton, for example, the Marian accounts contain no reference to the once celebrated shrine of St Brannoc. With some possible exceptions, like the 6d and 8d donated to 'St Piran's foot', few offerings to cult objects are recorded.[16]

Relics that reappeared in Mary's reign seem usually to have been destroyed by the royal commissioners in 1559. The East Newlyn assemblies failed to survive into Elizabeth's reign, and former relics were absent from Bodmin and Tavistock inventories of the 1560s. At Oxford the Frideswide cult was publicly denounced, and her relics were irretrievably dispersed. It was probably at this time that Piran's head was buried at Perranzabuloe, where it lay until its rediscovery in 1835. Only a small number of relics, like those associated with Chad and Thomas Cantilupe, survived the reformation and remain today. Reliquaries, like Eanswythe's at Folkestone, are similarly few. The only intact shrines are at Westminster and Whitchurch Canonicorum; those at Chester, St Albans and elsewhere have been reconstructed from fragments in modern times. Westminster's is the only great shrine to retain the relics of a saint.[17]

Sacred trees, like St Breward's and St Illick's, were also destroyed in Elizabeth's reign. Stone chairs and wells were harder to demolish – several, like the Germoe chair and the Laneast well, survive today – and some wells would long continue to be visited. Their religious significance, however, had been largely effaced. One Elizabethan sneered that pilgrimages to St Nun's well at Altarnun belonged to 'our forefathers' days, when devotion ... exceeded knowledge'. Another reported that the St Madern cult at Madron had similarly lost its ancient appeal, and that people were now 'coy of coming to his conjured well'.[18]

Interlude

The evidence surveyed would suggest that in 1530 the traditional religion was still accepted by the great majority of English people. Levels of enthusiasm, however, showed considerable variation, and overt hostility was by no means unknown. The evidence suggests also that although the subsequent official assaults on traditional institutions and practices were sometimes evaded or delayed, in most cases their local implementation was effective and relatively swift. Resistance occurred, but was usually less common than acquiescence and cooperation.

These conclusions must be tested by several additional forms of evidence. The first is contemporary observation. Although Elizabethan Protestants often looked back on the pre-reformation era as an age of 'devotion', their view is only partly supported by pre-reformation observers. In about 1500 an Italian visitor thought that the English omitted no 'form incumbent upon good Christians'; but he noted also that 'many ... have various opinions concerning religion'. In 1506 Richard Pynson complained that even basic Catholic beliefs were unknown to many men and women. In 1510 John Colet observed 'evil heresies and ill Christendom in the people', and in 1528 Richard Whitford saw 'faith dispersed', 'sanctity annulled' and 'religion decayed'.[1]

Some contemporaries, especially in the south-east, noted a continuing decline of Catholic zeal during the Henrician and Edwardian reformations. 'No love, not the least devotion, remains in the people', lamented a Suffolk monk in 1534. 'There be a hundred thousand worse people now than there was this time twelve months in England', complained a Sussex priest in 1538. A 'lack of devotion' throughout London was observed by the Greyfriars chronicler in 1553. In Edward's reign, recalled Cardinal Pole, 'all light of true religion seemed utterly extinct'. Observers noticed also the English tendency to comply at least outwardly with anti-traditional decrees.

'There is no shire in the realm more conformable to be ordered further', wrote Sir William Godolphin of Cornwall in 1537. 'They a little whisper and rown one to another ...', it was reported from the Midlands in 1539, 'but little they say, and soon that is sunken out of their heads and forgotten.' In 1550 Martin Bucer observed that the Edwardian ordinances were obeyed by 'the majority', albeit (he thought) 'very grudgingly'.[2]

Contemporaries confirm also that the Marian 'revival' was only partial. A conservative priest, Robert Parkyn, thought that it was received joyfully by 'holy church'; but even he conceded that 'heretical persons, as there was many, rejoiced nothing thereat'. Other traditionalists saw the epidemics, harvest failures and military reverses of this reign as divine judgements on English ingratitude for the Catholic restoration. Miles Huggarde believed that England's chief sin was 'infidelity, whereby God is most heinously dishonoured'. The government lamented the 'want of the fear of God in men's hearts', and Bishop Bonner noted the 'want and lack of steadfast and constant faith'.

The superficiality of Catholic revival, particularly in the south-east, was equally apparent to foreign observers like the imperial ambassador Renard and the Venetians Soranzo, Michieli and Suriano. In 1554 Soranzo thought that most English people were dissatisfied with the restored religion. In 1557 Michieli concluded that 'with the exception of a few most pious Catholics ... in the midst of so much error and confusion ..., all the rest make this show of recantation, yet do not effectually resume the Catholic faith'. This year Ralph Allerton told Bonner that, in addition to those 'clean contrary' to the old religion, many an Englishman was now 'neuter' or 'indifferent' – 'that is to say, observing all things that are commanded outwardly, as though he were of your part, his heart being yet wholly against the same'.[3]

Observers noted also the rarity of opposition to the Elizabethan assault. After their visitation of southern England, from Middlesex to Cornwall, in 1559, the royal commissioners reported that 'we found everywhere the people sufficiently well disposed towards religion – and even in those quarters where we expected most difficulty'. In 1564 Norfolk was in 'good quiet', and Sussex was 'free from all violent attempts ... to disturb the established good orders of this realm'. Even the province of York was 'in good quietness, the common people (being rightly handled) both tractable and corrigible touching religion. ... And although the nobility remain in their wonted blindness, yet the gentlemen begin to reform themselves, and the clergy also.' Elizabethan Protestants like Richard Carew and John Hooker could rejoice that the age of 'blind devotion' was now past. Catholics like William Allen, Augustine Baker and Robert Parsons agreed that the common people of early Elizabethan England had mostly been severed from the old religion, and 'knew not the Catholic verities'.[4]

The most systematic of contemporary observations were compiled by the bishops – with the aid of local gentlemen – in 1564. They classified fewer than 31 per cent of the JPs in England and Wales as unfavourable to the established religion. The remainder were neutral or (more often) favourable. In none of the 17 adequately recorded dioceses were over 74 per cent of justices unfavourable. In three the percentage was 50–74; in six, 25–49; and in eight, below 25. In only one of the 18 adequately recorded towns were over 74 per cent of aldermen unfavourable. In five the percentage was 50–74; in another five, 25–49; and in seven, below 25.[5]

A second form of evidence is the memorial brass, traditionally erected to attract intercession for the dead. In the southeastern county of Surrey, and the western or southwestern counties of Cornwall, Devon, Gloucestershire, Somerset and Wiltshire, some 233 brasses bear a death date between 1490 and 1569. 77 date from 1490–1509, and 81 from 1510–29; but only 42 date from 1530–49, and only 33 from 1550–69. These figures suggest a declining willingness among substantial families to invest in prayer-attracting memorials for their dead. Even more significant was the number of brasses with traditionalist depictions or inscriptions. This slumped from 73 in 1490–1509, and 77 in 1510–29, to only 31 in 1530–49 and 15 in 1550–69. Brasses like the Bletchingley example of 1541 – which shows the deceased in prayer to the Trinity, and requests prayer for their souls – were generally ousted by brasses like the Charlwood example of 1553, from which all such pictures and exhortations are omitted.[6]

A third form of evidence is the bequest. In ten counties the percentage of charitable giving directed to religion stood at 61 in 1480–90 and 71 in 1491–1500. Then, however, it steadily fell – to 57 in 1501–10, 50 in 1511–20, 43–4 in 1521–40, 28 in 1541–50 and a mere nine in 1551–60. In 1561–70 it recovered only to 12. These statistics imply that financial support for traditional religion began to weaken after 1500, declined markedly after 1540, and failed to recover its pre-reformation levels in Mary's reign.[7]

A fourth index of commitment to traditional religion was willingness to defend it forcibly against opponents. Throughout Henry's reign a number of people either voiced hostility to 'heretics' or assisted in their detection, trial and execution. At Exeter in 1532 spectators stoked the flames of a heretic's fire, and the capital punishment of dissidents was advocated by the northern rebels and by individuals in Essex, Worcestershire and elsewhere. In Edward's reign conservatives wanted to kill a minister for suppressing intercessions at Poole, and a layman for removing the pyx at Stratford-at-Bow, while the southwestern rebels demanded the death penalty for refusal to worship the host. In Mary's reign, moreover, some people reported heretical spouses or neighbours, as at Boyton, and many constables, justices, sheriffs and other officials cooperated in the persecution. In Essex the Tyrrels were particularly energetic. Sometimes, as at Cambridge and St Albans, spectators spoke against heretics at their burnings. [8]

On the other hand there were increasing signs of sympathy for persecuted dissidents. At Exeter in 1531–2 the mayor and council were reluctant to search out a heretic, and refused to allow his execution within their walls. Some spectators at his burning called him 'God's servant' and 'a good man'. Even more sympathetic was the reaction of the large crowd attending a burning at Ipswich in 1545. Mary's reign, moreover, saw widespread reluctance to support the official persecution. In 1555 the Venetian ambassador reported that it was 'odious to many people'. Two London burnings evoked 'the displeasure, as usual, of the population here'. Renard noted that Londoners were 'murmuring' against the persecution, and feared that it might cause revolt. Some gaolers allowed heretics to escape, and some gentlemen had to be pressured to assist at burnings. In 1557–8 the sheriffs of Essex and Hampshire were punished for failing to burn heretics, while the sheriffs of Essex, Kent, Staffordshire and Suffolk, the bailiffs of Colchester and the mayor of Rochester were all required by the council to explain why heresy sentences had not been carried out. This growing local reluctance to persecute will largely explain the falling number of burnings after 1556.[9]

The trend is discernible also in remoter regions of Marian England. Cornish justices angered Sir John Arundell by granting bail to overt anti-Catholics. One mayor of Exeter, despite his conservative sympathies, proved conspicuously tolerant of heretics, 'and did, both friendlily and lovingly, bear with them and wink at them'. At Hull the mayor and aldermen compelled the vicar to bury a heretic in consecrated ground. [10]

Demonstrations of sympathy for executed heretics were recorded not only by anti-Catholics like Foxe but also by Catholics like Huggarde, Pole, Michieli and Renard. Though strongest in London, they occurred also in southeastern towns like Colchester and Hadleigh and occasionally in more distant communities like Gloucester. The council tried to stop the Smithfield demonstrations by ordering the imprisonment of anyone 'aiding, comforting or praising' the victims, and by instructing householders to keep servants and apprentices at home. Pole lamented that Londoners had 'sore offended God by giving favour to heretics', and Huggarde complained that the burned were always surrounded by supporters eager to collect their bones. Fear of protests explains why executions were increasingly conducted at dawn, and why, by 1558, Bonner wanted them performed 'very quickly and without tumult'.[11]

A fifth type of evidence is offered by the actions and words of parliaments. On occasions, particularly in 1559, the Lords attempted to oppose the reformation; but peers and bishops constituted only a minute percentage of the English people. More representative – at least of the gentry and substantial merchants – was the Commons. Under Henry, Edward and Elizabeth this body usually cooperated with the crown's assaults on traditional religion, and sometimes actively propelled them. 'What say the Commons here but "down with the church!"', complained Bishop Fisher in 1530. In 1532 its *Supplication* attacked ecclesiastical jurisdiction, and in 1559 it successfully supported Elizabeth's religious settlement against opposition from the Lords. Under Mary, it is true, it obediently passed most of the crown's religious legislation. Nevertheless it opposed the surrender of church revenues, blocked the return of church lands in lay possession, and prevented the confiscation of property from religious exiles. The Venetian ambassador described Mary's third parliament as 'quite full of gentry and nobility, for the most part suspect in matters of religion'.[12]

A sixth type of evidence is the extent of recusancy. Under both Edward and Elizabeth some people, like the Staffordshire Fitzherberts, abstained from the official services in favour of clandestine Catholic worship. Before 1569, however, the number of recorded recusants was seldom high: most men and women conformed at least outwardly to the established religion. The rising number of recusancy cases thereafter was due partly to a tightening of official vigilance, and partly to an upsurge of Catholic dissent after the papal excommunication of the Queen. At the same time it should not be assumed that absence from official services was necessarily indicative of Catholic belief. Often it was patently the result of religious indifference.[13]

The final form of evidence is the level of physical resistance to the reformation. Only in October-January 1536–7, and then only in the north and Lincolnshire, did the Henrician regime encounter extensive insurrections. At their height they allegedly involved 35 000 men. Their grievances, however, included not only the religious changes but also the statute of uses, enclosures, entry fines and the recent taxes. Many were attracted by the prospect of plunder. They were actively opposed by several local peers and gentlemen, with their dependants, and by townspeople at Hull, Newcastle and elsewhere; and their defeat was welcomed by a number of people within the region.[14]

Outside it, substantial anti-rebel forces were raised by peers. Although the Duke of Norfolk, to excuse his inaction, claimed that his recruits were sympathetic to the rebels, expressions of support for them were no more than sporadic. They came from priests, monks and (less frequently) laymen. Often they were reported to the authorities and countered by expressions of hostility. A Kentish weaver announced his desire to 'tussle with some of the northern knaves'. When the abbot of Pershore criticized the executions, William Harrison retorted that 'his grace might justly have put 4000 more to death'.[15]

Above all, the south-east, south-west and Midlands failed to rise. A Bedfordshire priest lamented his people's lack of sympathy for the rebels – 'their opinion is good', he complained, 'and yours is nought' – while attempts to raise Norfolk and Cornwall proved abortive. The Walsingham conspiracy of 1537 recruited about 27 people and was easily suppressed by local gentry. Norfolk, reported Richard Southwell, remained in 'as good and due obedience as ever it was'. Cornwall, according to a government agent in 1536, was 'as quiet, and true to the king our sovereign lord, as any shire within his grace's realm'.[16]

In addition to the rebellions, some 562 cases of treason were reported in 1532–40. After rising steadily from four in 1532 to 128 in

1537, their number then fell – to 30 in 1540, and an annual average of 15 for the rest of the reign. If the rise indicates an increasing opposition to the official reformation as it became progressively more destructive, the fall implies a declining willingness to risk protest or resistance.[17]

The Edwardian reformation provoked some riots, most notably around Helston in 1548 – though this was suppressed 'with small trouble' by southwestern loyalists. Major rebellion was limited to Cornwall and Devon in June-August 1549, and even this was by no means solely motivated by religion. Also important were secular grievances, especially the taxes on sheep and cloth, and the lure of spoils: the rebels brought pannier-laden horses to Exeter in order to sack it.

According to eye-witnesses, moreover, they recruited no more than 7000 people. Exeter withstood a six-week rebel siege, and Plymouth castle was 'valiantly defended and kept from the rebels'. Money to sustain the anti-rebel forces was raised by merchants of Exeter and Totnes and parishes like Ashburton and Tavistock. Other loyalists came from towns like Chagford, Crediton and Cullompton, ports like Exmouth and Teignmouth, and a number of rural areas where the gentry and their servants actively opposed the insurgents. The royal army also recruited 'a great number of men' within the region. Finally, the rebellion won little support from other counties. In fact its suppression was largely financed by merchants of Bristol, Lyme, Taunton and elsewhere.[18]

Despite her anti-Catholic policies, the first decade of Elizabeth's reign was wholly free from insurrection. Only in November-December 1569, in the north-east, did rebellion erupt. The rebels claimed to seek 'the setting forth of [God's] true and Catholic religion': they paraded a banner of the five wounds, organized masses, and destroyed Protestant bibles and service books. Recruits, however, were attracted also by the offer of wages and the hope of spoils: again there is evidence of extensive plunder.

A priest promoted the rising by claiming 'that he had travelled through the most parts of England, and did find the most part of the common people most inclined thereunto'. 'Which', a rebel subsequently wrote, 'we (by experience) find to be most untrue'. Sir George Bowes' enquiry concluded that the rebels totalled no more than 5500 men. They were opposed, moreover, by an army of over 7000 northern loyalists, who expelled them from Yorkshire 'before any one man was raised in all the south'. Sir Ralph Sadler's fear that northerners were still 'blinded with the old popish doctrine' thus proved unjustified. The Midlands and south sent an army of over 5000 against the rebels, and the south-west remained in 'very good and dutiful obedience, peace and quiet'.[19]

Examination of these risings thus shows that only a limited and diminishing minority of English people was prepared to fight in defence of the old religion. The other mid-Tudor rebellions, moreover, proved either indifferent or hostile to it. In 1549 the 16 000 Norfolk rebels were concerned primarily with enclosures and rents; they made no protest against the suppression of Catholic practices, accepted the new service and were less than respectful to priests. The 1554 rising attracted 3000 Kentish recruits and many London sympathizers. While its avowed aim was to prevent Mary's Spanish marriage, anti-Catholic motives were discerned by contemporaries like Christopherson and Proctor and reportedly admitted by Sir Thomas Wyatt. Anti-Catholicism was also one factor behind the conspiracy, treason and 'rebellious murmuring' so often reported in this reign.[20]

The additional evidence thus tends to confirm that support for traditional religion was substantial, but far from total, before the reformation; that it declined markedly in 1530–70, with only partial remission in 1553–8; and that resistance to the official assault was less frequent than acquiescence or cooperation. Within this general framework, nevertheless, a number of significant variations may also be discerned.

Firstly, support for the different components of the old religion did not necessarily decline at a uniform rate. Some late Henrician testators requested prayers and masses but failed to invoke saints; others retained traditional preambles but omitted intercessory bequests. In a period of religious transition, simple categories like 'Catholic' and 'non-Catholic' were increasingly difficult to apply.[21]

Secondly, support for traditional religion appears to have declined more rapidly in the south and east than in the north and west. This variation was observed by conservatives like Robert Parkyn and non-conservatives like Bishop Bird, and is attested by the evidence relating (for example) to church building, chantry foundation and altar destruction. Other evidence points in the same direction. In 1480–1540 the percentage of giving channelled into religion varied from 70 in Lancashire and Yorkshire, and 68 in Somerset, to 60–1 in

Buckinghamshire, Kent and Norfolk and only 45 in Middlesex. 'Catholic' risings occurred in the north and south-west; non- or anti-Catholic risings in Norfolk and Kent.[22]

With some exceptions, the highest proportions of JPs unfavourable to the established religion in 1564 were usually in the north and west, especially Carlisle and Chester dioceses, and the lowest in the south and east, especially Canterbury, Ely, Lincoln, London and Norwich dioceses. Eighteen Yorkshire justices were unfavourable, though even these were outweighed by 38 favourers. All but four of the Norfolk justices were 'very well affected, and given to the executing of the orders and laws of this realm established for the ecclesiastical policy'. The towns with the highest proportions of unfavourable aldermen were also mainly in the north and west, particularly Chester, Hereford, Ludlow, Warwick and York. York had 11 who were 'no favourers of religion', and only two 'favourers'. At Leicester, more typically, four 'hinderers' were outnumbered by four 'indifferent' and seven 'earnest in religion', while at Brighton, Hastings, Lewes and Rye the governors were all 'earnestly given to maintain godly orders'.[23]

Under Mary, in 13 dioceses, the percentage of clerics deprived for an Edwardian marriage varied from four to 25. By 1560–2, in ten dioceses, archdeaconries and counties, the percentage of married clergy ranged from seven to 62, and the average was significantly higher than under Edward. In both periods, nevertheless, the highest percentages were usually in the southern and eastern dioceses, especially Canterbury, London, Norwich and Rochester, and the lowest in the northern and western, especially Chester, Exeter and York.[24]

It is therefore valid to posit a broad distinction between north-and-west and south-and-east. It is also evident, however, that innumerable variations existed within both areas. Although the number of parishes visited in Canterbury and Lincoln dioceses in 1556–7 was almost equal, the number of individuals charged with offences against traditional religion was two-and-a-half times greater in the former. Bequests to traditional religion feature in 43 per cent of the Cornish wills from 1520–69, but in only 35 per cent of the Devonian; and Devon provided most of the south-west's active loyalists in 1549. Even counties were seldom homogeneous. The percentage of Sussex wills with traditional preambles or bequests stood at 81–3 in 1530–46, and slumped to 16–26 in 1547–53. Under Mary it revived to 54 in the west, but only 41 in the north and 31 in the east.

At Hereford, in 1564, 21 of the councillors were religiously unfavourable, ten neutral, and none favourable; but at neighbouring Leominster the figures were nil, one and six.[25]

Was there a distinction between rural communities and major towns? In 1536 Andrew Borde met 'many rural fellows ... that love not our gracious King', and the 'Catholic' rebellions of 1536, 1549 and 1569 seem to have recruited primarily from hamlets, villages and small towns; loyalists came largely from the greater towns. The rural areas of six counties saw the number of new chantries fall from 98 in 1350–99 to 56 in 1400–49, but recover to 72 in 1450–99 and 83 in 1500–48. The urban communities, namely Boston, Canterbury, Colchester, Coventry, Hull, Lincoln, Salisbury and York, saw continuous decline – from 31 to 27, 21 and eight.[26]

An analysis of charitable bequests in 1480–1540 suggests that the proportion directed to religion was significantly lower in urban than in rural groups. Percentages of 91 for husbandmen, 81 for yeomen and 70 for the lower gentry compare with 64 for artisans, 57 for tradesmen and only 48 for merchants. In the reformation decades, in Durham and York dioceses, urban testators were usually less ready to arrange intercessions, while in Coventry and Worcester dioceses their wills were less likely to contain traditional preambles or bequests.[27]

At the same time both rural and urban communities were often divided. In 1550 a holy day caused 'division through all London'. 'Here among you in this city', observed a preacher at Bristol in Mary's reign, 'some will hear mass, some will hear none ...; some will be shriven, some will not ...; some will pray for the dead, some will not. I hear of much dissension among you.' The inhabitants of Exeter displayed differing attitudes to heretic burning in 1532, iconoclasm in 1536, rebellion in 1549 and Catholicism in 1553–8. Poole, Rye, Salisbury and other towns were similarly split.[28]

Some social variations may also be detected. In Durham and York dioceses the clergy was consistently readier than the laity to arrange prayers for the dead. Priests, monks and friars constituted less than 5 per cent of the population, but 55 per cent of the people delated for treason in 1532–40. 'If inveterate obstinacy was found anywhere', the commissioners reported in 1559, 'it was altogether among the priests.'[29]

In several towns, including Exeter, the wealthier citizens were generally less conservative than their inferiors. At Rye, on the other hand, the minor townsmen were less conservative than the mayor and jurats; and other social groups were similarly divided in religious attitudes. Gentlemen, yeomen, husbandmen, merchants, clothiers, shoemakers and mariners all contained both traditionalists and non-traditionalists. At Bristol in 1533 the 'great strife and debate' about religion divided 'all manner of sorts of people, from the highest to the lowest'.[30]

Many traditionalists came from the older generations. They included William Maldon's parents in 1539; 'old Thomas White' at Poole in Edward's reign; and the 'old women and men' who decried a heretic at St Albans in 1555. In 1557 the Venetian ambassador thought that of the 'few most pious Catholics' still remaining, none were under 35. Conversely, many anti-traditionalists were relatively young. They included the 20-year-old William Maldon at Chelmsford in 1539; the young scholar Philip Nichols in Devon in 1547; and the 19-year-old John Leafe, Yorkshire-born apprentice to a London tallow chandler, in 1555. Boys provided some of the most vehement anti-Catholics in Edward's reign, and apprentices were regarded as particularly sympathetic to persecuted heretics in Mary's. John Christopherson complained that children were increasingly liable to call their parents 'blind papists'; 'yea, and make a merry mocking stock of them and say, "my father is an old doting fool, and my mother goeth always mumbling on her beads"'.[31]

Again the distinction was far from absolute. Some young people remained Catholic, like Agnes Priest's children in Mary's reign. More important, wills suggest that even the older age groups tended to drift away from traditional religion in the reformation decades.[32]

Finally, did religion correlate with gender? Cranmer decried 'fond women, which commonly follow superstition rather than true religion'. Women were noted in 1500 for devotion to the rosary, and continued to use it at Dover in 1557 and in some Sussex parishes in 1569. Many financed traditional religion, like the glass-erecting wives of St Neot in 1523 or their manual-buying counterparts at Morebath under Mary. Some sought to resist the reformation, like the rioters at Exeter or the viragos of Stratford-at-Bow. Women, moreover, provided only five of the 52 offenders against traditional religion in Lincoln diocese in 1556, and only 54 of the more than 137 in Canterbury diocese in 1557. On the other hand, they also provided only 16 of the 562 people delated for treason in 1532–40; and a significant number of females in fact proved resolutely hostile to the old faith. They included Alice Cooper, who denounced saints, images and pilgrimages in London diocese before the reformation, and Agnes Priest, who died for her outspoken attacks on Catholicism at Exeter in 1558.[33]

Part Three: Motivations

15

SPIRITUAL CONVICTIONS (1)

What factors motivated the responses of the English people to the English Reformation? Were they primarily spiritual – that is, related to the worship of God and the eternal welfare of the human soul? Or were they more often secular – that is, related to the emotional, material or even physical needs of men and women on this earth? What impelled some to support traditional religion, and others to abandon it?

Support for the old faith might be motivated by a variety of spiritual considerations. One was the inner urge to serve and worship God. The rebuilding of Probus church in 1520–3 reportedly sprang from the parishioners' 'good minds and devotions', and one reason for northern support of the abbeys in 1536 was (according to Robert Aske) that they 'laudably served God'. The innate desire to worship might also be directed towards saints. In about 1500 St Mabyn people celebrated the completion of their church by singing a hymn in praise of Mabyn herself, while in 1526 John Lane erected a chapel at Cullompton 'in the honour of God and the assumption of Our Lady'.[1]

Often, however, people practised traditional religion in order to gain specific spiritual benefits for themselves, their families or their local communities. One was protection from demonic forces. This explains the carrying of holy water to local households, the distribution of candles at Candlemas, and the expulsion of evil spirits by crosses, bells and hymns in Rogationtide processions. Bells bore inscriptions proclaiming their power to repel evil, and for this reason were sometimes (as at Ashburton in 1509–10) rung in times of storm.[2]

Even more powerful, particularly in an age of short lives and sudden deaths, was the urge to acquire spiritual merit for the soul – and thus to speed its journey through purgatorial pain and into eternal bliss. Purgatory, said More's *Supplication of Souls*, 'passeth in heat all the fires that ever burned upon earth'. Its inmates were described as sleepless and restless, and unceasingly tortured by 'cruel, damned sprites'. Similar fears were evoked by contemplation of the final judgement, with its eternal separation of mankind into the saved and the damned. Its horrifying reality was emphasized by doom paintings over chancel arches, as at Salisbury St Thomas's, and by the Corpus Christi plays.[3]

Fears of this type seem often to have impelled the construction and furnishing of parish churches. These pious works not only earned indulgences for contributors, as at Thornbury in 1524, but also won spiritual merit for the principal donors and attracted prayer for their souls. An inscription on Cullompton church reminds the spectator that its south chapel was founded in 1526 by John and Thomasine Lane, asks her or him to say a *Pater Noster* and *Ave* for them, their children and their friends, and expresses the hope that God will have mercy on their souls. Inscriptions requesting prayer for donors were placed also on glass, fonts and screens. Similar beliefs about the after life explain why many pre-reformation people erected brasses or tombs, registered names on bede rolls and arranged intercessory prayers or masses.[4]

Prayer before pictures of Christ, or of his passion instruments, was believed to secure years or even centuries of remission from purgatory. Prayer to saints, especially Mary, was thought particularly effective in obtaining protection from divine wrath at the last judgement. Murals at Bovey Tracey and elsewhere showed rosaries tipping the judgement scales in favour of Mary's devotees. Sculptures, like that of 1517 at Tiverton, depicted donors in prayer to an ascending Mary. 'Jesus, mercy; Lady, help' was inscribed on brasses and bells. 'O blessed Lady of pity', pleads a Carshalton brass of about 1524, 'pray for me, that my soul saved may be.'[5]

An Exeter merchant, making his will in 1501, asserted his belief in the Catholic faith and the Trinity, but also admitted his terror of death, 'the which no manner of person living in this world cannot escape'. After commending his soul to its creator, he turned to Mary: 'I ask for charity, Our Lady, St Mary the virgin: with [the] saints, all the company of heaven, be mine advocate in the hour of my death and at the day of the great judgement.' In 1558 a Cheshire gentleman besought Mary and the saints to 'pray unto almighty God that it will please him (the rather through their intercession) that my soul may come and be in heaven amongst the blessed company there'. Pilgrimage and offering were similarly motivated. 'Who seeketh saints for Christ's sake', explains the pilgrim in a Heywood play, 'and namely such as pains do take on foot to punish thy frail body, shall thereby merit more highly than by anything done by man.' In 1535 a Canterbury friar taught that one penny offered at Becket's shrine was more meritorious for the soul than eighty given to the poor.[6]

That support for traditional religion was often impelled by spiritual considerations is thus beyond dispute. What remains debatable is the motivation of that increasing number of people who ceased to support it. To what extent were they driven by alternative forms of spiritual conviction?

Native heresy, or 'Lollardy', unquestionably remained alive in early sixteenth-century England. Although multiform, its characteristic features included lay bible-reading, prayer without visible aids, and worship without ritual, miracle or priestly control. From about 1520, moreover, it was reinforced by a newer version of the Christian faith. Originating in several parts of Germany and Switzerland, and influenced by a variety of reformers including Luther, Zwingli, Bucer and Calvin, this 'Protestantism' inevitably diversified into differing forms. Trinitarianism, predestination, infant baptism and episcopacy, though accepted by most English Protestants, were challenged by minorities; and even the mainstream divided on issues like clerical dress and the liturgy. The movement was united, nevertheless, by two central beliefs.[7]

The first concerned the location of spiritual authority. Scripture, declared Philip Nichols, is 'alone sufficient to teach us the true worship of God, faith in his promises and ... the way to everlasting life'. It is 'the touchstone and trial of all other doctrines', superior to all merely human 'laws, decrees and customs or ceremonies'. He rejected prayers and masses for the dead because 'the scripture speaketh not of them', and images because 'all the scriptures cry out upon them'. Philip Gammon objected to obligatory fasts because of what was 'written in the gospels', and John Bougin required burial without 'feigned ceremonies contrary to holy scripture, which is God's word and commandment'.[8]

The second belief concerned the means of spiritual salvation. Thomas Bennett declared the true church to exist 'where the true faith and confidence in Christ's death and passion, and his only merits and deservings, are extolled, and our own depressed'. He repudiated sacrificial masses because they devalued Christ's 'only sacrifice upon the cross, once for all', and dismissed saint veneration because 'Christ is our only advocate, mediator and patron before God his father, making intercession for us'. Philip Nichols denounced prayer for souls in purgatory on the grounds that 'the blood of our lord and Saviour Jesus Christ is ... able to wash away, to cleanse, to remit and to cover all the sins of as many as live and die in his faith'. Agnes Priest's rejection of prayers for the dead sprang similarly from her certainty that 'God's Son hath, by his passion, purged all'.[9]

In some men and women, therefore, abandonment of traditional religion was indisputably impelled by alternative types of spiritual conviction. But how typical were they of the English people as a whole?

A partial answer is provided by contemporary observations. Catholics noted the pre-reformation persistence of native heresy. 'We are ... nowadays grieved of heretics, men mad with marvellous foolishness', lamented the Dean of St Paul's in 1510. In 1515 the people of London were described by their bishop as 'maliciously set in favour of heretical wickedness'. By 1528 the Bishop of London was anxious also about the spread of Protestantism, by which (he feared) 'Catholic faith may be greatly imperilled'. In 1530 the Bishop of Norwich noticed its success among 'merchants, and such that hath their abiding not far from the sea', while a royal proclamation against heresy lamented 'the inclination of people to erroneous opinion'.[10]

Further progress was reported during the Henrician and Edwardian reformations, especially from Middlesex, Kent, Essex and Suffolk but also from more distant counties like Warwickshire, Wiltshire, Gloucestershire and Devon. It was fastest in towns. 'All Bristol', complained a Catholic in 1533, was 'knaves and heretics'. By 1547 most of the people of Poole had 'embraced God's word'. Protestants were found at Exeter in 1531, and increased after 1537. By 1549 a significant number, including the merchants Budleigh, Midwinter and Periam, 'wholly [applied] themselves to the reformed religion': they actively opposed the 'Catholic' rebellion. By 1553

John Hooper could rejoice that God 'hath mercifully inclined the hearts of the people to wish and hunger for the word of God as they do. Doubtless it is a great flock that Christ will save in England.' Mainstream Protestants were indeed concerned by the spread (particularly in Essex and Kent) of heresies more radical than their own. 'New ones are springing up every day', complained Hooper. Radicals, thought Micronius, existed 'in great numbers'. A Spaniard, Antonio Guaras, believed that the regime's support for Protestantism was due in part to 'seeing the people inclined to it'.[11]

Such observations did not cease in Mary's reign. Bonner described England as 'sore infected with many and sundry sorts of sects of heretics'. Another Catholic, Sir Henry Bedingfield, noted in 1554 that the Woburn area was mostly inclined to Protestantism, and that between London and Windsor 'men ... be not good and whole in matters of religion'. 'The detestable sort of schismatics were never so bold ... as they are now at this present', complained an Essex priest in 1557. 'We have such obstinate heretics, anabaptists and other unruly persons here as was never heard of', agreed another Essex observer in 1558. Foreign Catholics were similarly alarmed. Renard feared that England had 'drunk deep of error': Protestants, he thought, were numerous. 'These English', agreed a Spanish nobleman, 'are a barbarous and heretical race, with no fear of God or his saints.' Orthodox Protestants like John Clement were disturbed by the burgeoning of radical groups, who were 'swarming everywhere' and 'deceiving many a simple soul'. Enthusiasm for the new religion continued to be reported in Elizabeth's reign. At Coventry, in 1559, Thomas Lever found 'great numbers zealous for evangelical truth'. At South Molton, in 1562, many of the town officers, and of the the burgesses, merchants, victuallers, craftsmen and labourers, were 'in the Lord, and promoters of the kingdom of God and Christ'.[12]

Contemporaries, both Protestant and Catholic, were thus aware of the significant advances of non-Catholic Christianity. At the same time, however, they realized its limitations. In 1530 Bishop Nix noted its relative rarity among the gentry and commonalty of East Anglia, and in 1533 Sir Thomas More claimed that it had won no more than 'some ... in corners here and there'. In as late as 1561 Nicholas Sander believed that fewer than 1 per cent of English people were infected with the new religion. Other Catholics agreed that although the people of early Elizabethan England had mostly been detached from the old faith, 'neither knew they the contrary thereof, being heretical conceits; but rather remained in a kind of heathenism'.[13]

While such statements by committed Catholics were sometimes tainted by wishful thinking, convinced Protestants acknowledged that they remained a numerical minority in a generally conformist and often indifferent nation. One recalled that in the south-west, in 1531, 'few or none ... knew anything of God's matters'. In 1549 William Paget thought that the new faith was 'not yet printed in the stomachs of the 11 of 12 parts in the realm – what countenance soever men make outwardly, to please them in whom they see the power resteth'. 'We cannot but lament the people's wickedness ...', declared the council in 1551; 'for, the more we study for to instruct them in the knowledge of God and his most holy word ... so much the more busy is the wicked spirit to alienate their hearts from all godliness.' Ridley agreed that although 'many' of the common people had sincerely accepted Edwardian Protestantism, 'a great number received God's true word and high benefits with unthankful hearts'. 'Many', observed John Jewel at the start of Elizabeth's reign, 'will believe neither side, whatsoever they allege. Bring they truth, bring they falsehood; teach they Christ, teach they antichrist: they will believe neither, they have so hardened their hearts.'[14]

Contemporary observations must be supplemented by the heresy cases recorded in visitations and church courts. An examination of registers from Lincoln, London and elsewhere convinced John Foxe that a substantial number of early sixteenth-century men and women had been imprisoned or executed as 'faithful martyrs and professors of Christ', and that from 1520 'the light of the gospel began more to appear, and the number of [its] professors to grow'. Diocesan records undoubtedly suggest an upward trend before the reformation. In a sample of 461 heresy accusations from 1480–1522, 75 per cent occurred in 1500–22. London diocese saw some 40 accusations in 1510, 37 in 1517 and 200 in 1527–32; Berkshire, 120 in about 1500; Kent, 55 in 1511–12; Lichfield diocese, 74 in 1511–12; and Lincoln diocese, 350 in 1521 alone. Since there is no reason to believe that early sixteenth-century people were less tolerant than their parents, the rise in accusations probably indicates an actual expansion of heretical beliefs.

Of the sampled 461, 295 originated in southern or eastern dioceses – primarily Canterbury, Lincoln, London and Rochester, and to a lesser extent Chichester, Norwich and Winchester. Only 166 came from northern or western dioceses, mainly Coventry/Lichfield and Salisbury and to a lesser extent Bath and Wells. In most dioceses of the far north and west, namely Carlisle, Durham, Exeter, Hereford, Worcester and York, heretics were apparently few. Their main centres were towns like Bristol, Colchester, Coventry, Maidstone and London itself. They were predominantly weavers, smiths, shoemakers, tailors and other craftsmen or tradesmen, and occasionally merchants or clerics; but husbandmen – the bulk of the rural population – were relatively rare.[15]

Court and visitation records confirm also the spread of heresy in the reformation decades. Even in York diocese the number of accused rose from two in 1510–19, and six in 1520–9, to nine in 1530–9, 16 in 1540–6 and 47 in 1554–8. The west and east ridings, with their cloth-making and trade, supplied 54, the agrarian north riding only ten. As many as 55 came from towns – particularly Beverley, Hull, Leeds and York, and to a lesser extent Halifax, Rotherham and Wakefield. Apart from four clerics and three gentlemen, all were non-gentle layfolk; and all but five were male. South-eastern levels were generally higher. At least 206 Londoners, mostly lay and male, were presented for heresy in 1540. Ninety-four Ipswich people, again mostly lay, were named by a heresy inquest in 1556, though here as many as 41 were women.[16]

Court and visitation records, however, suggest also that only a minority of non-traditionalists were inspired by Lollard or Protestant beliefs. Of 52 offenders against traditional religion in Lincoln diocese in 1556, only six were explicitly accused of heresy; and of over 137 in Canterbury diocese in 1557, only 20. Thomas Moore, who 'defended many heresies', was less typical than the Maidstone butchers, whose sabbath trading can hardly have sprung from Protestant belief.[17]

Another type of evidence is the support accorded to heretics when arrested, in prison or at the stake. In 1547 as many as 1000 Salisbury people were allegedly prepared to pay sureties for a Protestant minister. In Mary's reign imprisoned heretics were sustained by London sympathizers, and fugitive heretics harboured by men who 'feared God' in Gloucestershire and Wiltshire. In London, in 1557, Essex Protestants were supported by a demonstration of 'about a thousand persons'. Even more significant were crowd reactions at executions, which increasingly expressed not only distaste for persecution but also identification with the victims' faith. This was reported not only by Protestants like Foxe but also by Catholics like Noailles, Pole and Renard. At Ipswich, in 1545, spectators encouraged the victim by 'giving shouts and praising God, with great admiration of his constancy'; and such reactions became frequent – particularly in the south-east – in Mary's reign. 'When any heretic shall go to execution', complained Pole to the Londoners in 1557, 'he shall lack no comforting of you, and encouraging to die in his perverse opinion ... by those that come out of your house.' At John Rogers' London burning, some spectators 'prayed God to give him strength, perseverance and patience to bear the pain and not to recant'; others wept, collected his ashes and bones, or threatened the bishops. At one Colchester holocaust the onlookers ('by estimation, thousands') shouted prayers to encourage the heretics, while in Suffolk the execution of Rowland Taylor evoked tears and similar prayers. When Derek Carver died at Lewes, 'the people called upon him, beseeching God to strengthen him in the faith of Jesus Christ'.[18]

16

Spiritual Convictions (2)

A fourth indicator of heretical belief is sometimes the phraseology of wills. The 'Protestant' preamble not only failed to commend the testator's soul to Mary or the saints, but also asserted her or his confidence in its salvation through God or Christ alone. Three Plymouth wills are typical. 'I commend my soul unto Christ Jesu, my maker and redeemer', declared William Amadas in 1553, 'in whom and by whom is all my whole trust of clean remission and forgiveness of my sins.' In 1560 William Lake expected Christ's merits to provide 'a full redemption and satisfaction for the trespasses that I have done or committed ..., so that my most wretched soul may be saved amongst thy saints'. In 1562 Joan Lake expressed her assurance of salvation 'by no other means' than the suffering of Christ.[1]

In most dioceses, including Canterbury and London as well as Durham and York, such preambles were apparently unknown before the 1530s. In Durham and York dioceses they were used by 1 per cent of testators in 1534–46; in Canterbury diocese, by 1 per cent in 1535–40 and 4 per cent in 1541–6; and in London, by 6 per cent in 1530–9 and 13 per cent in 1539–47. In Edward's reign the percentage rose to 32 in London, about 17 in Northamptonshire and seven to eight in Canterbury, Durham and York dioceses. Under Mary it fell to 20 in London, and six in Durham and York dioceses, but remained stable in Canterbury diocese and rose to four in Hull. After 1559 it again rose – to 23 in Northamptonshire by 1566–9, 31 in Durham and York dioceses in 1558–70, and 49 in Hull in 1558–68.[2]

These statistics suggest a long-term rise – with a temporary downturn under Mary – in testators' willingness to declare Protestant beliefs. That many were indeed convinced Protestants is beyond doubt. Some, like William Amadas, financed Protestant preaching. Others, like John Bougin, replaced unbiblical burial rites with psalms 'in the honour of God, and with thanksgiving that it hath so pleased him to call me to his mercy and grace'. In many Edwardian and Elizabethan cases, however, it is less certain that Protestant preambles reflect personal conviction rather than conformity to official norms. Some testators seem not to have appreciated the implications of their avowed belief. Ashburton's John Forde commended himself to God, 'trusting ... by the merits of his passion to have the fruition of his godhead in heaven', but then arranged prayers and masses for his soul.[3]

The statistics suggest also that before 1570, Protestant convictions remained limited to a minority of English men and women. Although traditional preambles experienced a drastic decline, the forms which replaced them were less often 'Protestant' than neutral or non-committal. Typical was that used by Cuthbert Strangeways of Leake in 1563: 'I commit my soul to almighty God, my maker and redeemer'. Such formulae, asserting neither confidence in saints nor faith in Christ alone, were increasingly common after 1530 and decreased only partially in 1553–8. By the 1560s, in Durham and York dioceses as well as Kent and Northamptonshire, they constituted the most frequent of preamble types.[4]

A fifth indicator is financial investment. The Edwardian and early Elizabethan years saw Protestant preaching sponsored by a number of peers, gentlemen, corporations and substantial townsmen, and the apparatus of Protestant worship purchased by the great majority of parishes. Accounts show that English prayer books were bought almost everywhere when officially required. Ashburton obtained 'a new book in which they read the epistles and gospels' for 3s 4d in 1549, 'a new book called a communion book' for 4s 4d in 1552–3, and the revised prayer book for 5s in 1559–60. Psalters, for congregational psalm singing, were also acquired, and 'bread and wine for the parish', for congregational reception in both kinds, became regular items of parochial expenditure. Wooden tables for the new communion were generally erected, as at Woodbury in 1550, and provided with cloths and benches or kneeling mats for communicants' use. Elizabethan parishes also supplied their clergy with desks from which to read the new service, and surplices in which to perform it.[5]

Expenditure, however, was seldom impressive. Surplices cost 15s at Stratton in 1562–3 and 10s at Crediton and Morebath in 1566–7. Edwardian communion tables cost less than 6s 8d at Ashburton, 1s 8d at Exeter Holy Trinity and a mere 6d at Woodbury. Early Elizabethan tables were acquired for 13s at Barnstaple, 5s 8d at Coldridge and 3s at Stratton. In 1559 Woodbury simply spent 4d on a 'plank to lie before the high altar', and Crediton pressed a broken Easter sepulchre into service. Although some finely-carved Elizabethan tables survive, few are datable to before 1570.[6]

Communion cups were designed for congregational use; but few Edwardian examples remain, or are recorded in accounts and inventories. At Exeter St Sidwell's the communicants had to drink from a redundant pyx. Extant Elizabethan cups date mostly from 1562 in Kent, 1567 in Norfolk and Suffolk and 1569 in Buckinghamshire, but from 1570 or later in most counties of the north and west. Many parishes were consequently compelled, like Woodbury and Crediton, to use an old chalice.[7]

Few testators financed the purchase of prayer books, tables, cups or other Protestant objects under Edward and Elizabeth, and relatively few parishes resisted their suppression under Mary. Elizabethan expenditure on tables implies frequent Marian destruction or sale, as happened at Stanford in 1554. Some books were stored – a communion book and two English psalters remained at St Breock in 1557 – but others were surrendered in response to an order of 1555. Dartmouth delivered its communion book into confiscation at Totnes.[8]

A sixth index is the level of active involvement in heretical groups, especially when officially proscribed. At Plymouth in 1535–7 a 'confederate band' of Protestants included several merchants like William Hawkins. By 1541 London contained a group 'favourable to the word of God', and such bodies appear to have multiplied in Mary's reign. The London 'congregation', which met in houses, inns and even ships, had a membership of 40–200; towards the reign's end it 'greatly increased'. Much Bentley dissidents assembled in houses on Sundays, forming 'privy conventicles and schools of heresy', while other gatherings were reported at Brighton, Colchester, Stoke-by-Nayland and elsewhere.[9]

A degree of personal conviction is indicated also by voluntary participation in Protestant activities under Edward and Elizabeth. These included psalm-singing sessions, like those held by Exeter citizens in

1559, and funerals with preaching, bible reading and new style congregational singing, like that attended in London by 'a great company of people' the same year. Occasionally they included involvement in a separatist congregation, like that formed by Londoners 'of the lowest order' in 1568.[10]

Under Edward and Elizabeth the official services appear to have been performed by the great majority of clerics and attended – at least sometimes – by the great majority of lay people. In 1549 even the Norfolk rebels 'procured a priest to minister their morning and evening prayer in the English tongue, then newly begun to be frequented', while in 1552 'the new service of bread and wine' was performed in 'all London'. After the Elizabethan Act of Uniformity Sir John Chichester could report that even in Devon 'the service in the church is well received and done for the most part of the shire', and at Exeter it attracted 'great resort of the people'. Performance and attendance, however, could owe as much to conformism as to conviction. There is, moreover, substantial evidence of non-attendance, which seems to have sprung much less often from Catholicism than from indifference. A proclamation of 1550 attempted to close London victualleries and taverns during service times, and in 1552 the government complained that 'a great number of people in divers parts of this realm', 'following their own sensuality and living either without knowledge or due fear of God', were missing church.[11]

'Come into a church on the sabbath day', lamented Bishop Pilkington in 1560, 'and ye shall see but few ...; but the alehouse is ever full.' 'The common people in the country universally come so seldom to common prayer and divine service', agreed Nicholas Bacon in 1563. In five Norfolk deaneries, cases concerning work or other activity in service time had risen from two in 1538–9 to 33 in 1569–70, and cases of non-attendance from one to 47. At York in 1561 the council had to order constables and other officials 'to see that every person come to the service in the church every Sunday and holy day'. At Exeter in 1560 the aldermen were instructed to ascertain whether apprentices and journeymen were attending church, and the subsequent decade saw individual or multiple absences in a number of other southwestern communities. Luppitt's John Parker had 'been at no church almost these twelve months'. At Stoke Gabriel Edward and Mary Sweetland repeatedly absented themselves, while at Launceston it was said that several recalcitrants 'do not come to church to serve God, not in long time'. One absentee was possibly associated with a Catholic gentleman, but most were motivated by preferences for work, sport, music, cards, drink or dance. John Parker was a violent reprobate who 'regardeth neither God nor man'.[12]

Nor did attenders always treat the new service with respect. Two men profaned the communion table at St Cleer, and a group of men mockingly parodied the new communion (with a handful of raisins) at Morchard Bishop. These subsequently explained that they had acted 'merrily', and were 'heartily sorry for their doings'.[13]

A final indicator of commitment to the new faith was willingness to endure imprisonment, exile or even death for its sake. In 1555–8 some 273 people refused to recant their heresy and were burned at the stake. 89 per cent died in the southern and eastern dioceses, principally Canterbury, Chichester, London, Norwich and Rochester, and only 11 per cent in the north, west and Wales. A high proportion came from towns, especially London but also Bocking, Colchester, Maidstone and elsewhere. Only 8 per cent were clergy, and 4 per cent gentry. Of the non-gentle laity whose status is known, 12 were husbandmen or their wives; the other 82 were mostly in trade or industry, including cloth. 81 per cent of the martyrs were male, and over half those with recorded ages were 30 or less.[14]

In the same reign some 642 adults, with 146 children and adolescents, endured exile for the new religion. Most took refuge in Germany or Switzerland, at Frankfurt, Geneva, Strasburg and elsewhere. Fifty-nine per cent came from the south and east, principally Essex, Kent and Middlesex, and 41 per cent from the north and west, principally Devon, Lancashire, Lincolnshire and Yorkshire. Of the adults 79 per cent were men. 15 per cent of these were priests, and 26 per cent theological students; but 37 per cent were peers or gentlemen, and 22 per cent lesser laymen. This last group was mainly urban: the three yeomen were outnumbered by 13 lawyers, physicians or printers, 32 artisans and 40 merchants.[15]

Mary's reign also saw considerably larger numbers suffer less severe penalties in the Protestant cause. Aylsham, for example, provided only one martyr; but 200 of its inhabitants were also suspected of heresy, and punished with public penances.[16]

The various types of evidence leave little doubt that abandonment of the old religion was often – and increasingly – motivated by alternative forms of spiritual conviction. Some sources in fact may underrepresent them. Wills were made usually by the old, who were generally less open to new ideas than the young or middle-aged. Under Henry and Mary, moreover, Protestant preambles were discouraged by memories of the William Tracey case. Executions, too, are no more than a very partial index of heresy's strength. In London diocese, for example, the 112 Marian martyrs were only the most zealous of a much larger corps of dissidents, the majority of whom fled, submitted to penance or outwardly conformed. Of 94 Ipswich heretics in 1556, 43 had 'fled out of the town, and lurked in secret places'.[17]

The evidence, however, shows also that convinced Protestants remained a minority of the English population. They were undoubtedly strongest in the south-east – from Sussex and Kent, through Middlesex and the Thames valley, to Essex, Suffolk and Norfolk. In a sample of some 3000 apparent Protestants in 1525–58, over 70 per cent of locatable individuals came from this region. In contrast, as Nicholas Sander observed in 1561, it was 'the most distant parts of the kingdom' – among which he instanced Cumberland, Northumberland, Westmorland and Devon, as well as Wales – that were the 'most averse to heresy'. But there were also areas of relative strength in the west, particularly Gloucestershire, and the north, particularly the west riding and south-east Lancashire. Counties might also contain significant variations. Protestant wills were markedly more frequent in the east of Sussex than in its west.[18]

Committed Protestants were usually more common also in major towns, ports and industrial areas than in smaller rural settlements. 'Heresy', thought Sander in 1561, 'does not live in country districts'. Its strongholds included London, sizeable centres like Bristol, Coventry, Ipswich and Norwich, and substantial communities like Colchester, Hadleigh, Maidstone and the Yorkshire clothing towns. In one Bristol parish in 1536, seven followers of 'the old fashion' were already outnumbered by 27 supporters of the new. In Coventry and Worcester dioceses under Edward, Protestant preambles or bequests appeared in 22 per cent of urban wills but only 11 per cent of rural. This does not mean that towns were religiously homogeneous – many were conspicuously divided – or that they accepted Protestantism at a uniform rate. In Mary's reign 53 per cent of Brighton's wills had Protestant preambles or bequests, but only 3 per cent of Lewes'. Some Protestants, moreover, lived in rural parishes, like Boyton and Broadclyst.[19]

Protestants seem to have been proportionately more numerous in the upper and middle strata of the social pyramid than at its lowest levels. In 1540 people worth £20 or more constituted about 10 per cent of all Londoners, but over 50 per cent of those accused of heresy. Throughout England they were generally stronger among gentlemen, yeomen, merchants and (especially) artisans than among husbandmen, rural labourers and the poor. Sander identified craftsmen like weavers and cobblers as particularly 'infected by schism'. In the sample of 3000, 34 per cent were clerics or theological students, 28 per cent skilled craftsmen like tailors or clothworkers, 11 per cent gentry and 6 per cent merchants. Husbandmen and unskilled labourers provided only 3 per cent. Exceptions were again many. In 1547 Protestants reportedly existed 'as well among the poor creatures as the rich and worshipful', and in 1554, at Woburn, Christopher Cooke was both a 'plain husbandman' and a 'very Protestant'.[20]

Several statistics suggest that Protestants were more often men than women. On the other hand John Budleigh's wife (for example) was 'wholly affected' to the new faith, while Anne Askew endured imprisonment, torture and eventually burning on its behalf. John Careless rejoiced that 'in these our days', God had given 'unto many godly women ... most excellent gifts of knowledge and understanding of his truth'.[21]

At least in its earliest decades, Protestantism seems to have appealed more strongly to the young than to the old. In 1538 a conservative derided one of Latimer's preachers as 'a foolish puppy and a boy', while the Marian exiles included 'youths ... in great numbers': many were students or apprentices. In 1555, nevertheless, Alice Potkins was converted to the new faith at the age of 48, and by 1560 London's sermon-attending and psalm-singing Protestants included both 'old and young'. Many young people, in contrast, showed little enthusiasm for either faith. At Morchard Bishop in 1567, the three mockers of holy communion were aged 20, 23 and 24.[22]

17

EMOTIONAL LOYALTIES

Responses to the reformation seem often to have been motivated less powerfully by spiritual convictions than by emotional loyalties. One such loyalty was to former generations. This, by nourishing a reverence for tradition and a fear of innovation, might subconsciously strengthen commitment to the old faith and engender suspicion of the new. A Sussex priest, in about 1538, longed for 'the old fashion again', while the southwestern rebels, in 1549, sought to restore the religion of 'our forefathers'. Protestantism was dismissed by an Oxford preacher in 1536 as a 'new sect', and by the northern rebels in 1569 as a 'new found religion'.[1]

On the other hand, such sentiments might be appeased by representations of Protestantism as a return to ancient Christianity. In the eyes of one convert, in Hampshire in 1538, it was a restoration of 'the antique and apostolic church, not yet fallen to antichrist, being pure and uncorrupt of all popish ceremonies'. Philip Nichols told the southwestern rebels that the English service was older than the Latin, because it was 'appointed out of the bible, whereof no part was unwritten these 1500 years'. 'The other, that ye call old, is new – and some of it made within 100 years.' In 1562 Robert Hill wanted to demolish the Cornwood rood loft, 'that we may be like Christian men again of holy time'.[2]

It is also evident that not all felt a sense of obligation to former generations. In 1536 Edward London was warned that 'our forefathers, ancient well learned and holy men, could not have erred these many hundred years': but this failed to deflect him from the new faith. Philip Nichols, in 1547, insisted that traditions inherited from 'our forefathers' should be overthrown. Some may indeed have been attracted to Protestantism by its newness. In Henry's reign an Essex priest complained that the people were susceptible to 'new fangled' preachers with a 'new story', and one reason for the crowds at Latimer's Exeter sermons was reportedly 'the novelty of the doctrine'.[3]

This may partly explain why traditional religion was abandoned more rapidly by young people (like London and Nichols) than by their elders. It may help also to explain the greater speed of reformation in the south-east than in the north and west. The greater security of existence in the prosperous lowlands appears to have made them more willing than the highlands to risk both social and religious innovation.[4]

While villages and many towns were small, and inter-communications limited, the individual's loyalty to his local community remained another powerful motive force. In several respects this favoured traditional religion. It helps explain the popularity of some saint cults, which focused on local wells, shrines or images, and of Rogationtide processions, which asserted the parish's boundaries against adjacent settlements. It partly motivated the construction and furnishing of parish churches. These were visible symbols of the community's status and wealth, and of its superiority to rival parishes. Inscriptions and arms ensured that they also expressed the local pre-eminence of specific families.[5]

Communal sentiment explains the residual power of excommunication, which barred offenders from law courts and from assemblies in the parish church. If, under Catholic monarchs, this encouraged conformity to the old faith, under non-Catholics it induced submission to religious change. In Elizabeth's reign, for example, it persuaded hesitant parishes to demolish rood lofts. At South Tawton in 1562–3 the Four Men were excommunicated 'because the rood loft was up': it was then pulled down. At Cornwood in 1562 the excommunication of their leaders impelled the parishioners to arrange their loft's destruction. 'Forasmuch as we be excommunicate for not plucking down of the rood loft', said one, 'let us agree together and have it down.'[6]

Men and women felt allegiance not only to their parishes and towns but also to their counties and regions. Evidence from the rebellions of 1536 and 1569 suggests that regional sentiment in the north, and its concomitant antipathy to the south, increased its hostility to the religious changes imposed by London. Regional feeling is similarly discernible in the southwestern revolt. Conversely, the reluctance of the south-east and Midlands to assist these risings – and the willingness of many to oppose them – must be attributed in part to the contempt and fear with which lowlanders viewed the highland zones. The north, in particular, was perceived to be materially empoverished, culturally inferior and militarily dangerous.[7]

Local and regional sentiments did not preclude a sense of allegiance to the national group, or of enmity towards its foreign rivals. Geographical insularity and historical experience – particularly of war against the Scots and French – ensured that chauvinism and xenophobia were already important components of the English psyche. 'The English', observed a visitor in about 1500, '... think that there are no other men than themselves, and no other world than England'; 'they have an antipathy to foreigners'. These emotions were sometimes expressed in anti-alien violence, like the May Day riots of 1517.[8]

They sometimes worked against the reformation, deterring English people from ideas originating in Germany and Switzerland. A Grantham priest dismissed the new faith as 'the Saxon contagion', and some English Protestants were anxious to minimize their debt to the German Reformation. Racial sentiment, in the form of Celtic antipathy to the language and culture of the Anglo-Saxon, also contributed to Cornish distaste for the Protestant prayer book. 'We Cornishmen', declared the 1549 rebels, 'whereof certain of us understand no English, utterly refuse this new English.'[9]

On the other hand, chauvinism and xenophobia eroded allegiance to the Bishop of Rome. They also eased acceptance of key features of the new religion, particularly its vernacular bibles and forms of worship. Indeed it was regarded increasingly as more English than its Catholic rival. In 1537 Hugh Latimer rejoiced that God 'hath showed himself God of England, or rather, an English God', and the concept of England as an 'elect nation' was subsequently popularized by Protestant propagandists like John Bale and John Foxe.[10]

In Mary's reign the virulence of anti-Spanish feeling was noted by observers like Renard and Suriano and expressed in hostile outbursts and assaults. Many Catholics, including Mary, feared its power to damage their religion, and 'to ground in the hearts of all people ... many abominable heresies'. A number of people, including John Cowlyn and Sampson Jackman, certainly identified Catholicism with foreign domination. Bartholomew Traheron saw the loss of Calais as a judgement on 'idolatry and popery', and De Feria thought that it dissuaded many Englishmen from attending mass. In Elizabeth's reign this hostility to Spain would increasingly nourish antipathy to the religion of which it was the global champion.[11]

The rise of chauvinism and xenophobia entailed a waning of respect for Christendom. Thomas More's papalism sprang from his refusal to 'conform my conscience to the council of one realm against the general council of Christendom', and the fear that 'all realms christened have forsaken us, but only the Lutherans', was voiced by a Yorkshire priest and some London and Newcastle friars. By the 1530s, however, such expressions of international loyalty were already rare.[12]

Associated closely with allegiance to the English nation was allegiance to the English crown. Writers and preachers of all faiths habitually represented the Tudor dynasty not only as a protector against foreign invasion, and a bulwark against internal disorder, but also as an institution appointed and approved by heaven itself. Obedience, in consequence, was widely regarded as a moral obligation, and resistance as a sin. 'He that regardeth not his obedience to his prince', declared the conservative Stephen Gardiner, 'regardeth not much his obedience to God and his truth.' 'Princes and magistrates', agreed the Protestant Philip Nichols, 'are the ministers of God, and therefore thoroughly to be obeyed.' 'No man ought to speak evil of them, much less to resist them or arise against them.' The *Mirror for Magistrates*, published in 1559, taught its many readers that 'who that resisteth his dread sovereign lord, doth damn his soul by God's own very word.' In 1557 the Venetian ambassador concluded of the English people that, in matters of religious behaviour, 'the example and authority of their sovereign can do anything with them'. In religion, agreed Foxe, 'the manner ... of the multitude' was 'commonly to frame themselves after the humour of the prince'.[13]

Before 1529, and in 1553–8, this worked in favour of the old religion. In 1553, for example, it was a major factor behind support for the legitimate heir, Mary Tudor, against her usurping rival, Jane Grey. It explains why most Protestants accepted Mary's accession, and avoided involvement in Wyatt's rebellion or later conspiracies. John Hooper simply prayed for God's strength 'to endure any sufferings whatever for the glory of his name'. Hugh Latimer had taught that although an evil command should be disobeyed, 'yet for all that I may not rise up against the magistrates or make any uproar; for if I do so, I sin damnably'.[14]

Under Henry, Edward and Elizabeth, however, this sense of obligation to the crown induced widespread acquiescence in its religious changes. It explains why even a traditionalist Southampton friar, when preaching in 1534, exhorted his hearers to retain their old faith but to offer no resistance to their prince. It explains why a similarly conservative London friar, when writing in 1537, acknowledged that the northern rebels deserved to die. And it explains why many who disliked the changes conformed to them. 'My heart in religion is free to think as I will', said the friar John Forest; but he insisted that 'laws must be obeyed, and civil ordinances I will follow outwardly'.[15]

It helps also to explain why so many people informed to the authorities against real or imagined opponents of the Henrician reformation. 'My duty bends me to disclose it', wrote Sir Piers Edgecumbe when reporting sedition. The vicar of Ashlower's recalcitrance was reported by parishioners who feared 'that they, in not uttering of it, should not do their duties according as your true subjects ought'. It was 'according to our duties and allegiance' that two magistrates investigated a conservative priest in Warwickshire. In Bedfordshire Sir John Gostwick – a purchaser of monastic land, but in most other respects a conservative – advised his heir to report offences immediately to a justice or councillor; 'for the longer you keep it, the worse it is for you, and the more danger toward God and the King's majesty'.[16]

Conformity to the Edwardian reformation is also largely attributable to this sense of duty to the crown. Nicholas Ridley thought that most clerics and magistrates were 'never persuaded in their hearts', but conformed outwardly 'for the King's sake'. According to John Hooker, who knew them, the resistance of Exeter's mayor and aldermen to the 1549 rebellion was motivated mainly by 'their duty to God' and 'their obedience to the King': they remembered that they had 'sworn their fidelity and allegiance to their King and prince'. These considerations outweighed the fact that they were 'not yet fully resolved and satisfied in religion'; some, indeed, were 'well affected to the Romish religion'. Most citizens similarly subordinated their religious preferences, and remained 'dutiful and obedient' throughout the siege. The same attitude weakened support for the northern rebels in 1569. They were actively opposed by 'the dutiful sorts' of Richmondshire and County Durham, who (thought Sir George Bowes) behaved 'according to their bounden duty'.[17]

Not all Englishmen were moved by such emotions. At Exeter, in Henry's reign, Peter Strache 'set not a turd by the king, neither by his council', while at Bledney John Tutton refused to obey a royal command that he considered 'naught'. Thomas Poole, however, worked on a saint's day because (he said) it was the King's command; and his attitude towards the established authorities was undoubtedly the more common. This sense of obligation, and the habit of obedience that it engendered, was evident in most regions of the Tudor realm. Among the justices of Kent in 1564, even 'the furthest off in favourable affection toward the state of religion' were 'outwardly men conformable'. The people of Devon were said to be 'conformable' in 1553, and in a 'dutiful obedience' in 1569, while even the Cornish impressed observers by their 'conformity' in 1536–7 and their 'conformable order' in 1569.[18]

18

Material Interests

The factors behind support for the old religion were not only spiritual and emotional but also material. For many sixteenth-century people – though more directly for rural peasants than for townsmen – the most urgent of material concerns was the fertility of their crops. This largely explains the popularity of Rogationtide processions, with their 'saying of the gospels to the corn in the field ... that it should the better grow'. Similar functions were performed by some saint cults. Walstan, Bawburgh's reaper saint, was revered as 'the god of their fields in Norfolk, and guide of their harvests'. Bury St Edmunds abbey possessed 'relics for rain, and certain other superstitious usages for avoiding of weeds growing in corn'. Livestock, too, was protected by relics and images. At Ripon, St Wilfrid's bones cured cattle. 'Offer up a candle to St Loys for thy horse, and to St Anthony for thy cattle', advised a Sussex priest in 1538.[1]

Equally urgent, especially for the lowest classes in the poorest regions, was the need for charitable relief. Northern support for monasteries was due largely to the fact that 'much of the relief of the commons was by succour of abbeys'. Aske defended 'the abbeys in the north parts' on the ground that they 'gave great alms to poor men', and the popularity of houses like Sawley owed much to their charity. On the other hand, monastic alms were less important to the propertied classes and the wealthier regions. Aid was dispensed also by some guilds, but usually was limited to their members.[2]

A related concern was the financial welfare of the region or locality. Northern opposition to the suppression of abbeys was due partly to a fear that their revenues would flow to new owners outside the region. The 1536 risings were sparked also by a determination to defend local wealth – particularly the plate of parish churches – from the depredations of the central government.[3]

Similarly crucial was employment. Fear of dismissal induced one monastic servant to conceal his prior's treason, and possibly others to oppose the dissolutions. A fear of losing work or promotion may also have deterred adherence to the new faith. In 1538 a Protestant was told that to gain preferment at Oxford he should 'leave this new trade', and in Mary's reign known heretics made little progress in government careers. The Venetian ambassador reported that people conformed outwardly to her religion for fear of losing their estate. In 1564, 'fear of loss of their farmholds' still made the tenants of northwestern noblemen reluctant to be known as Protestants.[4]

Other financial factors could work against the reformation. The Statute of Mortuaries angered many clerics. It cost the vicar of Halifax 80 marks per annum, and moved him to protest that 'if the King reign any space, he will take all from us of the church that ever we have'. The taxation of priests provoked some to join the 1536 revolt. Others resented the reduction of their incomes by the Edwardian attack on intercessions.[5]

Iconoclasm, too, had financial implications. In 1536 a friar observed that whenever images received offerings, 'somebody hath profit thereby: either the parson, parish priest or somebody'. At Pilton and Rewe the only complainers against iconoclasm were lessees who had received the offerings. Other beneficiaries included the craftsmen who carved images and the farmers or shopkeepers who sold provisions to their pilgrim devotees. Latimer attributed local support for Our Lady of Worcester to the profitability of her pilgrim trade. Relics could be equally lucrative, especially to monasteries and cathedrals. According to the Henrician regime, it was 'for covetousness' that monks had maintained them.[6]

In 1536, 1549 and 1569, the old religion was employed by rebels to legitimize both economic protest and outright plunder. Under Catholic monarchs, in contrast, material gain motivated active support for the regime. Mary bestowed lands and annuities on the gentlemen, yeomen and other loyalists who had served her against Northumberland and Wyatt.[7]

Fear of material deprivation could induce involvement in a 'Catholic' revolt. Recruits were gained by threats of eviction from tenancies in 1536, and by threats of despoliation in 1569. It could also deter opposition to a Catholic regime. Opponents of Mary Tudor were sometimes punished by heavy fines or expensive years in exile. Officials who failed to act against heresy might also be fined.[8]

Financial prudence, caused by the uncertain future of religion, may partly explain why communities were often slow to endow Protestant sermons or to buy communion cups. Reluctance to sell Catholic apparatus may similarly have owed less to traditionalist zeal than to the realization that it might be required by the next regime. 'We know what we have had', a loft-removing warden was warned in early Elizabethan Kent, 'but we know not what we shall have'.[9]

Material considerations thus served frequently to induce support for the old religion, or to weaken opposition to it. More often, nevertheless, they appear to have worked against it. The English, observed a foreigner in 1557, 'will accommodate themselves to any religious persuasion, but most readily to one that promises to minister to licentiousness and profit'. Huggarde complained that anti-Catholics were impelled by greed, 'like common soldiers after the battle', and Latimer admitted that 'covetousness' led many to support the reformation.[10]

Antipathy to the monasteries was undoubtedly fuelled by their enclosures, rents and tithes, and resentment of the secular clergy by their exactions. 'There were few things within this realm', thought St German, 'that caused more variance among the people'. 'They look so narrowly upon their profits', complained Simon Fish, 'that the poor wives must be accountable to them of every tenth egg... . What money pull they in by probates of testaments, privy tithes, and by men's offerings to their pilgrimages and at their first masses? Every man and child that is buried must pay somewhat for masses and dirges to be sung for him... . What money get they by mortuaries; by hearing of confessions ...; by cursing of men, and absolving them again for money?' More objective sources confirm that rising taxes and inflation made early sixteenth-century priests increasingly insistent on their dues.[11]

As important as financial grievances were financial ambitions. These impelled gentlemen to buy monastic lands, and lower ranks to despoil suppressed houses. They moved common lawyers to covet the lucrative business of church courts. They also motivated a considerable number of people to defraud priests, embezzle church money, steal ritual apparatus, suppress lights or expropriate intercessory endowments. Such offenders were more often denounced by contemporaries for greed than for heresy. At St Austell, for instance, the expropriation of money from image lights was attributed to 'covetous minds'.[12]

The lure of government pensions will partly explain the acquiescence of most monks in the suppression of their houses, and of most mass priests in the dissolution of their chantries. Profit also encouraged parishes to sell their Catholic apparatus: proceeds were often converted to parochial uses, or invested in amenities like bridges, conduits, harbours and quays. Employers may have been persuaded to accept the reduction of holy days by the economic advantages of a more regular working week.[13]

Finance might also motivate cooperation with the official reformation. Informing against its opponents could bring reward. John Northbrook's denunciation of a gentleman at Exeter was due in part to his desire for his victim's house – with which he was in fact rewarded. Thomas Leigh's apparent denunciation of the master of a Burton Lazars hospital was inspired by his ambition to gain its mastership for himself.[14]

Even more lucrative was to provide a reforming regime with military aid against conservative rebels. Several magnates received monastic lands for their assistance against the northerners in 1536. In 1549 southwestern loyalists like the Carews and the Exeter corporation were granted land, or rebels' goods and ransoms. Many, moreover, had joined the loyalist forces for pay or plunder. A 'mass of money' had been used to recruit large numbers, and in several places they had also indulged themselves in 'spoil'.[15]

Payment similarly persuaded craftsmen and labourers to destroy altars, images, rood lofts and shrines. At Durham in 1541 John Simson received 2s for demolishing the shrines of Cuthbert and Bede, and four other labourers 1s 3d for removing the fragments. At Ashburton in 1559–60 a man was paid 8d for taking down the rood. 2s 2d was given to those who removed the images, and money and drink to those who carried the sacred figures to their burning.[16]

As potent as the desire for gain was the fear of loss. One gentleman's hostility to the southwestern rebels was inflamed by their determination to seize abbey and chantry lands from their lay owners. 'Wherein I for my part am so heated that if I should fight with those traitors, I would, for every two strokes to be stricken for treason, strike one to keep my lands: the which I bought too surely to deliver it at a papist's appointment!' Such fears extended beyond the gentry to a considerably larger number of middle-rank men, who had acquired either monastic land or (more often) the cheaper property of the chantries. 'I believe there be few in the realm', observed the gentleman, 'but it will make them smart to forgo [their] abbey and chantry lands.'[17]

Although some families with monastic land were, like the Cornish Arundells, later recusant, this fear undoubtedly limited support for a comprehensive revival of traditional religion. In 1554 the Emperor Charles V concluded from his agents' dispatches that 'the main difficulty' hindering Catholic restoration in England was 'the obstinacy of the holders of church property: who care more for temporal riches than for their souls' welfare, and fear to be dispossessed'. In 1557 the Venetian ambassador agreed that fear of losing church property was a major reason for wariness of 'the present religion'.[18]

Further down the social scale, fear of unemployment moved servants, apprentices and other employees to conform to the religion of their masters. This explains some informing under Henry VIII. In 1540 a traditionalist cleric complained that Archbishop Cranmer's servants would say whatever he wished, 'for fear of losing their service and in trust to obtain higher promotion'. It explains also why so many 'serving men' – like Foxe, the servant of Sir Hugh Pollard – actively opposed the 'Catholic' southwestern revolt of 1549.[19]

A reluctance to jeopardize their livelihoods similarly impelled clerics to submit to the religious policies of reforming regimes. 'I think you are not so very a fool as to refuse to subscribe', one London clergyman told another in 1559, 'and thereby lose so good livings as you have.' A minority objected, and were deprived; the great majority conformed.[20]

Resistance to reforming regimes was further deterred by a fear of financial punishment. The southwestern rebels lost not only lands and goods but also ransoms: one had to pay £140 for his release. Even non-violent recusancy entailed financial risk. From 1559 each failure to attend the new service was subject to a 1s fine, and this 'penalty of the statute' must partly explain the subsequent conformity of most English people.[21]

But equally important in undermining the old religion was the erosion of confidence in it as a repository for investment. From 1536 the officially sanctioned attack on monasteries inevitably stimulated a belief – among individuals in 1536–7, and 'among great estates and low' in 1538 – that total suppression was now imminent. This not only discouraged investment in the surviving monasteries; it also aroused a widespread apprehension that the government's next victims would be the parish churches. In 1536 such rumours were circulating in counties as far apart as Lincolnshire and Cornwall. Cornishmen believed that government agents, on Cromwell's orders, were about to 'take away the crosses, chalices and other jewels of the churches'.[22]

These fears will explain both the decline of investment in ritual apparatus and the rise of sales. At Thame the parishioners were persuaded to sell crosses and other treasures so that 'the King shall not have all his mind'. At Davidstow the parishioners' sale of their best chalice was induced by a rumour that commissioners were about to seize 'such ... jewels of churches as they listed to take'. In 1547 the Edwardian regime blamed the recent spate of selling on these 'vain bruits', but they were only increased by its own commissioners: one, in Cornwall that year, created the impression that church goods were about to be seized. Any remaining confidence was destroyed by the subsequent official confiscations, and was never fully restored in Mary's reign. When Thomas Morritt bequeathed copes and vestments to Sherburn church in April 1558, he cautiously arranged their reversion to his heirs if future monarchs should 'call such things into their highnesses' possession, as of late time hath been'.[23]

In Buckinghamshire, Norfolk, Northamptonshire and Shropshire the monastic dissolutions also aroused fears that parish churches might be stripped of their land or even demolished. At Aylesbury, in 1537, it was said that the church was about to be pulled down; at Wigmore, that churches would be halved in number. This helps explain the selling of church land and the drastic downturn in church construction. In some counties, including Norfolk, the dissolutions provoked anxiety also about the future of guild lands.[24]

Similarly corrosive of investors' confidence was the government's increasing hostility to intercessions. The restriction of soul masses in 1529–32, and the suppression of monastic intercessions in 1536–40, were followed by the chantry statute of 1545 and the activities of 'the King's visitors for the church's lands' – whom the Woodbury wardens (for example) had to meet in 1545–6. The uncertainties thus created both discouraged new investment and accelerated the conversion of existing endowments to other ends. At Davidstow, in about 1545, it was 'lest they be taken ... for the King' that the parish sold oxen that had been hired out to finance a chantry priest. From 1547 official hostility was increasingly apparent. In July a testator of Lanlivery requested a trental 'if it may be'. The chantry dissolutions not only halted investment in Edward's reign; they also created an expectation in Mary's that they would be repeated after her death. One Yorkshire testator left money for intercessions in May 1558, but arranged its diversion to the poor 'if the laws of the realm do not permit mass and *dirige* to be done'.[25]

Such apprehensions will help to explain also the increasing reluctance of communities and individuals to invest in fraternities, images, rood lofts and other components of traditional religion. The decline of financial support for images, for example, was largely a reaction to the Henrician iconoclasm. It was evidently in anticipation of an official confiscation of offerings that the parishioners of Rewe, on hearing of the 1538 injunctions, despoiled the sacred figures in their church. Even in Mary's reign, and particularly in 1557–8, confidence in the future of Catholicism was undermined by her age, her childlessness, and the prospect of her replacement by Elizabeth. In 1557 a Londoner 'trusted to see the lady Elizabeth's grace to restore God's honour, and to put away this popery that now is brought into this realm'.[26]

Finally, investment in traditional religion was eroded by two causes which made increasing demands on the financial resources of the local community. One was war. The French war of 1543–6 forced Plymouth to sell church goods worth over £41 to buy bows, arrows and gunpowder, and Dartmouth to sell silver chalices and other sacramental equipment 'for gunpowder and for the gunners' wages'. Similar sales or pawnings financed the purchase of guns and gunpowder at Kingswear and East Budleigh and the building of a bulwark at Salcombe. Monetary payments ranged from about £1 at Chagford, and £3–4 at Camborne and Modbury, to £7–8 at Dartmouth and Stratton and over £25 at Ashburton. The reigns of Mary and Elizabeth saw small scale but frequent expenditure on soldiers, arms and armour: Braunton spent £1 9s 9d on soldiers in 1557–8, £3 10s in 1562–3 and £1 6s 8d in 1568–9. Further outlay was necessitated by military operations against riots or revolts. These impelled a number of southwestern parishes to sell or pawn their ritual apparatus in 1548–9.[27]

But local resources were more seriously depleted by the mounting demands of poor relief. Enclosure, inflation, rack renting and the loss of monastic charity combined to create a crisis of poverty that contemporaries regarded with rising alarm. Philanthropy and a fear of social disorder together impelled the propertied to channel their surplus wealth increasingly towards the poor.

Almost everywhere the percentage of testators bequeathing to the poor experienced a long-term rise. In Exeter diocese it rose from 20 in 1520–9 to 43 in 1560–9, and in Durham and York dioceses from 19 in 1520–33 to 32 in 1558–70. At first such charity was often linked with intercession. In 1529, for example, a Tiverton merchant bequeathed £20 and a dinner to the poor men, women and children attending his funeral, 'to pray for my soul and all Christian souls'. Increasingly, however, it became divorced from the traditional benefactions. In 1565 a Morchard Bishop man bequeathed a half bushel of rye to each poor householder in his parish, and £4 to its poor box, but not a penny to a religious cause.[28]

Parochial resources, too, were increasingly consumed by poor relief. Churchwardens' accounts show that this trend began in the latter years of Henry VIII, accelerated under Edward and continued under Mary and Elizabeth. In 1550–1 Ashburton donated £5 'to the poor people for one whole year', and a further £5 on the Sunday before St Barnabas' day. By the 1560s many parishes had regular poor rates, with wardens to enforce them. Money might also be raised by ales, as at Rewe in 1569, or by sales of ritual apparatus, as at Exeter under Edward and at Plymouth and St Breock under Elizabeth. 'Relief of the poor people' was one reason for the demolition of York churches in 1548.[29]

If poor relief depressed investment in the old religion, poverty itself may have weakened the traditionalism of the lower orders. It helps explain the despoliation of religious houses by 'the poor people', as in Warwickshire and elsewhere, as well as the multiplication of church thefts and the laity's increasing resistance to clerical dues. In Buckinghamshire in 1549, for example, organized tithe refusal followed harvest failure. Poverty might also explain why some people, like Axminster's Thomas Perry or Landkey's John Smith, found Catholic services less attractive than gainful employment: Perry worked at an inn, and Smith span. Expenditure on images may have been reduced by the 'scarceness and penury of all things' that Latimer noted when attacking them in 1536. It was certainly 'necessity' that impelled an Exeter man to break the Lenten fast – by making soup from bacon scraps – in 1556.[30]

Empoverishment may also have caused some parishes to neglect their churches, and some towns, including Coventry, Lincoln and York, to reduce investment in chantry foundations. In the past, says the capper in the *Discourse of the Common Weal*, prosperity had enabled urban craftsmen to endow chantries; 'and now we are scant able to live without debt'. The suppression or expropriation of some chantries seems also to have been caused by the financial difficulties of their towns, as at Canterbury, Lincoln and York in 1536–45.[31]

19

Physical Drives

The appeal of traditional religion is attributable largely to one of humankind's most basic physical drives: the desire for health. Holy bread and water were valued as remedies for sickness and preservatives against disease. Sight of the host was believed to prevent sudden death, and certain candles (according to a Windsor priest in 1538) to 'mitigate and assuage the plague'. Cures were also sought from saints. Roche was shown with his plague sores, as on the Plymtree screen. A Mary figure at Canterbury was revered for healing a woman in 1525, 'by reason of the which miracle there is stablished a great pilgrimage', and in 1536 a London friar advocated offering to images on the ground that 'God hath given you your health of body for such causes'.[1]

Healing also drew pilgrims to the holy wells. St Cadoc's, for example, expelled 'venomous diseases', while St Nun's aided the insane. Relics had similar power: devotees left models of cured body parts at Bawburgh, Exeter and York. At Durham the lame and others prayed at St Cuthbert's shrine for 'his miraculous relief and succour'. Migraines were removed by Thomas of Lancaster's hood at Pontefract, and toothaches by Apollonia's jaw bone on St Michael's Mount: she appears on screens with her tooth between pincers. Several monasteries had girdles associated with female saints, 'which women with child were wont to gird with'.[2]

Although such objects were widely valued, resistance to their destruction was weakened by the availability of alternative modes of healing. One was medicine, though (as Latimer observed) only the wealthier classes could usually afford it. Another was hydrotherapy, which by Elizabeth's reign was practised at spas like Bath and Buxton and at some ancient wells shorn of their saints. A third was 'Protestant' prayer, addressed directly to God without tangible aids. But probably the most widespread was the use of charms. By 1570 the physical needs once met by saints were being satisfied by an apparently rising number of 'cunning men', 'wise women' and other local healers. Gloucestershire's Alice Prabury, for example, was said in 1563 to 'help Christian people of diseases strangely happened ... by the way of charming'.[3]

A second drive was the search for physical pleasure in food, drink, recreation, sport or sex. At times this limited support for the Protestant faith, at least in its morally rigorous manifestations. It was opposed by 'drunkards' at Rye in 1536, and by a 'very drunkard' at Kidderminster in 1538: the latter proved a 'despiser of the preachers and doctrine of Christ'. Adulterers and fornicators similarly had reason to resent it, especially when subjected to humiliating public penances by puritanical bishops like Coverdale of Exeter or Hooper of Gloucester. 'Envy and grudge of the people' was also provoked by the reformation attack on holy days, which drastically reduced the labouring classes' leisure time. Absence from the reformed services, moreover, was often due to a preference for drinking, dancing, football, bowls or other unspiritual recreations. A typical offender was Mary Sweetland, who in 1567 absented herself to enjoy 'the ale' and 'the dance'.[4]

This factor, nevertheless, was at least as effective in turning men and women from traditional religion. In 1557 the Venetian ambassador thought that English people's abandonment of the old faith was due largely to their desire for 'licence and liberty in their mode of life'. He feared that they sought freedom from the restraints imposed by confession, fasting, and 'all the external acts enjoined to Catholics'. Catholicism, agreed Huggarde, 'giveth rules and orders to frame man's frail nature', but Protestantism 'giveth rules to advance man's nature': it 'persuadeth [men] to embrace liberty, belly cheer and all pleasure'. Bonner believed that Protestantism had been advanced by its promise of 'loose liberty' – 'a thing indeed most delectable and pleasant unto the flesh, and unto all unruly persons'. Even supporters of the new religion admitted the relative weakness of its moral discipline. In Edward's reign, lamented Cranmer, sins like adultery and drunkenness were 'lightly punished, or else not punished at all'. Peter Martyr noted 'the gross vices of those who profess the gospel', and Johan Burcher agreed that 'every kind of vice (alas!) is rife among them, and especially that of adultery and fornication'.[5]

If many lay people favoured the new religion because of its weaker discipline, they resented the old on account of its more galling restraints. It was the attempt of a Marian church court to penalize his fornication that drove a Shute man to assault its summoner. Similarly it was a charge of sexual misconduct that provoked a Colebrooke man to attack a Marian priest. A desire for release from the sexual discipline of the Catholic church must also have impelled clerics to take wives, though Robert Parkyn was uncharitable in describing them as 'carnal priests, which had led their lives in fornication with their whores and harlots'.[6]

Anticlericalism was also due in no small part to sexual fears and jealousies. Suspicion was aroused by the unmarried state of priests and by their supposed influence over female parishioners. Simon Fish was not the only layman to believe that they 'apply themselves, by all the sleights they may, to have to do with every man's wife, every man's daughter and every man's maid'. Philip Nichols saw confession as a priestly device for 'moving men's wives to folly' and 'enticing men's daughters to lewdness and vice'.[7]

But the most powerful physical factor behind responses to the reformation was probably the fear of corporal or capital punishment. This certainly won recruits for 'Catholic' risings. In 1536 the abbot of Holm Cultram threatened to hang tenants who failed to join the revolt, while at Croft the priest warned his parishioners that refusers would be 'hanged and killed at their own door posts'. In 1549 'very many' were recruited 'by force, against their will'. One was allegedly told that failure to join would mean destruction for him and his family. In 1569 'great numbers of people' were levied 'more by coercion than favour'. The parishioners of Pittington were commanded to re-erect their altar and holy water stone on pain of hanging.[8]

More systematic was the exploitation of physical fear by the secular and ecclesiastical authorities. Under Henry VIII potential converts to Lollardy or Protestantism were deterred by the threat of imprisonment and death at the stake. Thomas Bennett was incarcerated, 'kept in stocks and strong iron with as much favour as a dog should find', then burned alive. The Act of Six Articles decreed death for denial of the sacraments: Philip Nichols shuddered at its 'extreme bloodiness'. Danger returned in Mary's reign, when 'fire and faggot carried the sway'. Some 273 died; many others suffered whipping or imprisonment.[9]

Such punishments, thought Foxe, were designed 'utterly to terrify and keep back all others from the true knowledge of Jesus Christ and his gospel'. Certainly they inhibited the public expression of heretical beliefs. In Mary's reign Latimer admitted that 'many' had been driven to recant by 'the pain of the law'. One Londoner 'revoked his opinion openly before all the parish', and two condemned heretics from Steeple Bumpstead were similarly compelled to recant. Fear, however, produced outward conformity more often than internal conversion. Protestants like Bradford and Clement lamented that many of their number had been driven to attend mass by 'the malice of this troublesome time'. A Catholic observed that some Bristolians attended confession merely 'for fear'. In 1557 the Venetian ambassador concluded that although 'externally, and in appearance, the Catholic religion seems day by day to increase and take root' – churches, for example, were being frequented, images replaced, and ancient rites performed – in reality these activities proceeded principally 'from fear'.[10]

Sometimes, moreover, persecution appears to have strengthened the new faith. Rowland Taylor's execution reportedly aroused anger in Suffolk, and Julins Palmer was converted by Latimer and Ridley's martyrdom. Renard concluded that the burnings were counterproductive. That the victims' fortitude was widely thought to prove their righteousness is shown by the anxiety of Catholics to refute this view. 'It moveth many minds', admitted a priest in 1555, 'to see an heretic constant and to die.'[11]

Physical punishments could work against the reformation; they could also work in its defence. Penalties for opposing the Henrician reformation included pillorying, stocking, whipping and ear cropping. On Cromwell's orders, and under Sir Piers Edgecumbe's supervision, dissidents were pilloried and stocked at Plymouth in 1533 – on market days, to maximize the impact on public opinion. At Gloucester in 1538 two speakers of sedition suffered pillorying and the nailing of their ears. Capital punishment – which the Treason Act of 1534 extended to words against the King – might include beheading, hanging, disembowelling, quartering and the public display of body parts. The period 1532–40 witnessed some 203 executions for rebellion or conspiracy. After the northern rising the Duke of Norfolk was ordered to cause 'dreadful execution upon a good number of the inhabitants, hanging them on trees, quartering them, and setting their heads and quarters in every town'. There were also some 110 executions for other types of treason. The south-west, in 1537–8, saw a Plymouthian executed, an Exeter man hanged and quartered, and a St Keverne man hanged in chains. London, in 1540, saw three priests hanged, beheaded and quartered, 'and their quarters set about the city'.[12]

Although the Treason Act was partly repealed in 1547, equally sanguinary retribution was visited upon the Cornish rioters of 1548 and the southwestern rebels of 1549. About 4000 of the latter were slaughtered in the field, some after surrender. 'A great many' were subsequently executed by Lord Russell and Sir Anthony Kingston, ringleaders dying in London and the others in the south-west. Lesser offences against the Edwardian reformation, like attending mass at Princess Mary's court, were punished by imprisonment. After the 1569 rising Sir George Bowes and other loyalists executed large numbers of rebels and their supporters, 'in divers places of the country': 66 died at Durham alone.[13]

The purpose behind such painful, humiliating and usually public punishments was to terrify potential resisters into submission. Henry VIII's avowed aim was 'the terrible example of others'. The Council of the West was instructed to punish dissidents 'extremely, for example', and Sir Roger Townsend used the stocks as 'a warning to other light persons in such wise to order themself'. Protector Somerset executed rebels so that 'their example should be terror this great while to all the country, and not to attempt such kind of rebellion again'. Such actions proved effective. 'The counties in the north was never in a more dreadful and true obeisance', reported Sir Arthur Darcy after the executions of 1537. In Cornwall even papists had been forced to 'do show outward, for avoiding of danger of the law'. 'We may say nothing openly', a traditionalist friar warned his hearers in London in 1536, 'for the knaves have our heads under their girdle. But we must be obedient unto our King and obey his commandment and take all things patiently.' 'Fear compelled us to bear with the time', the conservative Edmund Bonner would later explain, 'for otherwise there had been no way but one.'[14]

Fear also led many to cooperate actively with the Henrician reformation, particularly since failure to report treason was punishable by imprisonment or death. William Fielding admitted that this moved him to report a delation to Cromwell in 1535. In 1537 the Duke of Norfolk expected many delations from northerners, who were 'in such fear'. In 1539 two Exeter men denounced a gentleman for treason because they feared that he might denounce them. 'Wherefore', they allegedly argued, 'let us prevent him and play sure, and go to Mr Mayor, and first accuse him; and so shall we save ourselves.' In 1535 Richard Reynolds believed that it was largely 'from fear' that most people had conformed to the official reformation.[15]

The effect of the 1549 executions on the south-west is indicated by its failure to mount another revolt, or even a riot, against the anti-Catholic regimes of the next two decades. The events surrounding the 'commotion' were long remembered in the region. The north-east was similarly traumatized by the executions of 1569–70. 'And sure the people [are] in marvellous fear', reported Sir George Bowes in 1570; 'so that I trust there shall never such thing happen in these parts again.'[16]

Fear of the Tudor regime should not be overstated. Its coercive capacity was limited by its lack of a permanent army and a professional police force. Some of its subjects were not afraid to criticize it, conceal treason from it, or even rise against it. One London priest, in 1535, spoke in favour of the recently executed Fisher and More, and blithely declared that he 'cared not a fart' for the Tower. The evidence nevertheless indicates that fear was one of the powerful physical drives which, alongside spiritual convictions, emotional loyalties and material interests, induced the majority of English people to accept or even support the religious revolution.[17]

Part Four: Influences

20

Families, Employers, Neighbours, Strangers, Foreigners

Writers like Richard Whitford expected Catholic parents to teach their children the elements of the faith – including the *Ave Maria* as well as the *Pater Noster*, *Credo* and commandments. Parental instruction, particularly when reinforced by personal example, could certainly prove effective. In 1548, for example, the traditionalist rioters in Cornwall included both John Tribo and his son. The Catholics at Exeter in 1549 had been similarly indoctrinated: they remained unable to 'abide nor hear of any other religion than that as they were first nowselled in'.[1]

Increasingly, nevertheless, the influence of Catholic parents was rejected by their offspring. At Holsworthy Thomas Newcourt had donated land to maintain a chantry; in about 1540 it was re-appropriated by his heir. At Cullompton John Trotte had founded an almshouse with bedesmen; in about 1544 it was dissolved by his sons. At Exeter the mayor and aldermen had been 'nowselled in the Romish religion', but in 1549 they stoutly resisted those who rose in its defence. And although Robert Hooker and William Hurst were Catholics, Hooker's son became a Protestant and Hurst's daughter married one. Inter-generational conflict was even more frequent in the south-east. At Barking Hugh Buck's parents had taught him the *Pater Noster*, *Ave*, *Credo* and other elements of traditional religion. By 1538, however, he had rejected their 'idolatry', and lamented their failure to give him 'knowledge of eternal life'. In 1555 two Essex men justified their abandonment of the old religion on the ground that 'they have now read more scripture than ... their parents and kinsfolk'. Many Catholics, like John Christopherson, concluded that filial obedience was eroded by the reformation.[2]

Other senior members of the family found their Catholicism challenged by the young. In 1536 Edward London ignored his uncle's warnings to abandon Protestantism, and indeed informed against him. At Brodford in 1538 the vicar was accused of treason by his nephew, while at Worcester in 1546 an uncle was so shocked by his bible-reading and priest-mocking nephew that he denounced him as a heretic.[3]

An increasing number of parents, moreover, exerted an anti-Catholic influence on their young. At Hadleigh, from about 1530, Protestants' children were 'trained ... diligently in the right knowledge of God's word'. Five of the Ipswich heretics in 1556 had heretic parents, while the Marden dissidents in 1557 included John Ham senior, John Ham junior and James Ham. In Marian London the martyrdom of John and Elizabeth Warne was shared by their 20-year-old daughter, and the young martyr William Hunter had similarly been 'instructed in true religion' by his parents. Cardinal Pole indeed complained that London's 'youth' had been 'perversely and perniciously brought up in ill opinions'. Even in the south-west, fathers like Thomas Bennett, John Budleigh, Robert Kede and Philip Nichols – usually with the assistance of similarly committed wives – appear to have transmitted their convictions to their young. Kede's sons, for example, both espoused their father's faith. Not all such parents were successful: Agnes Priest failed to convert her children to the new beliefs.[4]

A powerful influence might be exerted by a husband or a wife. Many pre-reformation couples, like John and Joan Greenway, appear to have consolidated each other's Catholic faith: at Tiverton a sculpture of about 1517 shows them in prayer together before Our Lady. At Alphington in 1567 the Catholic activities of Thomas Stephens were abetted by his wife, while at York in 1568 both Robert and Isabel Willie absented themselves from the official services.[5]

Some wives remained more actively traditionalist than their men. At Exeter, in 1536, women rioted against iconoclasm without their husbands, while at York, in 1568, Cecilia Archer – but not her husband – was charged with non-attendance. On the other hand, an increasing number were more overtly anti-Catholic than their spouses. Agnes Priest exhorted hers 'to leave idolatry and to worship God in heaven'. Ten wives, without their husbands, were accused of religious offences at Ipswich in 1556, and 18 in Canterbury diocese in 1557. At Goudhurst the absentees from Catholic services included Richard Dallington's wife and daughter but not Richard himself.[6]

An increasing number of couples consolidated each other's opposition to traditional religion. Thomas Bennett's wife was 'contented to bear the cross with him', and sustained him in prison; he, in turn, 'comforted her, and gave her many good and godly exhortations'. In Mary's reign Martin and Joan Alley of Kenton both showed contempt for sacraments, while William and Alice Mount of Much Bentley both died at the stake. Fifteen women from Ipswich, and 14 in Canterbury diocese, were accused of religious offences with their men. Of the 125 women exiles, as many as 100 accompanied their husbands.[7]

Religious attitudes might be influenced not only by parents and spouses but also by employers. The substantial householder was expected to provide religious instruction not only for his wife and children but also for his servants, apprentices and other dependants. Catholics inevitably sought to encourage traditional practices among their employees. In 1554 the Exeter alderman John Tuckfield bequeathed 5s to his servant Roger Robinson, 'to pray for me', and additional sums (on the same condition) to another servant, an apprentice and each of his maids. The employer's Catholicism, nevertheless, was sometimes rejected by his employees – like the Chelmsford apprentice Thomas Jeffrey in 1539. Increasingly, moreover, the employer's influence was anti-Catholic. At Hadleigh, from about 1530, masters instructed their servants in Protestant doctrine. Some 58 of the Marian exiles accompanied their employers: the merchant John Budleigh took several servants, including his maidservant Eleanor, as well as apprentices like John Boggens and Richard Vivian. Similarly anti-Catholic was the Axminster innkeeper who, in 1556, commanded his ostlers to serve guests instead of attending the revived rites.[8]

Neighbours, too, could be persuasive. Sampford Courtenay's resistance to the 1549 prayerbook was initiated by a small group, whose stand was then emulated by their fellow parishioners. On the other hand, the example of neighbours encouraged some to plunder monasteries. 'Might I not, as well as others, have some profit of the spoil of the abbey?', a Yorkshireman subsequently asked; 'for I did see all would away, and therefore I did as others did.' Neighbours could also infect each other with heresy. At Axminster in

1535–6 a shoemaker's eagerness to discuss religion caused conservatives to fear that 'erroneous and heretical opinions' were 'like to increase daily and grow in the said town'. In London, under Henry VIII and Edward VI, the bricklayer John Harridance proclaimed the new faith from his house window and in his garden: as many as 1000 hearers were attracted. At Aylsham, in Mary's reign, people flocked to hear a Protestant glover, while at South Molton, by 1562, Protestants had disseminated their faith throughout the neighbourhood. There were also failures. Heretics were sometimes reported by resistant neighbours, and Harridance's preaching evoked local complaints: one neighbour threatened to throw a bowling ball at him if he continued.[9]

Attitudes might also be shaped by contact with inhabitants of other regions. In 1537, while visiting Hampshire to sell fish, two Cornishmen were persuaded by local conservatives to plot a Catholic rising. On the other hand, the ability of the north and the south-west to reinforce each other's Catholicism was seriously weakened by the distance between them and by their cultural and linguistic differences. These factors largely explain why the two regions failed to support each other's rebellions. In the south-east, in contrast, communications were facilitated by the superior road system of the lowland zone. This, together with the mobility of the clothworkers, will help explain the more rapid spread of Lollardy and Protestantism in south-eastern counties, especially in the clothing areas of Suffolk and Kent. Thomas Man preached Lollardy throughout this region – and allegedly won 700 converts – before his burning in 1518, while the Londoner Nicholas Field carried Protestantism into Buckinghamshire in 1530.[10]

Western and south-western heresy was also stimulated by contact with the capital. Bristol's Protestantism owed much to its seaborne trade with London, and two of Exeter's leading Protestants, John Budleigh and John Periam, were merchants with metropolitan connections. In 1559 a number of London merchants, while visiting Exeter for a fair, assisted Periam and other citizens in restoring 'godly' worship. Other Devon Protestants with London links included Totnes's Philip Nichols and several Plymouth merchants. In the north, too, especially in south-east Lancashire and the west riding, the new faith was promoted by commercial and industrial contacts with the south-east. In 1543, after working in Suffolk, the clothworker William Bull returned to Dewsbury with hostile opinions about confession, extreme unction and holy water. In Edward's reign John Leafe migrated from Yorkshire and became an apprentice in London, where he was converted by John Rogers' preaching. Under Mary a Yarmouth man read the English Bible in a house at Hull.[11]

English people might also meet inhabitants of other countries. The Irish, Spanish and Portuguese, and to a lesser extent the Welsh and French, remained predominantly Catholic. Although their influence was sometimes felt in the south-east – in Essex, for example, a French priest failed to erase the Pope's name – geography and commerce ensured that it was stronger in the south-west. Catholicism here was sometimes reinforced by Welsh immigrants – like Tiverton's John Ap Price, who ordered intercessions in Mary's reign – and by Irish traders and fishermen: one, in 1539, purchased his registration on the Stratton bede roll. Two Spaniards, after landing at Dartmouth in 1541, travelled to Salisbury and spoke in favour of monasteries and the Pope. Brittany gave the region several saints: an image of Armil was commissioned by Stratton in 1531, and his picture remains on the Torbryan screen. Bretons also erected the region's rood lofts, as at North Petherwin in about 1520, and welcomed its pilgrims to Breton shrines. One spread disaffection in the region in 1538, and others supported its 'Catholic' risings in 1548–9.[12]

In the north the old religion was sometimes sustained by Irishmen or Scots. Two Irish priests, carrying seditious letters, landed at Shields in 1538–9. A Scotsman, 'of the same sort and fashion as the Maid of Kent was', was arrested in 1534, and Scottish friars were employed by the vicar of Newark to denounce the Henrician reformation.[13]

These contacts, however, did not always advance the old faith. A shipowner from Torre, making his will in a Breton port in 1556, left nothing to religious causes. Contact with Spaniards was increasingly liable to result in conflict rather than conversion to their religion. The influence exerted by these nations, moreover, was sometimes anti-Catholic. Some Bretons supported the iconoclasm at Exeter in 1536. Scots preached in favour of the reformation at Bristol, London and Salisbury under Henry, and proclaimed the new faith in northern England under Edward. In 1549 the southwestern rebellion was opposed by 1000 Welshmen under Sir William Herbert.[14]

Contact with Scandinavia, Germany, the Netherlands and Switzerland, in contrast, was strongest in the south and east, and was increasingly likely to bring experience of the new religion. In some cases the connection was forged by foreign visitors or immigrants. By 1526 the Hanse merchants in London were maintaining Lutheran heresies and importing Lutheran books. In the 1530s some foreign heretics were expelled or burned, particularly in London and at Colchester, though in 1539 the Oxford 'favourers of God's word' still met in the house of a Dutch or German bookseller. Edward's reign saw the establishment of Protestant communities by Germans and Frenchmen in London and by Walloons at Glastonbury. Fagius rejoiced that they would advance 'the doctrine of eternal life', though Micronius blamed German refugees for the rise of radical religious groups. The Marian regime would complain that 'innumerable heresies' had been spread by foreigners. Not all such immigrants, of course, were Protestant: one 'Dutchman' repaired images for Exeter cathedral in Mary's reign.[15]

In other cases the connection was forged by Englishmen, as sailors, merchants, visitors or emigrants. Sailors from Hull, visiting ports in Germany and the Netherlands in 1527, saw and apparently liked the vernacular worship of the Lutherans. In 1530 a Londoner attacked fast days and festivals on the ground that he had been in Germany – 'and there they used not so to fast, nor to make such holy days'. In Mary's reign, moreover, some 800 English exiles gained firsthand experience of the new religion in its Swiss and German homelands. Many returned to England with beliefs markedly more radical than those approved by the Elizabethan regime.[16]

21

LAY AUTHORITIES

The religious behaviour of a local community could be powerfully influenced by its local peers and gentry. The authority of this élite sprang not only from its wealth and status but also from its virtual monopoly of important office: sheriffs, commissioners and justices of the peace were almost always recruited from its ranks.

Before the reformation its influence was predominantly supportive of traditional religion. The construction and furnishing of parish churches was financed by aristocratic dynasties like the Beauforts, who largely rebuilt the fabrics at Bovey Tracey, Sampford Peverell and Uplowman in about 1500, and by a much larger number of gentry families like the Evanses, who donated the benches at Coldridge in 1511. Some gentlemen played leading roles in parochial religion: at Stratton a Chamond was warden of the High Cross guild in 1518, and helped to commission the rood loft in 1531. Others, however, were less supportive. Three Devon gentlemen robbed churches in 1517–20, and three Cornish gentlemen led an attack on Tavistock abbey property in 1527.[1]

What influence was exerted by this élite in the reformation decades? In 1536 many northern peers and gentlemen, including the Nevilles and Percies, led their dependants into 'Catholic' revolt; but they were seldom emulated by the aristocracy of other regions. In 1549 only a handful of southwestern gentry – 'not past two or three', thought Somerset – took arms against the official reformation. In 1569, too, only a minority of the northern élite led their servants and tenants into rebellion: they included the Earls of Northumberland and Westmorland, and several Nortons.[2]

A significant number of gentry attempted non-violent resistance to the reformation. Under Henry VIII one in Derbyshire had church bells rung on abrogated days, and prevented royal injunctions from being read, while in Kent several dissuaded people from reading the Bible. Under Elizabeth some in Herefordshire held masses in their homes, and some in Sussex proved 'mislikers' of the official religion: Broyle's James Gage, for instance, was 'a common harbourer of obstinates'. 'Whose example', feared their bishop, 'draweth a number of people after them.' On the other hand, none of the Kent justices were guilty of 'maintaining the perverse and ungodly'; and even in Cornwall and Devon, by 1569, only three refused to attend the new services and receive communion. The great majority of English peers and gentlemen thus failed to lead their inferiors into effective resistance to the reformation.[3]

Some, it is true, cooperated diligently with the Marian reaction. In 1554, for example, the council thanked certain Essex justices 'for their travails in the well ordering of the shire'. A larger number, however, actively enforced the Henrician, Edwardian and Elizabethan reforms. Henry's reign saw suspected supporters of the Pope, monasteries, saints' days and other prohibited elements of the old religion assiduously examined, punished and reported to Cromwell by local gentlemen. One justice boasted of his ceaseless efforts in detecting and punishing 'fautors of the venomous papistical faction of Rome'. Southwestern activists included Sir Thomas Dennis, Sir Piers Edgecumbe, Sir William Godolphin, and Hugh and Richard Pollard; the Pollards participated also in the destruction of local image cults.[4]

Most of these served under Lord Russell on the short-lived Council of the West, a body intended to 'give strait charge and commandment to the people to conform themselves' to the Henrician reformation. Similar roles were performed by the lords and gentlemen of the Council in the Marches and the Council of the North. Among the dissidents arrested, tried and executed by the latter were York's John Ainsworth and the vicar of Muston. Peers and gentlemen also raised forces against the risings of 1536: the Earl of Derby, for example, led 'a great number of men'.[5]

Under Edward it was largely the gentry who, as royal commissioners, implemented policies like the suppression of chantries, the removal of images and the confiscation of church goods. The chantry commissioners for Devon included members of the Bluett,

Cary, Harvey, Haydon, Pollard and Prideaux families, while the compilation of church inventories in Cornwall was supervised by a Chamond, a Godolphin, a Grenville, a Killigrew and a Reskymmer. Accounts attest the impact of such commissioners throughout the realm. Ashburton had to send representatives to meet them at Exeter, Totnes and Paignton in 1547–8, at Newton Abbot in 1548–9 and 1549–50, and at Exeter in 1550–1. Meetings were invariably followed by actions like image destruction or book buying: in 1548–9, for example, a 'new book' was bought 'at the King's command'. Sometimes, as at Hull, images or other objects were destroyed by the commissioners themselves.[6]

Gentlemen also quelled dissent. The Helston riot was suppressed by 'the gentlemen of the country', while the southwestern rebellion was opposed, defeated and punished by members of local families like the Bluetts, Carews, Champernownes, Chichesters, Courtenays, Dennises, Grenvilles, Pollards, Raleighs, Russells and Yardes. Among the most active were Lord Russell and Sir Gawen and Sir Peter Carew. Such figures were usually followed by their numerous dependants. Servants accompanied their masters into battle at Fenny Bridges and elsewhere, and the government subsequently expressed its gratitude to the gentlemen and serving men 'who have so valiantly acquitted themselves in the service of his majesty'.[7]

Elizabeth's religious policies were similarly implemented and defended by local gentlemen. Commissioners like Sir Peter Carew and Sir John Chichester organized the suppression of altars, images and other Catholic elements in 1559, and accounts throughout England again record the general speed and effectiveness of their activities. In 1569 the northern revolt was actively opposed by peers like Lord Scrope and gentlemen like Sir George Bowes, invariably with the support of their dependants: Scrope sent 'all his tenants and servants' to Sir George's aid.[8]

While they remained legal, elements of the old religion were supported by some of the élite. In Henry's last years, for example, Stratton church received a gift of vestments from an Arundell, and a South Petherwin guild was defended from predators by a Tremayne. In Mary's reign, according to Parkyn, many priests restored mass because they were 'commanded by lords and knights Catholic'. Some gentlemen bequeathed ritual equipment to parish churches, as at Woodbury, served as store wardens, as at Braunton, or attempted to protect churches from exploitation, as at North Lew.[9]

On the other hand, the influence of traditionalist gentry could be resisted. Thomas Bennett and Agnes Priest both ignored the gentlemen who urged them to recant, and in 1537 a Warwickshire man refused his landlord's command to denounce a Protestant. Frequently, moreover, the example provided by the gentry for its inferiors was either indifferent or hostile to traditional religion. The Emperor Charles V, in 1554, was one of many who thought that popular attitudes to Catholicism were being poisoned by the church-despoiling gentry. 'They are very numerous', he lamented, 'and seduce the people.'[10]

In Henry's reign they sometimes led local opposition to monastic houses. In 1533–8 they organized an attack on the prior of Bodmin's servant, a raid on his weir, and a petition against the abbot of Torre. Sometimes they attempted to seize income from guilds, as at Exeter, or from parish churches and chapels, as at Pelynt and St Giles in the Wood. They were also conspicuous in the expropriation and suppression of chantries, as at Colebrooke, Colyford, Exeter, Halberton, Lansallos, St Michael Penkevil, St Winnow, Thornbury and Tretherf. Under Edward and Mary they seized ritual apparatus at Barnstaple and Exeter, led opposition to holy water at Menheniot, and encouraged fast-breaking at Tavistock and image-mocking at Silverton.[11]

Particularly striking was their willingness to despoil the clergy. Many proved ruthless in acquiring episcopal and cathedral lands, either on favourable leases or in outright possession. In 1542–51 the see of Exeter's annual income was reduced from some £1600 to £500: beneficiaries included the Carews, Dennises, Killigrews and Russells. Lesser clerics were also exploited. By the 1550s gentlemen were blackmailing them at North Lew, detaining rent from them at Cornwood, and seizing their houses or lands at Bovey Tracey, Gulval and High Bickington. One Marian cleric complained of the gentry 'who never did the church good, nor peradventure intend'.[12]

At St Cleer in 1534 the justices failed to protect a priest from physical attack, because his assailants were supported by 'men of authority and power in that country'. In Edward's reign the plundered parson of Bittadon found that the gentry 'rather mocked [him] than caused him to have any restitution': he described his despoilers as 'belonging to certain gentlemen'. Others encouraged their inferiors to resist offerings and mortuaries, as at Lamerton and Portledge, to refuse clergy rents, as at Stokenham, and even to seize clergy property, as at Bridestowe, Hartland and St Just. At Lamerton in 1551 it was a justice, Mr Tremayne, who commanded the parishioners to reduce their traditional offerings to the vicar.[13]

A number not only weakened the old religion but also promoted the new. Though most frequent in the south-east – Sussex, for instance, had 20 such 'favourers of religion and godly orders' in 1564 – they existed also in the north and south-west. In Yorkshire, by 1564, they included Sir George Bowes and Sir Thomas Gargrave. In Devon Sir William Carew shielded heretics in Henry's reign, while his son proved 'a great favourer of all Protestants' and 'an earnest promoter of God's true religion'. Sir Peter Carew patronized John Hooker and Philip Nichols, and Nichols attributed the growth of southwestern Protestantism to his protection. In Mary's reign it was sustained by families like the Raleighs and Tremaynes – the exiled merchant Peter Willis was a Tremayne dependant – and in Elizabeth's it continued to be led by gentry like the Chichesters, Fortescues, Parkers and Pollards.[14]

If the growth of the new faith owed much to zealous lords and gentlemen, its weakness in some areas was due partly to a scarcity of such powerful patrons. The south-west was 'not stored' with 'well persuaded magistrates' in 1549, and Gloucestershire (thought Hooper) needed more 'good justices' in 1552. In 1564 some Exeter diocese justices were still 'not so earnest to maintain the ecclesiastical policy as they are wished to be', and similar attitudes among the Somerset justices were believed to encourage 'grudge and doubt among the common people'.[15]

In major towns, in contrast, a stronger religious influence was usually exerted by the corporation. In as late as 1564 some Sussex towns were governed by the 'frowardly superstitious', and two-thirds of the Hereford council were 'no favourers of religion'. On the other hand, Exeter's mayor and aldermen suppressed opposition to the Henrician reformation, organized resistance to the 1549 revolt, and helped confiscate ritual equipment in 1552 and 1559. At Plymouth their counterparts assisted the campaigns against monasteries and images, while at Lostwithiel it was the mayor who ordered the defacement of St George's chapel in 1549. Some urban oligarchies provided their inferiors with a 'perilous example' by refusing tithes, as at Helston in about 1540, and detaining church goods, as at Exeter in 1555. Anti-traditionalist influence is discernible also in the north. At Hull in 1559 the mayor and aldermen ordered the conservative vicar to perform the new service, 'according to the book authorized by parliament', while at Newcastle in 1564 their equivalents determined to remain 'obedient to the [religious] laws, and keep the town so too, with all their diligence'. But it was most powerful in the south-east. In London, for example, it was at the mayor's command that St Barnabas' day was suppressed in 1550.[16]

Although the authority of oligarchies was never total – one Exeter woman, incensed by an alderman's collusion with the Henrician iconoclasm, 'gave him a blow and sent him packing' – in most cases it promoted obedience to the official reforms. Sometimes its influence was positively Protestant. By 1564 Brighton, Hastings, Lewes and Rye were all 'governed with such officers as be faithful favourers of God's word', and similar enthusiasts were to be found in the corporations at Exeter, Plymouth, South Molton and elsewhere.[17]

Religion could also be influenced by parish constables. One headed the traditionalists at Axminster in 1535–6, and a number supported conservative revolts in 1549 and 1569. Most, however, appear to have enforced the religious policies of the crown. At Ashlower, Wootton and elsewhere they detected and reported opponents of the Henrician reformation. In 1537 a Suffolk man complained that if two or three people talked, 'the constable come to them and will know what communication they have, or else they shall be stocked'. Constables also cooperated in the compilation of church inventories, as at Germoe in 1549, and enforced attendance at the new services, as at York in 1561. Sometimes they took the lead in the denunciation of priests, as at Paul and St Breock, or in the embezzlement of church property, as at Davidstow.[18]

Churchwardens could sustain the old religion by purchasing apparatus, raising altars or erecting images. Their accounts, however, leave no doubt that the great majority of sixteenth-century wardens were unwilling overtly to resist a royal decree. It was largely their dutiful collaboration that made possible the effective local implementation of official reform.

22

Clerics (1)

Pre-reformation clerics influenced adult layfolk through personal contact and in the rite of confession. They also instructed the young, not only in parish churches – hence the Creed sequences on rood screens – but also in cathedral and chantry schools and in the universities. Formal education, however, was usually restricted to the relatively wealthy by the cost of books and by the peasant's need for his children's labour.[1]

Clerics might also reach congregations, or even large crowds, by public preaching. Parish churches retain some 200 pre-reformation pulpits – Holne's, for example, is datable to 1504–19 – and innumerable contemporary benches. Sermons were also delivered in churchyards, as at Exeter St Mary Major at Easter, in chapel yards, as at East Newlyn in Rogation Week, and even in remote locations like St Breage's Beacon on St Petrock's day. Preachers included bishops, canons, parish priests, monks and, above all, friars – like the Dominican and three Franciscans at Exeter in 1531. On the other hand, pulpits may have been used as much for bedes biddings as for sermons, and a scarcity of preaching was noted by the Archbishop of Canterbury in 1528 and the Archbishop of York in 1535. Fewer than 12 of the latter's secular clergy were capable of it.[2]

The religion disseminated by such means was predominantly traditional. 'Ye spare not to make lying sermons to the people', Thomas Bennett told friars, 'to maintain your false traditions and foul gains.' Many sermons, like those at East Newlyn, celebrated local saints, and many schools, like that at Week St Mary, were taught by priests who prayed for founders' souls. The 1520s nevertheless saw the beginnings of attacks on traditional religion by preachers like Barnes and Latimer at Cambridge and Bilney in London and East Anglia.[3]

The reformation decades witnessed some changes in the methods of clerical instruction. Confession was suppressed by the Protestant regimes, but preaching increased in importance. Pulpits were made obligatory in 1547, and many were erected in these years: those at Affpuddle, Chedzoy, Bungay and Knebworth are dated 1547, 1551, 1558 and 1567, and Exeter St Petrock's new structure cost some £12 in 1561–2. Were there significant changes in content too?[4]

In 1536–40 the dissolution of all monasteries eradicated the Catholic example and instruction which (according to Robert Aske) they had provided for their neighbours. Conservative friars were also subjected to increasing pressure. In 1533–8 their teaching or preaching was reported to the authorities by local informants at Bristol, Cambridge, London, Newcastle, Norwich, Plymouth, Southampton and elsewhere. 1534, for example, saw a Cambridge Dominican and a Southampton Observant investigated for pro-papal sermons. The consequences might be imprisonment – a Plymouth Franciscan examined by Sir Piers Edgecumbe was subsequently incarcerated at Launceston – or even death. Friars' preaching, moreover, was everywhere halted by the suppression of their houses in 1538.[5]

Many secular clerics remained traditionalist. Some were reluctant to propagate official articles and injunctions, as in the south-west in 1536. Some used confession to urge layfolk to 'stand strongly in their old faith', as in London, St Albans and Salisbury, while others taught or preached in its defence, as at Aylesbury, Exeter, Grantham, Stanmore, Ticehurst and elsewhere. At Ticehurst the incumbent preached in support of images in 1538, while at Aylesbury the vicar retained sermons favouring Becket and the Pope in 1539. Although some appear to have evaded serious punishment, others suffered penance, prison or execution. Imprisonment was the fate of the Exeter preacher who criticized the royal supremacy in 1534. By 1540 those who still dared to openly controvert the official reformation were conspicuously few.[6]

A rising number in fact proved partly or wholly hostile to traditional religion. They included schoolmasters like Week St Mary's William Cholwell, and preachers like those patronized by Thomas Cromwell. In London, for example, he organized anti-papal sermons in 1534. Similar attacks on the papacy were (according to a conservative) preached 'daily' at Southampton in the same year, and were subsequently organized by many bishops – not only reformers like Cranmer and Goodrich but also theological conservatives like Lee, Longland and Veysey. 'As to the setting forth of the abuses of the bishop of Rome', boasted Exeter's Veysey in 1536, 'I suppose no one has preached more freely than I.' He was assisted by several cathedral canons and the dean, Simon Heynes. In Lincoln diocese Longland distributed 2000 anti-papal declarations for his clergy to proclaim.[7]

A significant number of preachers were not only anti-papal but positively Protestant. They were most frequent in London, and in towns like Bristol, Exeter, Gloucester, Oxford, Plymouth, Rye and Salisbury, though rural areas were sometimes reached. In London they included Bishop Hilsey, who preached vigorously against images and relics, as well as Barnes, Crome, Garrett and Latimer. Provincial preachers included Richard Croke, who spoke in 37 different churches in Buckinghamshire, Hertfordshire, Northamptonshire and Oxfordshire, as well as Ward in Essex, Bale and Parker in Suffolk, Vaws in Hampshire, Large in Warwickshire and Erley, Latimer and Rawlings in the west. In Devon the new faith was proclaimed by visitors like Latimer, who spoke at Exeter in 1534, and by local clerics like Heynes and the incumbents of Branscombe, Plymouth and Sampford Peverell.

Robert Ward, for example, decried ceremonies and holy water and taught the Lutheran view of justification. Edward Large attacked fasts and rosaries, and declared 'the pure and sincere word of God', while Dr Heynes was noted for his 'sincere and true preaching of the gospel'. Such men were sometimes supported by lay patrons. William Lucy used his authority as a justice to protect Large from heresy accusations. Several Londoners, like Humphrey Monmouth, arranged Protestant sermons at their burial, while Plymouth's leading townsmen commissioned their parson to preach 'the word of God' on four days every week. Although many such preachers were silenced by Cromwell's fall – Barnes, for example, was burned – some continued to minister. Heynes, though imprisoned for several months, was protected by Sir Peter Carew.[8]

In 1547 a number of clerics still reportedly preached 'to keep the unlearned in their blindness still'. These, however, were increasingly targeted by the Edwardian regime. Most of the conservative bishops were eventually deposed, some after periods of imprisonment. Some of the most traditionalist of parish priests were deprived, imprisoned or even executed, particularly in the south-west after the 1549 revolt. Catholic influence was further weakened by the dissolution of chantry schools. At Stratford-on-Avon, for example, control of the school passed to the corporation.[9]

Unlicensed preaching was banned in 1547. By 1548 few traditionalists were still preaching in London, and in 1549 Bishop Bonner himself was imprisoned for a Paul's Cross sermon. Also incarcerated were provincial conservatives like Drs Chrispin and Moreman – to the anger of the southwestern rebels, who demanded their release 'to preach amongst us our Catholic faith'. Among the relatively few to continue preaching the old religion after 1549 were the vicars of Ipplepen and Staunton. The latter, who had spoken in favour of the mass, was compelled to recant.[10]

The Edwardian suppression of Catholic preaching was accompanied by a major expansion of its reformed equivalent. The Marian regime would lament 'the evil diligence of the abused preachers in the time of the schism', and the Greyfriars chronicler noted their 'much preaching through all England'. In London they included Bradford, Cardmaker, Crome, Hooper, Latimer, Ridley and many others. Latimer spoke frequently at Paul's Cross, and Hooper spoke at least once each day. Other towns were also targeted. 'All the time of King Edward's reign', a Maidstone Protestant later recalled, 'we were diligently instructed with continual sermons.' 'No Sunday nor holy day passed', says Foxe of Hadleigh's Dr Taylor, 'nor other time when he might get the people together, but he preached to them ... the doctrine of their salvation.' Thomas Hancock proclaimed the new faith at Salisbury and Poole: he denounced mass, vestments, holy bread and water, images and 'superstitious' ceremonies.[11]

Even the peripheral regions were visited by itinerant preachers, some sponsored by the regime. Rough laboured at Carlisle, Berwick, Newcastle and eventually Hull, while Bradford operated in Lancashire, Hooper in Gloucestershire, and Coverdale, Gregory, Reynolds, Tongue and others in the south-west. Bishop Hooper devoted himself to 'going about his towns and villages ..., teaching and preaching to the people there', while Dr Tongue spoke 'throughout [the] whole diocese' of Exeter.[12]

Even the south-west, in consequence, heard Protestant sermons not only in the cathedral, where Bishop Coverdale spoke frequently, and in city churches like St Mary Major, but also in towns like Barnstaple, Crediton, Honiton, Plymouth and Totnes. Many were sponsored by urban élites. Totnes' John Bougin gave a preacher £6 to proclaim 'the true and sincere word of God ... to the edifying of all Christian hearts', while the Plymouth townsmen sponsored sermons in 1547 and 1549–50. In June 1553 the Plymouthian William Amadas paid his parson to read out 'the homily of the salvation of mankind by only Christ', and to deliver 'godly exhortations' at a dinner for the mayor and aldermen and at an assembly of the common people. There was also some preaching beyond the towns. The parson of St Teath, Nicholas Daniel, evangelized widely in Cornwall and Devon, and Sir Peter Carew maintained a chaplain to preach 'in the countries round about him'.[13]

Fagius was therefore exaggerating considerably when he claimed that 'there are scarcely 10 preachers in the whole kingdom of England who can do anything with effect'. Particularly in the north and west, however, and in rural communities, it is evident that they remained inaccessible to many people. In Cornwall, at the reign's beginning, they were absent even from towns like Bodmin, Falmouth, Launceston and Liskeard. Hooker lamented the scarcity of 'learned preachers ... to teach and instruct the people' in the south-west in 1549, and Hooper acknowledged the need for 'faithful ministers' in Gloucester diocese in 1552–3. Philip Nichols noted the gentry's reluctance to endow preachers with substantial livings. The problem was only partly solved by readings from the officially sanctioned homilies. Accounts in fact suggest that only a minority of parishes even purchased these.[14]

Mary's reign saw the old faith again preached in London, by clerics like Bourne, Feckenham, Gardiner and Watson, and in Essex, by Thomas Tye and others. The south-west heard similar sermons at Dartmouth, East Newlyn and South Tawton, and the St George's day sermon was revived at York. Catholic preaching, however, remained limited. 'In most parts of the realm', observed the government in 1554, 'there is overmuch want of good preachers.' Exeter cathedral (for instance) found it difficult to provide them. This shortage compelled the regime to order the use of homilies; but the accounts suggest that most parishes never bought them. It was more successful in silencing Protestant clerics, by burning, exile or deprivation. 'Godly ministers of the word' nevertheless continued to 'feed their flock faithfully ... as the private pastors of particular flocks', and it was during this 'perilous time' that William Ramsey began his preaching ministry at South Molton.[15]

In the early Elizabethan years, and especially in the north and west, some clerics still sought to promote the old religion. Several were reported from Herefordshire, Northamptonshire and Worcestershire in 1564, and one was the 'most earnest mover' of the northern rebellion in 1569. On the other hand, the official campaign of 1559 effectively ousted all but one of the Marian bishops, many deans, archdeacons and canons, and possibly 5 per cent of parochial incumbents. The great majority again conformed, though more rapidly in the south than in the north. Some, like the vicar of Bodmin, were made to publicly recant their former errors. In the subsequent decade, moreover, the proportion of clergy ordained as Catholic priests was progressively reduced by senility and death.[16]

Overt traditionalists were driven from the universities, and schoolmasters ordered to teach the established religion. Although some refused – in 1568 York children were still taught by a priest who advocated prayer to saints – the episcopal licensing system seems gradually to have excluded most Catholics from the schools. Parish clergy were also ordered to teach the new catechism to children and the essential formulae to congregations. Not all responded with enthusiasm. In 1562 a Rockbeare man reported that he 'never heard the vicar to move the parishioners to come unto the holy communion but once in a twelve months'.[17]

Unlicensed preaching was prohibited in December 1558, and subsequently punished by the council and its local agents. Preachers who tried to defend 'popery', as at Exeter in 1560, were forced publicly to recant. Such measures proved effective. Even Exeter diocese saw the end of traditional sermons, like that at East Newlyn, and in 1561 the Bishop's comprehensive report on his several hundred clergy found only three – including the unmarried, non-graduate and religiously conservative vicar of Morebath – who still dared to preach without official licence. Catholic preaching seems similarly to have dwindled in the north, though exceptions occurred in Carlisle diocese in 1564 and in parts of the rebellious north-east in 1569.[18]

How often was it replaced by its reformed equivalent? In 1560–2 the percentage of Canterbury province clerics who preached the new faith ranged from approximately four to five in Coventry, Exeter and Peterborough dioceses, and eight to nine in Norwich and Salisbury, to 16 in Winchester, 20–22 in Gloucester and Rochester and 42 in London. Protestant preachers were apparently more common in the south and east, and in Gloucester diocese, than in most parts of the Midlands, west and south-west. Even in Exeter diocese, however, they included Bishop Alley, a 'godly preacher', and canons like Richard Tremayne, a Marian exile, as well as parochial incumbents like Bradford's William Cavel – a graduate and a diligent preacher.[19]

Such men were again supported by lay patrons. The Earl of Bedford sent his chaplain to preach in Devon in 1560, 'for the better setting forth of God's truth and the Queen's majesty's godly proceedings', while a North Molton gentleman, John Parker, was described in 1562 as 'a sure work and strong defence of God's word, and lover of all true preachers'. A number of early Elizabethan towns, including Colchester, Coventry, Ipswich and Leicester, established lectureships for the maintenance of preachers; and others, like Barnstaple, Crediton and Dartmouth, sponsored occasional sermons.[20]

Protestant preachers were particularly conspicuous in the towns. London, in 1559, heard them denounce ritual apparatus, attack rood lofts, and urge support for the returning exiles. At Coventry this year they were invited by the townsmen to 'proclaim the gospel to them', while at Newcastle, by 1564, one had been hired by the 'poorer sort'. At Exeter the citizens listened to cathedral clerics on Sundays and at morning prayer. But some rural parishes also heard sermons from visitors or incumbents. George Manning not only served his cure at Bovey Tracey but also preached at Ilsington, South Tawton and Woodbury. At Stoke Climsland, in 1566, the vicar had 'done his diligence to have a sermon every month'.[21]

In many places, nevertheless, such preachers remained few. In the south-west this shortage was noted in 1559–60 by Philip Nichols, Sir John Chichester and the Earl of Bedford: 'the lack is great of such good workmen in God's harvest', Bedford complained. In 1561 Bishop Alley found that his approximately 600 parishes were served by 28 preachers. Typical was rural Honeychurch, where the rector, Richard Downe, was unmarried, non-graduate and non-preaching. The problem was mitigated in part by readings from the official homilies and injunctions. Many parishes bought both in response to the order of 1559, and homilies 'On Rebellion' were obtained during or after the 1569 revolt. In many parishes, such as Dean Prior and Stoke Climsland, these works were certainly read by clerics to their congregations. Inevitably there was also neglect: in 1569 the vicar of Ilsington read the injunctions 'very seldom', and the homilies only once a year.[22]

23

Clerics (2)

Why was the influence of clerics so much less Catholic in 1570 than in 1530? One factor was the suppression, by Henry VIII, of the predominantly conservative religious orders, and in particular of the preaching friars. To this must be added Mary's failure to revive them, and Pole's refusal to import Jesuit preachers in their place. A second factor was the removal of Catholics from university posts – especially at Oxford, where they had opposed the English Bible and failed to 'teach the youth why the bishop of Rome was expulsed'. A third was the unwillingness of gentlemen and corporations to sponsor Catholic preaching. A fourth was the bishops' reluctance to lead their clergy in resistance to reform. Most acquiesced in the Henrician and Edwardian assaults, and only 1559 saw concerted opposition.[1]

The willingness of clerics to defend the old religion was sometimes eroded by material inducements. Dr Tregonwell's role in the dissolutions was rewarded with annuities and land. More important, however, were their sense of duty to established authority, their reluctance to risk their livelihoods and their fear of punishment. Deprivations, imprisonments and executions not only silenced the most overtly Catholic priests, but also dissuaded their less heroic colleagues from supporting prohibited institutions and activities. In 1549 (for example) the vicar of Sampford Courtenay used the new prayer book in obedience to 'the laws set forth'. Even after Mary's accession many priests were slow to restore the Latin mass, because 'there was no act, statute, proclamation or commandment set forth for the same'.[2]

Why did an increasing number become positive promoters of the new faith? Apart from its spiritual attractions – which often were crucial – the reasons include the patronage of gentlemen and corporations, the support of bishops and the training of the universities. Patrons provided the new preachers with both advancement and protection. Sir Peter Carew was 'a patron to all godly preachers, in defence of whom he did oftentimes show himself both stout and hardy'. Bishops like Coverdale and Cranmer appointed Protestant officials and licensed Protestant preachers. The most influential Protestant educators included Cox and Humphrey at Oxford and Bilney, Bucer, Cheke and Lever at Cambridge. Cambridge converted Bradford, Latimer and other ministers, and partly explains the frequency of Protestant preachers in the south-east.[3]

Why, nevertheless, did only a minority of clerics enthusiastically promote the new faith? One factor was persecution, which deterred Nicholas Daniel (for example) from preaching it in Mary's reign. A second was possibly the hostility directed against its advocates by traditionalists like John Chapel of St Teath. A third, in some places, was the lack of gentry patronage. In 1564 some Sussex gentlemen were reluctant to 'have learned preachers of their own or others'. A fourth was the financial difficulties of the Edwardian and Elizabethan regimes, which limited their ability to sponsor preaching campaigns.[4]

A fifth, in some dioceses, was the theological conservatism of the bishops. In Lincoln and Winchester, for example, Protestant preaching was actively hindered by Longland and Gardiner. The percentage of southern and eastern sees occupied by committed reformers was approximately 33 in 1546, 44 in 1549 and 66 in 1552. After falling to nil in 1554 it rose to 78 in 1560. In the northern and western sees, however, the percentages were 23, 31, 46, nil and 46.[5]

But the most serious obstacle was probably education. Colet and More admitted that very many of the parish clergy were 'unlearned', and in Exeter diocese only 20 per cent were graduates in 1561. This was largely because – as the Archbishop of York complained in 1535 – the incomes of many benefices were too poor to attract graduates. Reformers like Simon Heynes thought that lack of learning caused the doctrinal conservatism of most priests; certainly it prevented them from studying scripture and preparing sermons.[6]

How did the influence of the clergy affect the religious attitudes of the English people? In many cases it was unquestionably powerful in sustaining the old faith. At Chichester, for example, 'the inculcation of certain of the clergy' moved 'men of simplicity' to venerate St Richard's shrine. The northern risings of 1536 were officially attributed to 'the solicitation and traitorous conspiracy of the monks and canons of these parts', and the southwestern revolt of 1549 to 'the provocation only of certain popish priests'. In 1564 Hereford and its neighbourhood reportedly followed the example provided by its conservative cathedral canons, while in Durham diocese priests expelled from Scotland were accused of 'dissuading the people' from the new religion.[7]

The power of priest over penitent could be particularly strong. 'Under confession', complained a ballad of 1549, 'these priests do bind the simple people, most earnest of all, on pain of damnation to follow their mind.' Schooling was sometimes equally effective. In about 1530 Thomas Harding studied at the Barnstaple chantry school; three decades later he remained a fervent Catholic. Preaching, too, was often influential. 'When you preach', Thomas Bennett told friars in 1531, 'God knoweth how you handle it: insomuch that the people of Christ knoweth no gospel well near but the Pope's gospel.' At Bristol in 1533 many townspeople were convinced by William Hubberdine's 'old manner of preaching', while at Marldon in 1547 a traditionalist sermon by Dr Chrispin 'did deceive the ignorant people, which have little or no knowledge': he 'persuaded them all (for the most part) that nothing could be said to the contrary'.[8]

The falling number of clerics promoting the old faith will therefore help to explain its long-term decline. At the same time their power to shape the religious attitudes of the laity appears to have waned. In London, St Albans and elsewhere, those who attempted to use confession for this purpose were reported to the authorities by unpersuaded laymen. Catholic teachers were also resisted. John Hooker was educated by Dr Moreman, and John Jewel by a chantry priest – but both became enthusiastic Protestants.[9]

In the 1530s preachers, too, met increasing resistance. The commons of Bristol were offended by Hubberdine's pro-papal sermons: thirteen informed the royal council. At Colchester a cleric who preached against the official propaganda was reported to Cromwell by a townsman. A preacher who defended intercessions at Grantham was contradicted and delated, while a friar who preached against the King's supremacy at Norwich angered many of his hearers and was reported. A conservative sermon by Bishop Rugge proved similarly offensive to the mayor, the aldermen and many citizens. The parishioners of Harwich informed against their parson for attacking the new learning, and Stanmore men were angered by their priest's defence of images. An Essex priest complained that people now 'would not regard nor believe the sayings of the captains of the church', and Henry VIII noted the 'railing' and 'taunting' to which such preachers were subjected by 'many light persons'.[10]

Disrespect grew in Edward's reign – Leighton's sermons, for example, provoked 'much controversy and much business' in London in 1548 – and was not suppressed in Mary's. When Bourne preached at Paul's Cross he was 'pulled out of the pulpit by vagabonds; and one threw his dagger at him'. When Watson spoke there he needed the protection of 200 guards, and another preacher in the same pulpit only narrowly escaped shooting. Agnes Priest told Catholic preachers that they taught 'nothing but damnable lies'. Equally significant was non-attendance. In Bristol the mayor and aldermen absented themselves from cathedral sermons, while in London Miles Huggarde admitted that fewer people attended Catholic sermons in a week than supported Protestant martyrs in a day.[11]

What influence, on the other hand, was exerted by the rising number of anti-traditional clerics? Protestant bishops could prove effective. In 1552, for example, Ridley ordered that St George's day should no longer be observed – 'and no more it was not'. Protestant teachers were also influential. At Week St Mary William Cholwell's pupils were 'virtuously trained up in both kinds of divine and human learning', and at Bodmin a number of scholars became vigorous partisans of the new faith. 'Children', complained Christopherson, 'when they had been brought up in school a while with some lewd Lutheran, then would they write letters to their Catholic parents, and exhort them in the Lord's name to leave their papistry and blind ignorance.' Some laymen owed their Protestantism to the universities: Thomas Bennett was influenced by Bilney at Cambridge, and Bartlet Green by Peter Martyr at Oxford. Reformers automatically associated the 'ignorant sort' with the old faith, and the 'learned' with the new.[12]

But even more powerful was Protestant preaching. In Henrician London, recalled Latimer, merchants and 'many others' had shown 'great hunger and thirst of the word of God'. In 1536 John Stanton defied a friar and rejected absolution after hearing Latimer preach that no man could forgive sins. He also refused to offer to images, because he had heard preachers denounce them as useless stocks and stones. The impact intensified in Edward's reign. Ridley's sermons attracted many Londoners, 'swarming about him like bees and coveting the sweet flowers and wholesome juice of the fruitful doctrine'. Bonner accused Hooper of 'teaching his audience heretically – being many in number, and assembling in great routs – to reprove, contemn and despise the ... blessed sacrament of the altar'. It was largely by 'following the preachers' that Edward Underhill was converted, and seven of the Smithfield martyrs would recall that 'during the time of King Edward VI they, hearing the gospel preached and the truth opened, followed the order of the religion and doctrine then used and set forth'. Elizabethan preaching also attracted crowds. In 1560 Veron's sermon at Paul's Cross was attended by the mayor and aldermen, 'with many more people': it ended with all singing a Genevan psalm.[13]

Kent, too, was strongly influenced. During the Henrician reformation an anti-Catholic preacher at Folkestone 'turned a hundred men's hearts to his opinion'. At Chartham, as a result of Richard Turner's sermons, 'innumerable of the people of the country ... changed their opinions and favoured effectually the religion received'. In Edward's reign, complained a conservative, 'evil disposed' preachers were able to 'do much hurt in Kent'. The Essex experience was similar. At Harwich, under Henry, a priest lamented the impact of 'these new preachers nowadays, that doth preach their three sermons in a day': they had caused 'such divisions and seditions among us as never were seen in this realm'. In Mary's reign the council complained that Essex people had been 'of late seduced' by Protestant preachers. In Suffolk the population in and around Hadleigh was Protestantized by the sermons of Bilney, Rose and Taylor. It was Rose's preaching against images that induced his parishioners to burn the rood of Dovercourt. In Norfolk the 1549 rebels were receptive to reformed preaching: indeed they wanted to remove any priest 'that be not able to preach and set forth the word of God to his parishioners'.[14]

Converts were won also in the Midlands and the west. At Fotheringay under Edward the preaching of Laurence Saunders 'drew many ignorant to God's true knowledge', while at Derby the Edwardian sermons and homilies persuaded hearers like Joan

Waste. In Warwickshire, in 1537, the sermons of Edward Large were supported by at least 23 of his parishioners: they asserted that 'God's word and his word were all one'. At Coventry, in 1559, 'vast numbers ... were in the habit of frequenting the public preaching of the gospel'. At Bristol in 1533 'many' townspeople, including the mayor and council, 'favoured Latimer and his new manner of preaching'. A Wiltshire conservative protested that Latimer alone 'hath done more hurt in this country than Luther and all his disciples hath done beyond sea'. At Salisbury, in 1547, 100 or more townsmen were reportedly willing to provide bail for the Protestant preacher.[15]

Southwestern preaching also bore some fruit. So many people wanted to hear Latimer at Exeter in 1534 that church windows had to be broken open. 'The more he was heard', says Hooker, 'the more he was liked.' A number of citizens were converted or consolidated by subsequent preachers like Heynes and Coverdale: Thomas Prestwood, for instance, was 'greatly affected to the hearing of the preaching of the gospel'. At South Molton the Protestant group was created by William Ramsey in Mary's reign, when, as he later reminded its members, 'ye favoured me and the word of my preaching'. They had been 'delivered from their vain superstition unto the true knowledge of Christ, by hearing and believing the gospel'. Town preachers might also convert the inhabitants of neighbouring villages. 'I have upon the Sundays visited the sermons', explained Boyton's Agnes Priest, 'and there have I learned such things as are so fixed in my breast that death shall not separate them.' Further successes were scored by itinerants like Dr Tongue, who, in Cornwall and Devon under Edward, 'did marvellously persuade the people'.[16]

Even in the north, by 1569, preaching had produced 'men of all states that made profession of the gospel'. They were particularly numerous in towns and industrial parishes like Halifax, 'which, by continual preaching, had been better instructed than the rest'. In the previous year a York woman was moved by a Protestant sermon to rebuke a conservative priest: 'You priests were to blame, that did not teach us the same before!'[17]

Because of 'the preachers of this new religion', thought Abbot Feckenham in 1559, 'all things are turned upside down'. Their supporters and their enemies agreed on their vital importance in the expansion of popular Protestantism. In several areas, nevertheless, and especially in the north, west and south-west, its progress was substantially restricted by the scarcity of clerics both able and willing to proclaim it. 'Through lack of preachers', lamented the Edwardian regime in 1547, 'in many places of the King's realms and dominions the people continue in ignorance and blindness.' At Falmouth, for example, its commissioners reported that for this reason 'the people thereabouts be very ignorant'; and Hooker thought that the southwestern rebels' hostility to the 1549 prayer-book was due in part to inadequate preaching. In the north, in 1541, the Bishop of Chester observed that the people of his diocese, 'for lack of doctrine and preaching', were 'much behind the King's subjects in the south'. Edmund Grindal attributed the northern rising of 1569 to 'papistry and ignorance of God's word, through want of often preaching'.[18]

Protestant preaching, moreover, could be resisted. Latimer's was abhorred by 'good Catholic people' at Bristol and Exeter in 1533–4: one Devon gentleman threatened to pull him from the pulpit by his ears. Heretical preachers were similarly obnoxious to the northern rebels in 1536. In 1537 Edward Large's preaching was challenged by a local gentleman and some Stratford townsmen; in 1538 a Kidderminster tailor complained about a 'foolish knave priest come to preach of this new learning, which I set not by'; and in 1539 the parson of Sampford Peverell's preaching was denounced as heretical by William Cater. In Edward's reign an Exeter preacher needed protection from the Carews as he stood in the pulpit, and Thomas Hancock's preaching was opposed by the mayor of Salisbury and a merchant of Poole: the latter urged his fellow parishioners to flee such 'devilish doctrine'. 'Thou art a heretic, and hast taught us nothing but heresy', the preaching parson of Adisham was told by a parishioner under Mary. By the 1560s such open hostility was apparently rare, though in 1561 a young man did penance at Paul's Cross 'for speaking of certain words against Veron the preacher'.[19]

Those who did not overtly object to the new preaching were not necessarily converted by it. One of Latimer's hearers at Exeter in 1534 was Robert Hooker, who, when subsequently drafting his will, continued to make traditional bequests. When Ridley gave a lengthy sermon at Paul's Cross in 1552, his audience reportedly grew 'weary of his long standing'. And when, in 1553, news reached Exeter cathedral that Mary had been proclaimed Queen, most of the congregation at Coverdale's sermon immediately trooped out and left him in the pulpit. Many, sighed Latimer, 'cannot be content to hear God's minister, and his threatening for their sin – though the sermon be never so good, though it be never so true'.[20]

24

PLAYWRIGHTS, PLAYERS

The potential of drama as a medium of religious instruction is demonstrated by the extant pre-reformation plays. Mysteries presented biblical history from Creation to the Last Judgement. Miracles dramatized the lives of saints, while moralities combined allegory with a spiritual message. Although most were apparently written by clerics, their language was English dialect or Cornish.[1]

The centres of religious drama were major towns like Chester, Coventry, Newcastle, Norwich, Wakefield and York. Urban authorities supervised its performance and entrusted each scene to an appropriate guild – the Last Supper, for example, to the bakers, or Noah's Ark to the shipwrights. Spectators included not only townsfolk but also, as at Norwich in 1527, 'the people of the country'. Smaller communities might also mount performances. Ashburton had an annual mystery. Bassingbourne staged a St George play in 1511, and Braintree plays about Sts Andrew, Eustace and Swithun in 1523–34.[2]

Miracles were acted on saints' days, and mysteries at the feast of Corpus Christi. In Cornwall they were performed in large earthen amphitheatres, like that at Perranzabuloe, but towns elsewhere used wagons which stopped in streets and squares. Costumes and properties were often elaborate. At Ashburton they included clothes, visors and wigs. New tunics and headcrests were added in 1528–9, gold skins in 1534–5 and a wig and gloves in 1536–8.[3]

Although the plays included comic interludes and spectacular effects, their primary function was the inculcation of religious beliefs. Action was interrupted by assertions of dogma – like 'Father and Son and Holy Ghost, three persons and one substance, that is the true faith, as holy church teaches us'. *Beunans Meriasek* showed the saint explaining difficult doctrines like the virgin birth and the atonement. Heywood depicts an early Tudor priest teaching the Creed articles to his parishioners and advising them to visit Coventry – where 'ye shall see them all played in Corpus Christi play'.[4]

The religion thus transmitted was invariably traditional. *Beunans Meriasek* was hagiographical and miraculous; it even depicted the legend of Constantine and Pope Silvester. The mysteries, though based on scripture, also contained post-biblical and legendary episodes like the harrowing of hell and Our Lady's assumption. The Cornish *Ordinalia* included the imprisonment of Nicodemus and Joseph of Arimathea, the harrowing of hell, the greeting of the Virgin Mary by the risen Christ, the healing of the emperor by St Veronica, the miracle of the robe and the death of Pilate.[5]

The plays were designed not only to extend religious knowledge but also to reinforce religious commitment. This purpose was implicit in the *Ordinalia*'s emotive portrayal of the suffering, death and eventual triumph of Jesus, and became explicit when an actor directly addressed the audience: 'You go, reflect on his passion, every man in his heart, and keep it steadfast and true. It was not for himself he suffered it certainly, but for love of mankind. Show love to him; with thy heart worship him; do, day and night. When thou be passed from the world, with Christ be thou dwelling, within his court.' *Beunans Meriasek* depicted the power of St Meriasek as an intercessor and (especially) as a healer: he was seen curing the sick, maimed, leprous, blind, deaf, crippled, demon-possessed and insane. One scene showed him at Camborne, establishing his church and holy well. 'Grievance and disease of the season', he promised, 'if a loyal Christian have it and remembers me in this place, Jesus, Lord, dear heart, his grievance will assuage. Likewise the water of the fountain: for a man insane certainly I pray that it be a salve to bring him again to his sense.' The play's message was overtly stated: 'Whoever trust in him and loyally pray to him, Jesu has granted to them their desire readily.'[6]

Such instruction was often effective. The *Ordinalia* appears to have strongly influenced the glazier who made the 'creation' window at St Neot in about 1500: even the play's treatment of the Holy Rood legend is reproduced in the glass. *Beunans Meriasek* helped to maintain the saint's cult at Camborne. Elizabethan Protestants would hold the traditional plays responsible for 'the derogation of the majesty and glory of God, the profanation of the sacraments, and the maintenance of superstition and idolatry'.[7]

On the other hand they were rejected by pre-reformation Lollards, like the author of *A Treatise of Miracles Playing* in about 1500. Guilds were not always enthusiastic in their support: in 1527 several failed to contribute to the Norwich Whitsun plays, which showed 'the lives and martyrdoms of divers and many holy saints'. The Canterbury mysteries apparently ended in 1520, and relatively few plays (notably *Beunans Meriasek* in 1504) were composed in the early sixteenth century. Apart from revisions, as at Coventry in about 1534, the important works were mostly products of the fourteenth and fifteenth centuries.[8]

Most plays continued to the end of Henry's reign. Ashburton bought tunics, rattlebags, devils' heads and gloves in 1540–6, and Chester still staged its plays in 1546. A Becket pageant at Canterbury, however, was suppressed in 1538, and a mystery play at Beverley seems to have ended after 1541. Under Edward, moreover, the traditional plays were usually censored or suppressed. There were performances at York in 1548 and Chester in 1551, but at York, on the corporation's orders, the Corpus Christi play was shorn of 'certain pageants' – 'that is to say, the dying of Our Lady, assumption of Our Lady, and coronation of Our Lady'. At Ashburton, after payment to the players at Corpus Christi 1548, such expenditure disappeared from the accounts for the rest of the reign.[9]

Ashburton, Chester, Coventry, Lincoln, Wakefield and York saw at least some of the old plays revived in Mary's reign. The York corporation, in 1554, specified that 'those pageants that of late were left forth shall be played again'. At Ashburton the costumes were repainted or replaced: gloves, for example, were bought for 'him that played God Almighty' in 1555–6, and for 'him that played Christ' in 1558–9. Wine was provided for the actor playing St Rumon in 1555–6. Dramatic activity was apparently less in the south-east, though Canterbury saw its Becket play in 1555 and London a passion play in 1557. At Lincoln and Wakefield the guilds had to be ordered to produce their Corpus Christi pageants – on pain, at Wakefield, of a fine. Some plays, including the Beverley and Canterbury mysteries, seem never to have been restored.[10]

The assault was renewed in Elizabeth's reign. Some plays were not finally suppressed until the 1570s, as at Chester, Coventry, Wakefield and York, or later, as at Kendal, Lancaster and Preston and in

Cornwall. Their 'superstitious' elements, however, had usually been already censored by the Protestant authorities. At Norwich a traditional play was revised on strictly scriptural lines in 1565. At York the 'pageants of the dying, assumption and coronation of Our Lady' were again removed from the Corpus Christi play in 1561. In 1568 the council ordered the Corpus Christi play book to be further 'perused and otherwise amended before it were played'. The manuscript of the Towneley plays shows similar changes: a passage on the seven sacraments (for example) has been corrected.[11]

Many plays, moreover, had been totally suppressed by 1570. In London and Lincoln the traditional drama apparently ended after Elizabeth's accession. At Coventry, despite some protests, the Hock Tuesday performance had ended by 1561, and all expenditure on the traditional play at Ashburton ceased after 1559–60. Norwich's Corpus Christi cycle was terminated in 1564. Even at York the Creed play was suppressed by the corporation in 1568: it had been prohibited by the Protestant dean as 'disagreeing from the sincerity of the gospel'. Despite some citizens' demands, the Corpus Christi play itself ended in 1569.[12]

Redundant apparatus was stored away or sold. At Canterbury the pageant wagon of Thomas Becket – which, on his feast day, had staged a re-enactment of his martyrdom – was sold for 2s 8d in 1564. This year also the Norwich corporation removed to London a splendidly painted and ornamented wagon which had staged the grocers' play of Adam and Eve. By 1570 it was in the street, where it rotted and fell to pieces. Copies of the plays were also destroyed. Little survives of the saints' plays, or of the Creed and *Pater Noster* plays at Beverley, Lincoln and York. Fragments apart, only four mystery cycles have survived.[13]

Popular Catholicism was undoubtedly eroded by this gradual suppression of traditional drama. At York, for example, the elimination of the Virgin Mary pageants was probably one reason for testators' decreasing eagerness to invoke Our Lady or the saints.[14]

Protestants not only destroyed the play as a vehicle of Catholic propagation; sometimes they employed it in the dissemination of their own religion. Richard Morison, in 1535–6, appreciated its power to weaken respect for popes, monks, nuns and friars – because 'into the common people things sooner enter by the eyes than by the ears'. Anti-Catholic drama was subsequently produced by writers like John Bale, whose *King John* appeared in 1538. 'Twenty thousand traitors I have made in my time', boasts a priest named Treason in this play, 'under *Benedicite,* between high mass and prime... . In the place of Christ I have set up superstitions: for preachings, ceremonies; for God's word, men's traditions... . If superstitions and ceremonies from us fall, farewell monk and canon, priest, friar, bishop and all!'[15]

Such plays continued to be performed under Henry and Edward. In about 1541 Londoners saw 'an interlude ... openly played, wherein priests were railed on and called knaves'. Actors, complained Christopherson in 1554, had 'set forth openly before men's eyes the wicked blasphemy that they had contrived for the defacing of all rites'. Nor were they wholly suppressed by Mary. 'Very naughty and seditious matter ... to the slander of Christ's true Catholic church' was acted by a troupe that toured the north in 1556. In 1557 the increasing number of such cases impelled the government to prohibit interludes: actors were arrested in London and Canterbury, and Essex justices reproved for letting performances continue. More anti-Catholic plays were mounted in London and elsewhere after Elizabeth's accession. Some were less polemical: the Lincoln corporation, seeking 'a standing play of some story of the bible', organized one about Tobias in 1564 and 1567.[16]

25

ARTISTS, CRAFTSMEN

In monasteries and cathedrals, and especially in parish churches, religious ideas were transmitted to the pre-reformation laity by sculptures, wood-carvings, screen-paintings, murals and stained glass. The last two were the largest, and instructionally the most effective. That such art forms were still produced in the early sixteenth century is indicated by details of costume or armour, as in the St George window at St Neot, and by heraldic devices, like Katherine of Aragon's pomegranate on the Bridford screen. Inscriptions date bench-ends at Monkleigh, Coldridge, Altarnun and Hartland to 1508, 1511, 1525 and 1530, screens at Marwood and Bradninch to about 1520 and 1528, and sculpture at Woodleigh to about 1527. There is also dated glass, notably that of 1523–9 at St Neot.[1]

Such work was either produced by local artists and craftsmen or imported from more distant workshops. Exeter had its school of woodcarvers, and possibly of sculptors too. Finance was provided by the parish – as at North Petherwin, where a glazier received over £3 from the wardens in about 1520 – or by a guild, a family or an individual. At Bodmin in 1507–8, the £12 paid to craftsmen 'for the painting of four histories in the rood loft' was supplied in part by guilds; and the three stained-glass windows erected at St Neot in 1523–9 were donated by the wives, young men and young women. Such donors seem usually to have dictated the content of the work. At St Neot, several saints in the early Tudor glass were patrons of the donors depicted below them.[2]

At the same time, both wardens' accounts and artistic survivals – which frequently date from the fourteenth or fifteenth centuries, and sometimes before – show that many early sixteenth-century parishes were less enthusiastic about investment in art. These simply retained the work inherited from previous generations.[3]

Whether new or old, the art to be seen in 1530 was predominantly traditional in religious tone. The murals at Breage portray not only Christ but also Sts Christopher, Corentin and Thomas Becket. Those at Pickering include the coronation of Our Lady as well as Sts Christopher, Edmund, George, Katherine and Thomas Becket. The screen-paintings at Ashton juxtapose biblical figures with later and sometimes legendary saints, including Antony, George, Katherine, Margaret, Sebastian, Sidwell, Sitha, Thomas Becket and Ursula. Bench-ends sometimes portray episodes from Christ's ministry, passion or exaltation, as at Launcells, but saints are more frequent: a single end at Combeinteignhead shows George with his dragon, Agnes with her lamb, Hubert with his bow and Genesius in his jester's costume.

This interweaving of scripture and tradition is found also in glass. At St Neot a representation of *Genesis* intrudes the death of Cain and the legend of the holy rood. Also portrayed here, alongside the Trinity, Christ and other biblical characters, are apocryphal subjects like St Anne's daughters and Our Lady's coronation; celebrities like George, whose exploits and martyrdom fill a window, as well as Barbara, Christopher, Gregory, Katherine and Leonard; and local saints such as Clere, German, Mabena, Mancus and Meubred. One window, dated 1528, is devoted to Neot himself. Featuring his well, which stood within the parish, and his horn, which was preserved at Bodmin priory, it emphasizes his self-abnegating piety and miraculous power.[4]

Art, like drama, was designed not only to convey knowledge but also to reinforce commitment. If a Works of Mercy window, as at York All Saints, was intended to stimulate charity, a Weighing of Souls mural, as at Poundstock, or a Doom painting, as at Wenhaston, was intended to arouse repentance. Depictions of Christ's passion, as in a Breage mural, and of his passion instruments, as on many bench-ends, were meant to heighten devotion to the suffering saviour. Many representations, like the 'Neot' window at St Neot, were to raise confidence in the intercessory and healing power of saints. Often these various objectives were attained. In 1514 a London fishmonger not only requested burial before the Works of Mercy window in his parish church, but also showed that he had absorbed its message by donating money and clothing to prisoners and the poor. On the other hand, a newly painted picture of St Nicholas evoked only contempt from Richard Grace in 1521: he wanted it banished from the rood loft to the darkness of the tower. Lollards, recalled Gardiner, 'thought ... the crafts of painting and graving to be generally superfluous and naught, and against God's laws'.[5]

Official hostility began in 1538, when depictions of Becket were condemned. Under Edward and Elizabeth the assault became general: the eradication of all 'superstitious' pictures, paintings and glass was ordered in 1547 and 1559.[6]

Free-standing pictures were bought until 1547, and in 1553–8: Ashburton and South Tawton spent 13s 4d and £1 0s 8d on pictures of St Andrew in Mary's reign. Under Edward, in contrast, they were often removed. Some were consigned to storage, like Exeter St Lawrence's crucifixion or Dartington's Our Lady and St John: Marian expenditure on their 'mending' suggests damage or neglect. Others were lost by sale, like those which fetched 2s 8d at Stratton in 1549 or the 'plaster' sold by Exeter St Petrock's in 1550–1. 1559, moreover, saw organized public burnings of such art. At Exeter eight pictures were removed from St Mary Steps alone, and 'burned, by the commandment of the Queen's majesty's visitors', in the cathedral close. At Crediton two pictures of Our Lady were consigned to the flames. Of 143 Lincolnshire churches examined in 1566, not one retained a 'superstitious' picture undefaced. At Kelby a picture of St Peter had recently been burned, in public, by the churchwardens; elsewhere the destruction had been proceeding since 1559. Further north the process might be slower. One Yorkshire church had pictures of Christ, Mary and John discovered by the authorities in 1567.[7]

Reformers of this era seem also to have inflicted much of the damage still visible on medieval sculptures. Decapitation was the fate of Mary and other saints on the Paignton chantry screen. Destruction is also indicated by the empty niches on facades, as at York minster, on pillars, as at Tiverton, and on towers, as at Chittlehampton. Survivals like North Molton's Mary are relatively rare. And although the seven sacraments had been sculpted on some 40 East Anglian fonts between 1468 and 1544, their manufacture ceased thereafter and was not revived in Mary's reign.[8]

That many surviving bench-ends date from the reformation decades is indicated by renaissance features and by inscriptions: 1537 appears at East Budleigh and North Lew, and 1546 at Dowland

and Lewannick. They exhibit an increasing tendency to replace Catholic representations, particularly saints, passion instruments and the five wounds, with non-representational or secular motifs, particularly tracery, foliage, arabesques, grotesques, profiles, initials and heraldry. At East Budleigh the 63 ends of 1537 are (apart from angels) entirely destitute of religious figures or emblems. Catholic carvings are similarly absent from the mid-Tudor pulpits at East Allington and St Ives.[9]

A number of screens are also datable stylistically to these decades, though relatively few seem post-Henrician. Those at Burlingham St Andrew and Throwleigh were erected in about 1535 and 1544, and those at East Allington and Hubberholme are dated 1547 and 1558. Non-biblical saints appear at Burlingham and at Ugborough, where they may be Marian. On the other hand the Marian screen at Hubberholme has no provision for panel paintings of any type. The late Henrician screen at Throwleigh was painted with scriptural subjects, while the mid-Tudor screen at Lustleigh has biblical prophets and apostles. Probably from these decades also are the screen-paintings at Marwood, Sutcombe and Swimbridge, where saints are displaced by foliage and early renaissance decoration.[10]

Extant screen-paintings have often been defaced. Victims include figures of the Trinity, as at Kenn, and popes, as at Cawston, as well as many saints: the apostles at Ringland, for example, and Becket, Benedict, Cecilia, Edward the Confessor and John the Baptist at Burlingham St Andrew. Even paintings that appear whole have often been repainted in recent times. Elsewhere, as at Chivelstone, East Allington and South Pool, saints seem to have been obliterated and replaced by non-religious motifs. A similar fate evidently befell the original pictures on the Atherington loft, while at Wenhaston the Doom picture above the chancel arch was overpainted. Many such acts of destruction may be dated to the reformation years. Attacks on Becket figures must have followed the 1538 decree. The secular motifs at South Pool and elsewhere appear Elizabethan; so do the texts painted over the Wenhaston Doom.[11]

Extant stained glass is seldom datable to the reformation decades. At St Neot, significantly, the last inscribed date is 1529. Even when new glass was bought it was increasingly unlikely to bear traditional pictures. That erected at Dartmouth in 1541–2 was uncoloured. That erected at Tavistock in 1566–7 showed neither saints nor Christ – only the arms of Queen Elizabeth and the Earl of Bedford.[12]

Though destruction was inhibited by the cost of replacement, traditional stained glass was often subjected to defacement or neglect. The former occurred at Halberton, where glass was ripped from the windows by impious laymen in 1553. The latter occurred at Waghen, where it was reported in 1567 that 'the church windows are in decay'. Both occurred in eight parishes of Kent, where stained glass was defaced before 1553 and had not been repaired by 1557. At Wye, for instance, Marian visitors had to order the parishioners to 'make clean the images that be blotted in the glass windows'. Defacement and neglect are probably indicated also by the expenditure of innumerable mid-Tudor parishes on re-glazing and repairs. Under Mary, for instance, Easingwold paid a glazier £1 1s 7d 'for mending the glass windows', while in 1567 Stratton paid £1 2s 6d for 'new glass' and 13s for glass repair.[13]

Defacement and neglect, in these and later years, explain the fragmentary nature of medieval glass in most churches today. Only relatively rarely, as at St Neot or York All Saints, have extensive collections survived. The one virtually complete set, at Fairford, was removed during the reformation and not restored until the later seventeenth century.[14]

Few Catholic murals were painted after 1530. In Edward's reign, according to a London chronicler, 'all churches' were 'new white limed'; and accounts confirm the whitewashing of wall-paintings throughout the realm. At Long Melford, in 1547–8, John Kendall was paid £1 14s 8d for 'whiting of the church and chapels'. In the south-west such destruction occurred not only in Exeter parishes like Holy Trinity, St John's Bow and St Petrock's, but also in remoter communities like Antony, Ashburton and Stratton. At St Petrock's in 1548–9 the wardens paid for 'washing away of images, and for white liming of the same'.[15]

Mary's reign saw few attempts to repaint obliterated murals, and Elizabeth's accession renewed the assault on those that survived. At Long Melford in 1562 John Prince received 4s for 'the whiting of the chancel', and 1s 4d for 'the scraping out of the paintings all the length of the choir'. The south-west witnessed more whitewashing at Dartington in 1558–9, Ashburton in 1559–60, Kilmington in 1560–2, Woodbury and possibly Barnstaple in 1564–5, South Tawton in about 1565–6 and Chagford in 1567. Ashburton paid 6s 8d for lime, and another 6s 8d 'for washing the images in the church and the church house', while Dartington gave 1s 4d to Robert Edward 'for two days' labour, mending of the walls and whiting of the aisles and chancel'. Destruction may have been slower in the north. At Waghen in 1567 the authorities discovered 'painted pictures of Christopher and others on the church walls', though it was subsequently reported that these had been 'defaced'.[16]

The reformation years were therefore primarily responsible for the rarity of medieval murals in churches today. St Mawes was 'painted as a schoolmaster' in Henry VIII's reign; but no paintings of him have survived. Even those murals now visible were usually recovered only in the nineteenth or twentieth centuries.[17]

Although the survivals show that the destruction of Catholic art was never total, they represent only a small fraction of that displayed before the reformation. Most, moreover, are relatively limited in size. Glass and murals, the forms most effective in religious instruction, are usually only fragmentary.

If, in 1570, Catholic art had been largely suppressed, it had been only partly replaced by reformed equivalents. These included propagandist depictions of the royal arms – which were painted (for example) in Woodbury church in 1569–70 – and printed woodcuts, which appeared in books like Foxe's *Acts and Monuments.* Engravings of sadistic Catholics and heroic Protestants created stereotypes that would long influence the religious attitudes of the English people.[18]

26

Writers, Translators, Printers

Traditionalists sometimes used manuscript bills to promote their cause. Bills abusing Protestant preachers were posted in London in Edward's reign. Exeter saw the circulation of 'seditious bills' attacking iconoclasm and the King in Henry's reign; the fixing to doors, and scattering in streets, of 'most slanderous and seditious bills' in 1547; and the posting of bills in support of mass and the Pope in 1561. In 1536 and 1549 the northern and southwestern rebels issued manuscript copies of their demands, though government control of the press ensured that they were never printed.[1]

Catholics also used books. On the eve of the reformation a substantial number – sometimes in Latin but increasingly in English – were imported from the continent or printed in England. They included not only theological and mystical works but also guides to prayer and practical religion, like the primers and Whitford's *Work for Householders.* The most popular were celebrations of the saints, such as the *Golden Legend.* By 1530 the old faith was also being defended from its Protestant critics by treatises like More's *Supplication of Souls.* Catholic works continued to be published throughout the reign: Smith's defence of the mass appeared in 1546. But relatively few dared to oppose the official reformation, and these were largely suppressed. Abel was imprisoned for his *Invicta Veritas,* published abroad in 1532. Edward's reign saw a virtual cessation of Catholic publication.[2]

It resumed under Mary. Some works, like Bonner's *Profitable and Necessary Doctrine,* offered Catholic instruction; others, like Huggarde's *Displaying of the Protestants,* anti-heretic polemic. Catholics, nevertheless, authored only 64 of the 162 pieces of religious propaganda published in English in 1554–8. The regime proved slow to exploit literature, failing (for example) to publish the conservatives' successful debates with the Edwardian bishops. After 1559 such publication in England was again suppressed. Although exiles like Harding produced books abroad, in the 1560s these remained fewer than those authored by Protestants in Mary's reign.[3]

Catholic literature could be effective. In 1526 a book of Elizabeth Barton's prophesies was 'commonly sold and gone abroad amongst all people'. In 1564 Durham diocese was disturbed by exiles' books, which were said to 'disquiet the people', and in 1567 Harding's were read and praised by an Alphington man. Local disapproval, however, forced him to read them covertly, and landed him before the consistory court.[4]

Protestants proved even more energetic in the exploitation of the written word. Anti-Catholic bills were circulated or posted at Exeter (for example) in 1531, at Bristol in 1539 and in London in Edward's reign – when they appeared on St Paul's gate, in St Magnus' church and elsewhere. They were still disseminated under Mary, together with broadsheets, rhymes and ballads: one ballad celebrated the death of Robert Glover. More important were anti-Catholic books. Before the reformation these were read to neighbours by Lollard laymen like William Sweeting, in London diocese in 1511, and distributed by Lollard colporteurs, like John Hacker in London and Essex in about 1520. The 1520s, moreover, saw an influx of Protestant books and pamphlets from Antwerp and elsewhere. The authors were not only continental reformers, most notably Luther, but also English converts like John Frith and William Tyndale: the latter's output included *The Parable of the Wicked Mammon* and *The Practice of Prelates*.[5]

Their impact was greatest on the south-east. Their printing 'in great quantity' was lamented by the Bishop of London in 1528, and their readers included a number of London merchants. Books 'against the sacrament of the altar, with all other sacraments and sacramentals', were distributed covertly in London in 1544, and a 'great multitude' of English books were burned at Paul's Cross in 1546. A Chelmsford youth owned Frith's anti-sacrament book in 1539. 'Such as keepeth and readeth these erroneous books in English, and believe and give credence to the same', were worrying the clergy in Norwich diocese by 1530. Remoter regions also had some readers. At Exeter, in 1531, shearmen's houses were searched for heretical books, while at Wincanton, in 1539, a priest denounced the 'new fangled fellows which read the new books'.[6]

At the same time the official reformation was promoted by a government-sponsored literary campaign. Often published by Berthelet, the King's printer, its products were sometimes in Latin – like Gardiner's *De Vera Obedientia* – but more usually in English. These included learned works, like Marsiglio's anti-papal treatise, and more accessible sermons and pamphlets like Morison's *Remedy for Sedition.* Marshall's *Primer* criticized intercessions and the veneration of saints. Statutes and proclamations, with their propagandist preambles, were printed and sometimes distributed for display.[7]

Protestant literature exploded in Edward's reign, often in inexpensive pamphlet form. Protestants, indeed, were now commonly derided as 'two-penny book men'. Foreigners, especially Calvin, were translated, but most writers were English: they included Peter Moone, Philip Nichols and Luke Shepherd, the authors of *A Treatise of certain Things Abused, A Godly New Story,* and *John Bon and Mast Person.* Favourite targets were the priesthood and mass. Most were printed in London, some in Ipswich or elsewhere. Seven printers, including London's John Day, would be Marian exiles.[8]

Such literature was never wholly suppressed by Mary. Protestants in fact wrote some 60 per cent of the religious propaganda published in English in her reign. It included Knox's *Doctrine of the Mass* and less learned pieces like *Antichrist* and *A Sackfull of News.* Most was smuggled into England from abroad: Catholics complained of the 'three-half-penny books which steal out of Germany'. It was distributed by booksellers like Richard Hedley at Ipswich and preachers like George Eagles in East Anglia. Purchasers included both clerics and laymen, like the parson of St Teath and Kennington's Thurstan Wood. In London, 1554 alone saw some 60 householders, servants and apprentices imprisoned for owning or selling imported books. From 1559, moreover, English presses were again available to Protestants. Jewel's *Apology,* for example, was published in 1562, and Foxe's *Acts and Monuments* in 1563. South Tawton bought Calvin's *Institutes* in 1560–1, and 'a book of my lord Jewel's' had reached Alphington by 1567.[9]

The effectiveness of such literature was recognized by its opponents. These included the Bishop of London in 1528, Sir Thomas More in 1533, and the Bristolian who complained in 1536 that the 'new books' had 'brought in damnable darkness and endless damnation'. Marian conservatives agreed that 'devilish and erroneous books' had done 'great hurt [to] the ignorant people'. Their suppression was demanded by the 1536 rebels and attempted by the Marian regime, which eventually made death the penalty for possession.[10]

Undoubtedly they influenced many people. 'It pleased the Lord to work in them knowledge and understanding by reading a few English books', wrote Foxe of the Lincoln diocese Lollards of 1521. In 1529 the conversion of a London leather-seller was due partly to his reading of Tyndale's *Wicked Mammon*, and in 1558 a Cornish woman admitted that her knowledge of the new faith had been acquired in part from 'godly books, which I have heard read'. Calvin's *Institutes* taught Julins Palmer to despise popes, priests and images. In Mary's reign John Ponet rejoiced that 'ballads, rhymes and short toys – that be not dear, and will easily be borne away – do much good at home amongst the rude people'. Pro-reformation literature, however, was by no means always effective. In Henry's reign it was not infrequently opposed or reviled, and in 1567 Thomas Stephens remained unconvinced by his reading of Jewel's *Apology*.[11]

But the book of pre-eminent importance to Protestants was the Bible. Although vernacular translations were illegal, Lollard versions circulated in manuscript before the reformation. Tyndale's New Testament was printed (at Worms) in 1526, and emulated by Coverdale, Rogers and other translators. Patrons and publishers included the London merchants Humphrey Monmouth and Richard Grafton.[12]

Although copies were possessed by some pre-reformation laymen, like James Brewster in 1511, the reformation decades saw a major expansion of bible ownership. From 1526 Tyndale's Testament was smuggled into the south-east and widely sold. At Chelmsford, in 1538–9, English testaments were bought by a shopkeeper's son and apprentice and by a group of 'poor men'. Even in the south-west, Axminster townsmen had purchased testaments by 1535–6. By 1570 a number of lay people, such as Stratton's John Judde, owned entire bibles.[13]

Wills and inventories nevertheless suggest that these were a minority. Until 1538, moreover, vernacular scripture seldom featured in parish inventories and accounts. Then, however, all parish churches were ordered to buy and display an English Bible; and accounts throughout England show that by 1546 almost all complied. About half had done so by 1541: they included rural communities like

Morebath and Woodbury as well as urban parishes like Exeter St Petrock's. Morebath acquired in Exeter 'the church book called the Bible', and displayed it on a cord. The slower parishes were persuaded by the fines threatened in a proclamation of 1541. At Stratton, where the apparitor had to 'sue for the books' in 1540, a Bible was duly obtained in 1541. Some, like Woodbury, also bought desks 'to lay the Bible on'.[14]

In 1547 the parishes were ordered to exhibit not only bibles but also translations of Erasmus' paraphrases of the gospels. Most bought the latter – at Stratton, 'a book called Erasmus' arrived in 1547–8 – and some new desks or bibles. Some 22 per cent also adorned their walls or lofts with Bible texts. Long Melford spent £1 13s 4d on 'writing of the church and chapels'. Several, including Ashburton, Dartmouth and Long Melford, eradicated these in Mary's reign: Dartmouth paid for 'blotting out of the ten commandments'. Dover, Harrietsham and Headcorn, however, retained their texts in 1557. Bibles and paraphrases were removed from display. Some parishes, like Dartmouth and Morebath, delivered copies into confiscation, and several had to buy replacements in the next reign. Bibles or paraphrases nevertheless remained in ten Kent parishes in 1557, and both at St Breock at this date. Many of those owned by parishes in the 1560s seem not to have been purchased after 1558 – though Marian neglect is suggested by the mending sometimes needed.[15]

1559–60 saw the display of bibles and paraphrases restored in most churches with accounts. Exeter St Petrock's placed a desk 'in the body of the church, to set the Bible on'. Usually the Henrician or Edwardian copies were removed from storage or retrieved from confiscation: Exeter St John's Bow paid 2d 'for fetching home of the paraphrases'. Only a minority of parishes, including Morebath, had to buy replacements, though additional copies were purchased in the subsequent decade. The ten commandments, moreover, were displayed on tablets or boards. These were erected in most south-western churches in 1560–3, and at Ludlow (which retains its board) in 1561. By 1570 they were normally supplemented by painted wall-texts. Exeter St Petrock's spent £3 6s 8d on 'new writing of the scriptures about the church' in 1562–3, and Crediton 16s on 'painting [of] the scriptures' in 1565, though Woodbury did not paint its commandments until 1569–70.[16]

Where scripture was available it was often diligently studied. At Hadleigh 'a great number' of men and women became 'exceeding well learned in the holy scriptures', and knew portions by heart. Some read for themselves. Thomas Bennett's spare time was devoted 'wholly to his private study in the scriptures'. William Maldon and his friend hid their New Testament in their straw beds, 'and so exercised it at convenient times'. By the 1560s lay people like Alice Bennett were taking their bibles to church for use in 'godly prayer'. More, however, heard the Bible read. At Hughenden, in 1530, ten men assembled in a private house to hear a reading from the English scriptures. At Chelmsford, in 1538, townsmen read the New Testament in the church, 'and many would flock about them to hear their reading'. In London, in 1541, readings by John Porter and others drew 'great multitudes' to St Paul's.[17]

That bible-reading was increasingly frequent, particularly among the middle and lower middle orders, is confirmed by its opponents. 'Abominable heretics that readeth the New Testament in English' were denounced by the incumbent at Sturminster Newton in 1536. They 'infect the whole company with their new learning', he lamented. In about 1538 a Sussex priest deplored 'botchers, bunglers and cobblers which have the Testament in their keeping', and in 1539 a Buckinghamshire priest decried scripture-reading by serving-men and craftsmen. A statute of 1543 implied that scripture was being read by yeomen, husbandmen, craftsmen, apprentices, journeymen and labourers, and even by women. In 1545 Henry VIII complained that it was 'disputed, rhymed, sung and jangled in every alehouse and tavern'.[18]

Bible study often resulted in Protestant belief. 'The more he did grow and increase in the knowledge of God and his holy word', it was said of Thomas Bennett, 'the more he did mislike and abhor the corrupt state of religion then used.' By hearing scripture read, William Maldon received the 'glad and sweet tidings of the gospel'; and by reading it for himself, he was emboldened to quote texts at his conservative parents. In Edward's reign scripture-reading helped to convert Edward Underhill, and scripture-hearing taught Joan Waste to recite texts and use them in religious argument. 'The public knowledge of the Bible and holy scriptures', rejoiced Philip Nichols in 1549, 'hath confounded [the priests'] trumpery, and hath opened to the eyes of the world all their deceitful doctrine.' The southwestern rebels feared that unless the English Bible was suppressed, 'the clergy shall not of long time confound the heretics'. Lay bible-reading, agreed Cardinal Pole, 'maketh many to fall into heresies'.[19]

At the same time, study of the Bible was limited by its infrequent private ownership and its intermittent public display. In 1548 Nichols recalled that it had been 'an unknown thing within these twenty year here in England', and the reaction of Alice Bennett's vicar suggests that even in 1567 its study remained uncommon in Devon churches. Some lay people indeed regarded it with grave suspicion. Richard Drake assaulted a man for reading it in 1535–6, and William Maldon's father banned him from it in 1538. It was opposed by the mayor of Sandwich in 1541. 'We will have the Bible, and all books of scripture in English, to be called in again', demanded the southwestern rebels in 1549. By 1570 such hostility had waned, but respect was still not universal. Some parishes allowed their copies to become unusable or torn, as at Waghen and Welwick in 1567.[20]

The fact that only a minority of English people yet read the Bible will help to explain the limited expansion of the new faith. 'Alas', sighed Philip Nichols, 'how was it possible that we should be obedient unto the voice of our lord God, and walk in his ways, when we knew them not ...?' He told the southwestern rebels that their unawareness of scripture had kept them 'in such blindness and gross ignorance that ye know not what pertaineth to your souls' health or damnation'.[21]

The use of literature was made possible by two developments. One was the rising level of lay literacy. This phenomenon was due largely to the later medieval expansion of elementary and grammar schools, and is attested by the increasing frequency of inscriptions on church fabrics and furnishings. Signatures on legal depositions suggest that by mid-century the ability to read and write was possessed by most gentlemen and merchants, some 50 per cent of yeomen and 33 per cent of craftsmen. Only 10 per cent of husbandmen, however, were literate, and a smaller percentage of labourers and the poor. The proportion was higher for men than for women, and for towns than for rural communities. Exeter, for instance, contained enough literates to sustain at least one bookseller, and to ensure that 'many' could read (or hear read) posted bills. Its merchants needed literacy for business and had money to buy it. Tristram Hengescott, in 1537, provided for his son to be 'guided and kept to the school', where he was to have 'learning in writing and reading'.[22]

A related development was the expansion of printing, which substantially lowered the price of literature. This benefited Catholics – a few pence bought a Latin primer – but was more fully exploited by their enemies. A stream of Protestant works flowed from the presses in London and elsewhere. 'Two-penny books' were affordable to a substantial sector of the population, and even printed bibles (or parts of them) to the lower middle orders. Essex Lollards paid 3s 2d – a craftsman's weekly wage – for Tyndale's Testament in 1527. 'Either the Pope must abolish knowledge and printing', declared Foxe, 'or printing at length will root him out.'[23]

Religious literature was nevertheless inhibited by several restraints. One was official prohibition. Heretical books were forbidden in 1530, and unauthorized bible-reading in 1555. Pro-papal literature was banned in 1536, and unlicensed printing in 1559. A second restraint was clerical opposition. The pre-reformation clergy prohibited English scripture, so that (complained Nichols) 'none of us durst look upon it in the tongue that we understood'. Some continued to dissuade their congregations from reading it in Henry's reign, as at Enfield and Sturminster Newton, and even in 1547 were said to 'withdraw all men from reading and hearing it as much as they can'. Under Edward and Elizabeth, however, such dissuasion apparently declined. Increasingly it was Catholic literature that clerics detected and suppressed.[24]

Literature of any persuasion, moreover, was affordable only to a minority of the population. Protestant tracts cost 2s each in Marian Cornwall, and the Bible £1 at Crediton in 1559. In addition the cost of education, and its infrequency outside towns, combined with gender prejudice to ensure that illiteracy remained widespread among the lower orders, country-dwellers and women. This not only limited the popular impact of Catholic books; it also helped to concentrate Protestant commitment in towns, the middle and lower middle social strata, and the male sex.[25]

Conclusion

In one view, the Tudor assault on traditional religion was generally welcomed and supported. In the opposite view, it was generally resented and resisted. The evidence examined in this book suggests that the reality was considerably more complex than either interpretation would allow.

It seems that the reformation was resisted by some, supported by others, and accepted by most. Its progress, moreover, was usually more rapid in the south and east than in the north and west, in major towns than in rural parishes, and probably among the young and the male than among the old and the female. Exceptions to all these rules were numerous.

Equally complicated were the motives behind religious attitudes. Those which impelled support for the old faith were emotional, material and physical as well as spiritual. Those which impelled its abandonment included not only spiritual convictions but also (and more frequently) a variety of essentially secular considerations. Attitudes were shaped also by a wide range of influences. These included parents, neighbours and foreigners as well as teachers, preachers and writers. Though predominantly pro-traditional in 1530, they were predominantly non- or anti-traditional by 1570.

Or so it seems. For the historian sees through a glass darkly, and can seldom be confident that he has accurately reconstructed the minds and souls of generations long departed.

NOTES

Unless otherwise indicated, the following reference conventions have been employed:

- References to individual churchwardens' accounts and corporation accounts are to compilation date. Thus 'CWA Woodbury, 1546', refers to the account compiled by the Woodbury wardens in 1546, and 'CWA Woodbury, 1548–9', refers to the accounts compiled by them in 1548 and 1549.
- References to *Ancient Cornish Drama* and *Beunans Meriasek* are to line numbers.
- References to LP are to document numbers.
- Other references are to pagination or foliation.

Introduction

1. For the quotation (from R. Morison, *An Invective against the Great and Detestable Vice of Treason*, 1539), see Elton 1972, p.204. For accounts of the changing religious policies of successive regimes, see (for example) Dickens 1989; Haigh 1993.
2. For the former view, see especially Duffy 1992; Haigh 1993; Scarisbrick 1984. For the latter view, see especially Dickens 1989.
3. References to art and architecture are based largely on the present author's personal examination of parish churches throughout England. See also (for example) Anderson 1955; Bond 1908; Bond 1910; Bond and Camm 1909; Caiger-Smith 1963; Cave 1948; Cook 1954; Cox 1915; Cox 1916; Cox and Ford 1943–4; Morris 1989; Nelson 1913.
4. For documentary sources, both unofficial and official, see *Bibliography and Abbreviations*. For the *Acts and Monuments*, see also Mozley 1940, especially pp.118–203. For wills, *Foxe*, V, pp.31–2; Duffy 1992, especially pp.504–19; Mayhew 1983, especially pp.38–45; O'Day 1986, pp.155–9; Whiting 1989, pp.5–6; Zell 1977, pp.246–9. For churchwardens' accounts, Cox 1913; Whiting 1989, especially p.5. See also 'Description of Exeter', pp.25–6; *Grey Friars Chronicle*, pp.54–5.

1 The Papacy

1. *Acts and Monuments*, II, pp.1037–40; CWA Morebath, 1531; ER XV, fol.61.
2. EHD, p.671; ER XIII, fol.145; *Foxe*, IV, pp.177, 205; STAC 2 34/91.
3. LP, XI, 1246; Dickens 1967, pp.59–61; Dodds and Dodds 1915, I, II; Haigh 1993, p.143; Whiting 1989, p.118.
4. LP, VII, 522, App.26, 29; X, 346; *York Records*, III, p.170; Elton 1972, pp.28, 120–1, 221–30.
5. C 1 973/69–70; LP, IX, 100, 109, 510, 1059; X, 14; XI, 408; XII (2), 571; XIII (1), 275, 987, 1171; XIV (1), 76, 444; TRP, I, pp.275–6; Elton 1972, pp.131, 151, 236–8, 258; Finucane 1977, pp.211–12.
6. CWA Ashburton, 1538, 1545; *Leland*, I, p.216; Duffy 1992, pp.419–20; Finucane 1977, p.211, plate 16; Wall 1905, p.167.
7. Hooker, Commonplace Book, fol.342; LP, IX, 742; SP 1 106/134; Haigh 1993, p.122; Hutton 1987, p.116; Whiting 1989, p.116.
8. *Foxe*, V, pp.62–3; *Grey Friars Chronicle*, pp.37–8; LP, VI, 1077; VII, 754; IX, 51–2, 108, 204, 497, 510; X, 94, 164, 346, 774; XI, 392; XII (2), 864, 1212; XIII (1), 107, 615, 705, 822; (2), 887; XIV (2), 438–9, 454, 458–9, App.45; Elton 1972, pp.28, 32, 61, 85–7, 108, 124–30, 137, 152–60, 278–9.
9. *Acts and Monuments*, II, pp.1037–40; CWA Ashburton, 1539; *Foxe*, V, p.33; Holme, 'Fall of Rebellion', p.129; LP, VI, 1077; VII, 754; XIII (1), 822; (2), 1178; Stowe 142, fol.14; *York Records*, IV, pp.68–70; Elton 1972, pp.85–7, 101, 129–30, 278–9; Whiting 1989, pp.114–15.
10. 'Description of Exeter', pp.27, 35, 37; Nichols, 'Answer', fol.3; Rose-Troup 1913, pp.80n, 489; Russell 1859, pp.47–56.
11. *Copy of a Letter*, pp.24–8; CSPV, V, p.346; *Godly New Story*, pp.24–6; Loades 1970, p.105.
12. *Acts and Monuments*, II, p.2051; CSPS, XII, p.243; XIII, p.112; CSPV, VI (2), pp.1004, 1018; *Foxe*, VI, p.573; VII, pp.91, 94; *Narratives of the Reformation*, pp.209–10; SP 11 2/2; Strype, *Memorials*, III (2), p.390; *York Records*, V, pp.112–13; Haigh 1993, pp.222–3; Hutton 1987, p.130; Loades 1970, p.110; Loades 1991, pp.113, 267.
13. For example, *Rising in the North*, p.254.

2 Religious Orders

1. EHD, pp.198, 762–70, 783; Dickens 1989, pp.75–9; Gilyard-Beer 1976, pp.54–7; Knowles 1948–59, III; Morris 1979, pp.220–7; Rowse 1941, pp.162–93.
2. Dickens 1989, pp.40, 74–5; Knowles and Hadcock 1971, especially pp.42–7, 494.
3. *Acts and Monuments*, II, p.1039; C 1 900/34–5; PROB 11 20, fol.229v; 21, fols.32v, 128, 202v; 22, fols.8, 254v, 302; 23, fol.71; 24, fols.10, 19; 25, fols.95v, 280v; 26, fol.76; 28, fol.17v; Dickens 1989, p.40; Henderson 1923–4, p.260; Whiting 1989, pp.120–1.

4. Bowker 1981, p.177; Knowles and Hadcock 1971; Morris 1979, especially pp.177–81, 219–27, 237–80; Tanner 1984, pp.222–3; Turnpenney 1992, tables; Whiting 1989, p.277.
5. CWA Ashburton, 1522; CWA Chagford, 1524; CWA Exeter SP, 1523; EHD, p.783.
6. *Bodmin Register*, pp.298–302; C 1 382/1; 491/24; CCB 854, I, fol.257; *Exeter Records*, p.269; STAC 2 18/221; 22/353; 25/60; 29/169; 30/115; Clark 1977, pp.28–9; Dickens 1989, p.78; Haigh 1993, pp.46–8.
7. EHD, p.676; *London Wills*, pp.56–150; Bowker 1981, p.177; Bruton 1987, tables; Thomson 1965B, pp.178–95; Whiting 1989, p.277.
8. *Acts and Monuments*, II, p.1039; *Foxe*, IV, p.584; LP, XI, 133; *Readings in Church History*, pp.659–63; STAC 2 29/55; 31/38; Elton 1972, pp.195, 198.
9. *Bodmin Register*, pp.293–4, 304–5; C 1 686/45; 695/2; 714/39; 719/25; 785/1–5; LP, VIII, 743; IX, 1147; *Plymouth Records*, p.108; STAC 2 18/77; 21/96; 29/11; Rowse 1941, pp.89, 178.
10. 'Examination of Aske', pp.330–48, 550–73; LP, XI, 1246; Dickens 1967, pp.56–7; Fletcher 1973, pp.21–47.
11. Hooker, Commonplace Book, fol.343; LP, XI, 681; SP 1 102/33; Elton 1972, pp.321–2.
12. LP, VI, App.10; XII (2), 864; XIII (1), 529, 845, 904–5, 975; XIV (1), 295, 839, 1094; Elton 1972, pp.44, 71–2, 93–4, 137, 155–60, 329–31.
13. *Letters to Cromwell*, pp.246–7; LP, XIII (2), 354, 381, 389.
14. *Leland*, I, pp.37–8, 132; II, p.58; V, p.104; Dickens 1989, pp.181–8; Morris 1979, p.234; Whiting 1989, p.122.
15. CWA Morebath, 1537; EHD, pp.785–6; Hooker, Commonplace Book, fol.345; *Letters to Cromwell*, pp.211–12; *Tavistock Records*, pp.16–19; *Tudor Treatises*, pp.123–6.
16. *Godly New Story*, pp.24–6, 60; Nichols, 'Answer', fol.33v; Russell 1859, pp.47–56; Whiting 1989, pp.122–3.
17. APC, V, p.169; SP 11 2/2; Bruton 1987, tables; Haigh 1993, p.226; Loades 1991, pp.300–2; Turnpenney 1992, tables; Whiting 1989, p.277.

3 The Secular Clergy (1)

1. Bowker 1981, pp.40, 125; Haigh 1987, pp.69–71; Haigh 1993, pp.37–8; Moran 1983; Storey 1989.
2. CAB 3552, fol. 134v; ER XIII–XIX; SP 12 6/17; Bowker 1981, pp.40, 125; Haigh 1987, p.71; Haigh 1993, pp.182, 215–6, 249–50; Hughes 1950–4, III, p.53; Pill 1963.
3. *Testamenta Eboracensia*, 6, pp.10–11; Bowker 1981, p.177; Bruton 1987, tables; Knowles and Hadcock 1971; Turnpenney 1992, tables; Whiting 1989, p.277.
4. *London Wills*, pp.56–150; PROB 11 33, fol.116; 34, fol.86v; Bowker 1981, p.177; Bruton 1987, tables; Turnpenney 1992, tables; Whiting 1989, pp.132, 277.

5. *Bodmin Register*, pp.36–8; C 1 581/88; CCB 854, I, fol.202; 854A, I, 18 January 1541/2; *Foxe*, IV, pp.183–205; PROB 11 17, fols.60, 199v; 18, fol.238v; 20, fol.229v; 21, fols.19, 202v; 22, fols.84v, 254v, 302; 23, fol.71v; STAC 2 22/376; 35/74; Clark 1977, p.28; Dickens 1989, p.116; Haigh 1993, pp.45, 47–8, 50, 96; Lander 1987, p.42.
6. C 1 666/8; 900/34–5; CCB 855, fols.304, 331–2; CCB 856, fol.434v; CWA Crediton, 1565; Elton 1972, pp.329–31; Haigh 1975, pp.57–8; Prince 1701, pp.181–2.
7. TRP, I, pp.224–5, 398; II, p.121; Haigh 1993, p.182; Houlbrooke 1979, pp.273–7; Pill 1968, p.48.
8. C 1 900/34–5; 1011/50–2; 1020/4–9; 1117/16; 1170/43; 1300/41–4; CCB 855, fols.45v, 193v, 238, 375, 376v, 451–2; CCB 855A, fol.489; CCB 855B, 7 June 1565; CCB 856, fols.449v–53; CWA Credition, 1565–71; CWA Morebath, 1537; *Tudor Parish Documents*, p.208; Elton 1958, pp.175–220; Henderson 1923–4, p.267.
9. C 1 1011/50–2; CCB 856, fols. 449v–53; LP, XI, 1080; Brigden 1989, pp.52, 201, 203; Russell 1859, pp.53–4.
10. CCB 855, fols.50v–1v, 53; CCB 855A, fol.422v; CCB 855B, 24 July 1566; CWA Crediton.
11. C 1 636/24; 666/8; 721/36; 778/19; 1002/1; 1004/52; 1023/77; 1061/30; 1073/1–2; 1160/5–6; 1170/48; 1193/54–7; 1273/55–6; 1347/16–18; 1366/5–6; 1369/11–20; 1373/14; 1386/35; 1389/68–71; 1424/5; 1466/76–80; 1467/41; C 3 9/41; LP, V, 1217; STAC 2 7/93; 19/341; 21/163; 32/4; STAC 3 3/81; Russell 1859, p.48.
12. *Acts and Monuments*, II, p.1038; CCB 855, fol.158; CCB 855A, fol.62; CCB 856, fol.470; 'Description of Exeter', pp.65–8; Haigh 1987, pp.3–6, 22–3; Houlbrooke 1979; Lander 1987, pp.34–55.
13. EHD, p.654; Clark 1977, p.28; Dickens 1989, p.323; Haigh 1993, pp.49–51, 72–3, 86–7.
14. *Acts and Monuments*, II, pp.1038–40, 2050–1; CAB 3552, fols.140, 145–8; CCB 855, fols.127v–8v, 174v–5, 266; CCB 855A, fols.222, 234–4v; CCB 855B, 17 December 1566, 28 February 1566/7, 10 March 1566/7; CCB 856, fols.449v–53, 470; *Copy of a Letter*, especially pp.32–3; Hooker, Commonplace Book, fol.352.
15. *Acts and Monuments*, II, p.1038; C 1 892/17–18; CCB 778, 30 November 1533; CCB 779, letter at back of volume, *c.*1562; CCB 855, fols.115v–16, 186, 191–1v, 210v, 257v, 375, 376v; STAC 2 32/28; Collinson 1967, p.40; Lander 1987, pp.34–55; Pill 1968, p.51.

4 The Secular Clergy (2)

1. STAC 2 2/267.
2. CCB 854, I, fols.31, 212; EHD, pp.669–76; ER XIII, fols.144v–5; *Foxe*, IV, pp.177, 205, 234; Haigh 1993, pp.50–1; Houlbrooke 1979, pp.178–9; Lander 1987, p.37.

3. *Foxe*, V, p.535; VII, p.80; VIII, p.383; *Godly New Story*, pp.24–5, 59–62, 72; LP, XII (1), 687, 990; *Grey Friars Chronicle*, p.88; Nichols, 'Answer', fol.10; *Readings in Church History*, pp.659–63; *Reformation in England*, pp.118–19; SP 11 2/2; STAC 2 2/267; Strype, *Memorials*, III (2), pp.389–413; Elton 1972, p.66; Loades 1991, p.289n; Whiting 1989, pp.129, 140.
4. C 1 1144/28–30; CCB 854A, I, 10 January 1541/2; CCB 855, fols.174v–5, 498v–9, 505; CCB 855A, fol.22v; CCB 855B, 4 July 1565, 26 July 1565; CCB 856, fols.307v–9v, 318v–22; REQ 2 8/324; STAC 2 9/63.
5. C 1 1139/23–4; 1144/28–30; CCB 854A, I, 8 December 1541, 23 December 1541; II, 30 June 1541; CCB 855, fols.49v–50, 70v, 150v–1v, 184v–5v, 235; CCB 855A, fols.181, 215–17, 222–3, 234–4v; CCB 855B, 4 July 1565, 19 December 1566; CCB 856, fols.210v–11v, 307v–9v; STAC 2 31/11, 178.
6. C 1 1139/23–4; 1144/28–30; CCB 856, fols.271–3v; STAC 2 31/178.
7. CCB 855, fol.375v.
8. CCB 855, fols.36v, 190v, 275–5v, 287–7v, 356–6v, 361–1v, 366–6v, 369v–70, 470–0v; CCB 855A, fols.222, 234–4v; CCB 856, fols.297–7v; 'Description of Exeter', p.68; *Grey Friars Chronicle*, p.95; LP, VI, 87; STAC 2 15/316; 19/341; 21/163; 22/376; 25/310; 30/104; 31/178; TRP, I, p.407; Brigden 1982, p.57; Dickens 1989, pp.138, 320; Elton 1972, pp.373–4; Haigh 1993, pp.50–1; Prince 1701, pp.181–2.
9. C 1 1378/19–21; CSPS, IV (1), p.367; EHD, pp.652–60; *Foxe*, VIII, pp.125, 284; *In God's Name*, pp.70–1; LP, XII (2), 1114; *Readings in Church History*, pp.659–63, 665; Strype, *Memorials*, III (2), pp.484–5; Dickens 1989, pp.112, 117; Elton 1972, pp.100–7; Haigh 1993, p.28; Platt 1981, p.147.

5 Parish Churches, Chapels (1)

1. For the functions and development of medieval parish churches, see (for example) Cook 1954; Cox and Ford 1943–4; Morris 1989; Platt 1981.
2. *Leland*, I, p.127; Hoskins 1954, pp.259–60, 324; Whiting 1989, pp.87–9, 219–20.
3. PROB 11 23, fol.22; Bond and Camm 1909, especially II, p.281; Whiting 1989, pp.86–7, 89–90.
4. The data for this survey has been collated from Jordan 1960A, pp.298–301; Jordan 1961A, pp.183, 389–401; Jordan 1961B, pp.115–23; Jordan 1962, pp.84–9; Pevsner and Hubbard 1971, especially pp.15–16, 23; Pevsner and Radcliffe 1974; Slader 1968, p.62; Whiting 1989, pp.83–105. For the specific references, see ER XV, fol.33; PROB 11 23, fols.22, 29, 71; STAC 2 17/209; Bond and Camm 1909, II, p.334; Haigh 1993, p.34; Hoskins 1954, pp.324, 381, 412, 418, 432, 448, 472, 509; Pevsner 1952A, p.155; Pevsner 1952B, pp.44, 96–7, 182–3, 188, 196, 203, 221; Whiting 1989, p.87.

5. C 1 1138/88–92; *Dartmouth*, p.188; Cox 1913.
6. This paragraph is based primarily on analysis of extant churchwardens' accounts. For specific references, see CWA Ashburton, 1529; CWA Exeter HT, 1529; *Plymouth Records*, p.29; *Testamenta Eboracensia*, 6, pp.10–11. For ales, see Hutton 1987, pp.123–4. For bequests, see Bowker 1981, p.177; Bruton 1987, tables; Tanner 1984, pp.222–3; Turnpenney 1992, tables; Whiting 1989, pp.91–2.
7. C 1 536/62; CCB 854, I, fol.31; CWA Ashburton, 1520, 1526–7; ER XIII, fol.135v; *Foxe*, IV, pp.235, 585; *Kentish Visitations*, p.181; LP, XIII (2), 21; STAC 2 17/209; 21/158; 22/376; Lander 1987, p.42, n.36; Morris 1989, pp.322–5, 330–9.

6 Parish Churches, Chapels (2)

1. For pulpits and benches, see below, pp.167–8. For screens, see especially CWA Modbury, 1545; Bond and Camm 1909, II, pp.228, 330, 353, 388, 392; Pevsner 1952B, p.125. For the St Neot glass, see Rushforth 1927B, pp.150–90.
2. *Inventories, Exeter*, p.11; Moger, 22, John Hill, 1546; Hoskins 1954, pp.381, 416, 441, 489, 518; Pevsner 1952A, p.108; Pevsner 1952B, p.96; Slader 1968, p.62. For the survey of eight counties, see note 4 to Chapter 5.
3. C 1 1074/18; LP, XIII (2), 561; PROB 11 31, fol.151v; Elton 1972, pp.97–8; Henderson 1923–4, pp.139, 250–1; Henderson 1925, pp.115, 124; Hoskins 1954, pp.342, 460; Pevsner 1952A, p.88; Pevsner 1952B, p.231. See also note 4 to Chapter 5. For an effective refutation of the claim (on stylistic grounds) that post-reformation church building was more frequent than is usually believed, see Bernard 1992, pp.344–50.
4. CWA Exeter SP, 1551; CWA Morebath, 1551, 1558; CWA Woodbury, 1551; Phelps Brown and Hopkins 1956; Whiting 1989, pp.95–6.
5. C 1 996/12; 1091/32–5; 1094/22–3; 1348/86–8; 1378/39; 1482/97; C 3 192/5; 202/65; CPR, II, p.259; CWA Ashburton, 1531; CWA Exeter SP, 1569; STAC 2 21/94; 25/310; Whiting 1989, p.97.
6. CCB 855, fols.409–9v, 415–15v; CWA Antony; CWA Ashburton; CWA Braunton; CWA Chudleigh; CWA Dartington; CWA Exeter SJB; CWA Exeter SMS; CWA Kilmington; CWA Morebath; CWA Woodbury; HCWA Stratton; SWA Stratton; Haigh 1993, p.213; Hutton 1987, pp.123–4, 130–1, 136–7. For guilds, see also below, pp.46–51.
7. CCB 855, fols.174v–5, 203v–4, 206v; CCB 855A, fol.492; Hutton 1987, pp.123–4, 130–1, 136–7. For wax silver, see below, pp.85, 90, 92.
8. CWA Ashburton; CWA Exeter HT; CWA Exeter SJB; CWA Exeter SMS; CWA Exeter SP, especially 1568; CWA Morebath, especially 1542, 1558; CWA Woodbury, especially 1539.

9. *London Wills*, pp.56–150; PROB 11 48, fol.491v; 51, fol.51; Bowker 1981, p.177; Bruton 1987, tables; Turnpenney 1992, tables; Whiting 1989, pp.99–100, 276.
10. C 1 623/12; 1138/88; 1217/3; CCB 855A, fols.222, 234–4v; CCB 856, fols.15–15v, 25v–6, 351v–3; CWA Antony, pp.1, 33, 54, 56; *Melford Church*, pp.12, 34; STAC 2 29/156; Strype, *Memorials*, III (2), p.482; Whiting 1989, pp.100–1.
11. C 1 1160/75–6; 1348/86–8; 1482/97; CCB 855, fol.184v; CWA Morebath, 1558; 'Lives of Saints', fols.202v–3, 312v; PROB 11 39, fol.203; STAC 2 29/156; Strype, *Memorials*, III (2), pp.389–413; Haigh 1993, pp.182, 212; Henderson 1923–4, pp.196–7; Hoskins 1954, pp.272–3; Pogson 1987, p.155; Whiting 1989, p.102.
12. *Royal Visitation*, especially p.xxxv; *Foxe*, VIII, p.302; Strype, *Memorials*, III (2), pp.389–413, 482; Cook 1954, p.267; Haigh 1993, pp.212, 250; Houlbrooke 1979, pp.278–81; Whiting 1989, p.102.
13. *Grey Friars Chronicle*, p.55; *Leland*, I, pp.169, 175, 240; II, p.38; *York Records*, V, pp.28, 38–9, 100, 117, 147.
14. CWA Exeter SJB, 1550, 1561; CWA St Breock, fol.14; CWA Woodbury, 1560; E 315 122/15–28; *Foxe*, VI, p.679; SWA Stratton, 1541–2; Haigh 1993, pp.242–3. For glass, see below, p.192.
15. APC, V, pp.112–13; EHD, p.866; *Grey Friars Chronicle*, p.55; STAC 4 8/47; *York Records*, IV, pp.168–9, 179–80; V, pp.4, 53, 72, 106, 129.
16. CCB 854A, I, 11 November 1541; CCB 855, fols.43v, 115v–16, 140v–1, 150v, 151v, 174v–5, 188v, 266v, 360v, 470–0v; CCB 855A, fols.222, 234–4v; CCB 855B, 17 December 1566; CCB 856, fols.297–7v, 307v–8, 320–1, 449v–53; *Documents of Church History*, p.433; *Exeter Records*, p.308; STAC 2 10/244–56; 15/316; 23/95; STAC 3 1/58; STAC 4 9/38; TRP, I, pp.537–8; II, pp.177–9; Henderson 1923–4, pp.214–15; Houlbrooke 1979, pp.278–81.
17. LP, XVIII (2), 546; STAC 2 2/267, 269; Strype, *Memorials*, III (2), p.391.

7 Guilds

1. Scarisbrick 1984, pp.19–39; Whiting 1989, pp.105–12. See (for example) CWA Morebath; CWA N. Petherwin, especially fols.14, 22v, 32v, 38v; HCWA Stratton. For the Boston guild of Our Lady, see *Foxe*, V, pp.364–5.
2. CWA Morebath; *Exeter Records*, p.45; Duffy 1992, p.144; Henderson 1935, pp.75–9.
3. CWA Ashburton, especially 1526; CWA Camborne, especially 1535; CWA N. Petherwin, especially fol.38v; HCWA Stratton, especially 1519, 1527.
4. CWA Ashburton; CWA Chagford; CWA N. Petherwin; HCWA Stratton, especially 1530; Henderson 1935, pp.75–9.

5. E 315 122/15–28; HCWA Stratton, especially 1512, 1518; *Survey of Cornwall*, pp.322–3.
6. CWA Antony; CWA Ashburton; CWA Broadhempston; CWA Camborne; CWA Chagford; CWA Exeter HT; CWA Exeter SJB; CWA Exeter SMS; CWA Exeter SP; CWA Morebath; CWA N. Petherwin; CWA S. Tawton; CWA Winkleigh; HCWA Stratton; SWA Stratton; Craig 1955, pp.267, 299; Haigh 1993, pp.35–6.
7. PROB 11 19, fol.208; 22, fol.191v; Bowker 1981, p.177; Bruton 1987, tables; Tanner 1984, pp.222–3; Turnpenney 1992, tables; Whiting 1989, pp.107–8.
8. CWA Ashburton; CWA Camborne; CWA Exeter SJB; CWA Launceston; CWA Morebath; CWA N. Petherwin; CWA Woodbury; SWA Stratton; Whiting 1989, pp.109–10.
9. C 1 959/35–7; 976/32–3; 1029/46–50; 1042/7–9; 1162/52; 1185/31; CCB 778, 12 January 1533/4, 17 March 1533/4; CWA Antony, pp.69, 71–3, 75–7, 86; CWA Chagford, 1529; CWA Morebath, 1536; *London Wills*, pp.56–150; PROB 11 25, fol.227v; Bowker 1981, p.177; Bruton 1987, tables; Dickens 1989, p.238; Haigh 1993, p.36; Kreider 1979, p.158; Turnpenney 1992, tables; Whiting 1989, p.108.
10. CWA Antony; CWA Camborne; CWA Modbury; CWA Woodbury; *Documents of Church History*, pp.328–57; HCWA Stratton; STAC 3 2/14; SWA Stratton; Hutton 1987, p.122; Whiting 1989, pp.110–11.
11. CWA N. Petherwin, fols.3, 30–2; Bowker 1981, p.177; Bruton 1987, tables; Morris 1989, pp.375–6; Turnpenney 1992, tables; Whiting 1989, p.108.
12. CWA Coldridge; CWA Morebath, especially 1556; Hutton 1987, p.131; Whiting 1989, pp.111–12.
13. CWA Braunton; CWA N. Petherwin, fols.3v–4; HCWA Stratton; Bruton 1987, tables; Hutton 1987, p.131; Turnpenney 1992, tables; Whiting 1989, p.108.
14. CCB 856, fols.25v–6; CWA Braunton; CWA Chagford; CWA Chudleigh; CWA Coldridge; CWA N. Petherwin, especially fols.4–4v; Turnpenney 1992, tables; Whiting 1989, pp.108, 112.

8 Rites (1)

1. For 'seven sacrament' fonts, see below, p.190.
2. ER XIII, fols.144v–5; *Foxe*, IV, pp.173–9, 205, 221–46, 584–5; Duffy 1992, pp.70, 102–4; Hoskins 1954, p.450; Rushforth 1927A, pp.21–9.
3. CWA Ashburton, especially 1518; EHD, p.195; LP, IX, 1147; *Melford Church*, pp.5–6; PROB 11 23, fol.71.
4. *Dartmouth*, p.213; *Foxe*, IV, p.179; *Kentish Visitations*, p.160; Duffy 1992, pp.112–13, 118; Thomas 1973, pp.90, 200.
5. CWA Exeter SMM, fol.11; EHD, p.198; *Melford Church*, pp.10–25; Dunkin 1882, p.10; Pevsner 1952B, pp.64, 98.

6. CWA Morebath, 1531; PROB 11 23, fol.54; Pevsner 1952B, pp.28, 52, 307; Pevsner and Radcliffe 1970, p.122; Whiting 1989, pp.20–3.
7. C 1 246/48; CCB 854, 28 February 1507/8; CWA Ashburton, 1521, 1529; CWA S. Tawton, 1532. For fonts, see Bond 1908.
8. *Butley Priory*, p.67; *Foxe*, V, p.33; LP, XI, 1424; XIV (1), 1001; XVIII (2), 546; STAC 2 2/267–72, 287; 23/273; 29/111; Dickens 1989, pp.54–5; Duffy 1992, pp.391–2; Elton 1972, pp.88, 152.
9. *Foxe*, V, pp.32–9, 443–9, 530–3; LP, XI, 1424; STAC 2 2/267–72, 287; 23/273; 29/111; Duffy 1992, pp.391–2; Elton 1972, pp.88, 106.
10. C 1 712/8; CWA Antony, 1545–6; CWA Ashburton, 1539; CWA Camborne, 1538; CWA Chagford, 1532, 1536, 1539–40; CWA Exeter SP, 1541; CWA Iddesleigh, 1536, 1538–9, 1542; CWA Morebath, 1535, 1537, 1539, 1542, 1547; CWA Winkleigh, 1547; CWA Woodbury, 1539, 1543; PROB 11 25, fol.227v; 29, fol.151; 30, fol.333; 31, fols.15v, 36, 151v; SWA Stratton, 1546; Pevsner 1952A, pp.83, 149; Whiting 1989, pp.25–6.
11. C 1 1138/93–4; CWA Dartmouth, 1545; CWA Morebath, 1535; HCWA Stratton, 1545; *Melford Church*, pp.26–35; *Plymouth Records*, p.113; STAC 3 2/20; STAC 4 8/47; SWA Stratton, 1546.
12. C 1 900/34–5; CCB 854A, II, 24 November 1540; CWA Exeter SP, 1542; CWA Woodbury, 1543; *Foxe*, V, pp.443–9; LP, XVIII (2), 546; SP 1 106/135; STAC 2 7/93; 15/233–7; Thomas 1973, pp.190–1.
13. *Grey Friars Chronicle*, pp.61, 69; Harleian 352, fols.65v–6v; Dickens 1989, p.321; Loades 1970, p.185.
14. *Acts and Monuments*, II, pp.1305, 1308; 'Description of Exeter', pp.26–9; 'Life of Carew', p.lxxxvi; Nichols, 'Answer', fols.11–12, 14, 19–19v, 22, 25; Whiting 1989, pp.34–8. For the southwestern revolt, see also Cornwall 1977; Rose-Troup 1913; Youings 1979; below, p.108. For the Norfolk revolt, see Cornwall 1977; Russell 1859, especially pp.47–56; below, p.109.
15. CWA Ashburton; CWA Morebath; CWA Woodbury; *Grey Friars Chronicle*, p.56; HCWA Stratton; Parkyn, 'Narrative', pp.295–9; SWA Stratton; Duffy 1992, pp.462–3; Haigh 1993, p.208; Hutton 1987, pp.120, 122–3.
16. *Barnstaple Records*, I, pp.198–9; CWA Antony, pp.36–7; CWA Camborne, 1553; CWA Coldridge, 1552; CWA Morebath, 1548, 1552; CWA Woodbury, 1547, 1549, 1553; *Grey Friars Chronicle*, p.77; HCWA Stratton, 1551, 1553; *Inventories, Cornwall*, especially p.ix; *Melford Church*, pp.36–47; Parkyn, 'Narrative', p.306; Stowe 141, fol.67; Hutton 1987, pp.126–7; Whiting 1989, pp.38–9.
17. For bells, see CWA Credition, 1551; CWA Exeter HT, 1549; CWA Morebath, 1551; CWA N. Molton, 1549; CWA Woodbury, 1549, 1551; E 117 2/7; HCWA Stratton, 1552; *Prayerbook of 1549*, p.73; Ellacombe 1872, pp.225, 288–9; Rose-Troup 1913, pp.372–7. For books, see CWA Dartington, 1554; CWA Exeter SMM, fol.12; CWA Morebath, 1555; CWA Woodbury, 1550; *Melford Church*, pp.30, 50; Parkyn, 'Narrative', p.301; *Prayerbook of 1549*, pp.49, 127–9; Hutton 1987, p.125. For Marian expenditure, see below, p.63. For fonts, see (for example) CWA Coldridge, 1556; CWA Exeter SMS, 1554. For sepulchres, see (for example) CWA Ashburton, 1556; CWA Crediton, 1554; CWA

Dartmouth, 1554; CWA Exeter SJB, 1554; CWA Exeter SMS, 1554; CWA Morebath, 1554; CWA S. Tawton, 1559; CWA Woodbury, 1554; HCWA Stratton, 1558. For pyxes, see Parkyn, 'Narrative', p.297.

18. *Barnstaple Records*, I, pp.198–9; CWA Ashburton, 1552–3; CWA Crediton, 1551; CWA Exeter HT, 1551–2; CWA Exeter SJB, 1549; CWA Exeter SP, 1551, 1553; CWA Modbury, 1548; CWA Morebath, 1548, 1553, 1558; CWA N. Molton, 1549; CWA Woodbury, 1547–9, 1551, 1553; E 117 1/48, 52; 2/7; HCWA Stratton, 1548, 1551, 1553; *Inventories, Cornwall*, p.xii; *Inventories, Exeter*, especially p.xiii; *Melford Church*, p.29; SP 10 6/25; SP 15 3/29; *Tavistock Records*, p.22; Hutton 1987, pp.126–7; Whiting 1989, pp.27–8.
19. C 1 1217/3; CWA Morebath, 1549; CWA Woodbury, 1547; E 117 1/52; 2/7; *Exeter Records*, pp.363–4; *Inventories, Exeter*, especially pp.20–4, 66–70, 75–84; REQ 2 5/335; STAC 4 8/47; Duffy 1992, pp.487–90; Whiting 1989, p.29.
20. CWA Antony, 1549; CWA Ashburton, 1550–1; CWA Camborne, 1550; CWA Crediton, 1551–2; CWA Dartmouth, 1552; CWA Exeter HT, 1550; CWA Exeter SJB, 1550; CWA Exeter SP, 1550–1; CWA Morebath, 1551; CWA N. Petherwin, fol.32v; CWA Woodbury, 1550; ER XV, fols.119v–20; HCWA Stratton, 1551; Parkyn, 'Narrative', p.301; Hutton 1987, pp.125–7. For Marian re-erections, see below, p.63.
21. CWA Dartmouth, 1552; CWA Woodbury, 1550; *Harpsfield's Visitation*; STAC 4 8/47; Haigh 1993, p.177.
22. *Acts and Monuments*, II, p.1305; *Grey Friars Chronicle*, pp.55, 57; Nichols, 'Answer', especially fols.9v–10, 12–13v, 19v–20, 23, 25–6; Parkyn, 'Narrative', p.297.

9 Rites (2)

1. CWA Antony, 1554; CWA Ashburton, 1554; CWA Braunton, 1555; CWA Camborne, 1554; CWA Chagford, 1554–5; CWA Coldridge, 1553–4; CWA Crediton, 1554; CWA Dartmouth, 1553; CWA Exeter SJB, 1554; CWA Exeter SMS, 1554; CWA Exeter SP, 1556; CWA Morebath, 1554, 1556; CWA S. Tawton, 1554–5; CWA Woodbury, 1554; *Harpsfield's Visitation*, especially p.187; HCWA Stratton, 1553, 1556; SWA Stratton, 1557; *Tavistock Records*, p.24; Haigh 1993, pp.211–12; Hutton 1987, pp.127–9, 131–2.
2. CWA Coldridge, 1559; CWA Easingwold; CWA Exeter SJB, 1559; CWA Molland, 1557; CWA Woodbury, 1558–9; Hutton 1987, pp.129–30; Pevsner and Radcliffe 1970, p.46.
3. CWA Ashburton, 1554; CWA Camborne, 1554; CWA Dartmouth, 1554–5; CWA Easingwold; CWA Exeter SP, 1558; CWA Morebath, 1554; CWA S. Tawton, 1555; CWA Woodbury, 1554, 1558; E 117 13/105; *Melford Church*, p.30; PROB 11 37, fol.268; Duffy 1992, pp.549–50; Haigh 1993, pp.207–9, 213; Hutton 1987, pp.129–30.

4. APC, V, pp.112–13; CWA Morebath, 1555; *Foxe*, VIII, p.304; *Melford Church*, p.47; Strype, *Memorials*, III (2), pp.389–413; Haigh 1993, p.210; Hutton 1987, pp.129–30.
5. *Harpsfield's Visitation*, especially pp.186–90, 223; Duffy 1992, pp.555–63; Haigh 1993, pp.211–12; Hughes 1950–4, II, pp.236–43; Hutton 1987, p.132.
6. *Grey Friars Chronicle*, p.93; *Narratives of the Reformation*, p.81; Parkyn, 'Narrative', pp.308–9, 311; Haigh 1993, pp.206–7; Hutton 1987, pp.127–8, 130–1. For lights, see (for example) CWA Crediton, 1558; for vigils, CWA Crediton, 1554; for Candlemas, CWA Antony, 1555; for funerals, CWA Ashburton, 1554–9.
7. *Acts and Monuments*, II, p.2050; ER XVII, fols.24v–5v; *Foxe*, VI, pp.678–9; *Narratives of the Reformation*, p.81; Parkyn, 'Narrative', p.309; SP 11 2/2; Wriothesley, *Chronicle*, II, p.101; *York Records*, V, p.105; Duffy 1992, pp.527–8.
8. APC, VI, p.158; CCB 855, fols.111v, 150v–1v, 361–1v; *Foxe*, VIII, pp.598–600; *Grey Friars Chronicle*, p.97; *Harpsfield's Visitation*, p.189; Strype, *Memorials*, III (2), pp.389–413; Haigh 1993, pp.206–7, 220; Loades 1991, pp.384–5; Whiting 1989, pp.41, 43.
9. *Acts and Monuments*, II, pp.2050–2; APC, IV, p.395; C 1 1348/86–8; 1482/97; CCB 855, fols. 49, 63, 111v, 174v–5, 191–1v, 214v, 377v, 409–9v, 415–15v; *Foxe*, VIII, pp.383, 598–600; *Harpsfield's Visitation*, especially p.109; Strype, *Memorials*, III (2), pp.389–413; Haigh 1993, p.220; Loades 1991, p.116; Whiting 1989, pp.43–4.
10. *Acts and Monuments*, II, pp.2049–52; *Foxe*, VII, pp.192–3; VIII, p.383; Parkyn, 'Narrative', pp.308–9; Strype, *Memorials*, III (2), pp.389–413; Dickens 1982A, p.223; Haigh 1993, pp.206–8, 220.
11. CCB 855, fols.140v–1; EHD, p.866; *Foxe*, VI, p.678; VIII, pp.598–600; *Grey Friars Chronicle*, pp.89, 95; *Harpsfield's Visitation*; *Narratives of the Reformation*, pp.81–2; Dickens 1982A, pp.225–6; Duffy 1992, pp.544–6; Haigh 1993, pp.206–7, 220; Loades 1991, p.49.
12. *Foxe*, VIII, pp.598–600; *Harpsfield's Visitation*, p.192; Haigh 1993, p.220; Whiting 1989, p.43.
13. CCB 856, fols.143v-6; *Foxe*, VIII, p.564; Machyn, *Diary*, p.225; *Original Letters*, p.19; *Rising in the North*, especially pp.258–9; Strype, *Memorials*, III (2), pp.472–3; *Tudor Parish Documents*, pp.143–4; Aveling 1970, p.168; Loades 1991, p.394. For the 1569 rising, see also below, pp.108–9.
14. CWA Chagford, 1561; Hooker, Commonplace Book, fol.352; Machyn, *Diary*, p.196; Strype, *Annals*, I (2), p.436; Collinson 1967, p.32; Hutton 1987, pp.133–5.
15. CWA Exeter SMM, fol.16; DRO 1660 A 12; Machyn, *Diary*, p.208.
16. CWA Antony, p.9; CWA Ashburton, 1569–70; CWA Camborne, 1561; CWA Exeter SJB, 1570; CWA Exeter SMM, fol.16; CWA Kilmington, 1566; CWA Molland, 1562; CWA Morebath, 1560, 1568; CWA St Breock, fols.4v,16,21,23; E 178 517; *Exeter Records*, p.308; HCWA Stratton, 1570; *Inventories, Cornwall*, p.32; *Melford Church*, pp.70–1; *Plymouth Records*, pp.232–3; *Tudor Parish Documents*, pp.144–6; Whiting 1989, p.28.

17. *English Church Furniture*, pp.29–171. For Witham and Kelby, see pp.109–10, 165–7.
18. Birt 1907, pp.427–30; Cox and Harvey 1973, pp.28, 341; Haigh 1993, p.247; Hutton 1987, pp.134–5. For sales in the 1570s, see (for example) Whiting 1989, p.28 and n.47.
19. *Barnstaple Records*, I, p.213; CWA Antony, 1559; CWA Ashburton, 1560; CWA Chudleigh, 1568; CWA Coldridge, 1560; CWA Crediton, 1559; CWA Exeter SP, 1560, 1562; CWA Exeter SJB, 1559, 1565; CWA Exeter SMS, 1562; CWA Kilmington, 1560; CWA Molland, 1559–60; CWA Morebath, 1559, 1566, 1572; CWA S. Tawton, 1560–1; CWA Winkleigh, 1560,1566; CWA Woodbury, 1559; *English Church Furniture*, pp.29–171; Hooker, Commonplace Book, fol.352; Cox and Harvey 1973, pp.8–11; Haigh 1993, pp.245–6; Hutton 1987, pp.134–5, 137; Morris 1989, p.374; Whiting 1989, pp.45–6.
20. *English Church Furniture*, pp.29–171; Duffy 1992, p.584; Pevsner and Radcliffe 1970, p.110.

10 Intercession

1. C 1 900/34–5; CWA Ashburton, especially 1510; CWA Dartmouth, 1530; EDCL 2864; PROB 11 20, fol. 229; 23, fol. 29; Prince 1701, pp.324–5.
2. *Certificates, Yorkshire*, especially p.166; PROB 11 21, fols. 128, 202v; 22, fols. 8, 191v, 302; 23, fol. 29; 24, fol. 10.
3. Kreider 1979, especially pp.78, 87, 90–1, and additional data from Dr Kreider.
4. Bowker 1981, p.177; Bruton 1987, tables; Haigh 1975, pp.69–70, 194; Jordan 1959, especially pp.246, 375; Thomson 1965B, pp.178–95; Turnpenney 1992, tables; Whiting 1989, p.20.
5. EHD, p.674; ER XIII, fols.144v–5, 179v–81; *Foxe*, IV, p.584; Kreider 1979, pp.154–5.
6. CWA Woodbury, especially 1539; LP, XI, 876; XII (2), 534; PROB 11 27, fol.69v; 29, fol.201; 31, fol.115v; Elton 1972, p.250.
7. *London Wills*, pp.56–150; Bowker 1981, p.177; Bruton 1987, tables; Haigh 1975, pp.69–70, 194; Jordan 1959, pp.246, 375; Mayhew 1983, pp.38–67; Turnpenney 1992, tables; Whiting 1989, p.30. For the views challenged here, see Duffy 1992, pp.513–14.
8. HCWA Stratton, 1530–46; Kreider 1979, pp.78, 86–92, and additional data.
9. C 1 781/26; 786/54; 930/1; 959/35–7; 976/32–3; 986/44; 1042/7–9; 1068/15–16; 1200/10–11; *Certificates, Cornwall*, pp.21, 27, 34, 42, 48, 50, 53; *Certificates, Devon*, pp.xxi–ii, 23–4, 41; *Certificates, Yorkshire*, pp.168, 296; STAC 2 25/80, 142; 3 2/20; 7/45; *York Records*, IV, p.144; Dickens 1989, pp.232–3; Haigh 1975, pp.71–2, 147; Kreider 1979, pp.155–60; Whiting 1989, pp.30–2.

10. *Acts and Monuments*, II, pp.1037–40; *Foxe*, V, pp.38–9; LP, XI, 1424; Dickens 1982A, p.45; Elton 1972, p.88.
11. CWA Morebath; CWA Woodbury; E 117 1/52; E 178 518, 659; *Grey Friars Chronicle*, p.56; Nichols, 'Answer', fol.25; Haigh 1993, pp.171–2; Hutton 1987, p.122; Russell 1859, pp.47–56.
12. *Godly New Story*, p.47; HCWA Stratton; Moger, 39, John Southwood, 1549; Nichols, 'Answer', fols.25–6; PROB 11 33, fol.116; Bowker 1981, p.177; Bruton 1987, tables; Haigh 1993, p.172; Mayhew 1983, p.52; Turnpenney 1992, tables; Whiting 1989, p.32.
13. *Barnstaple Records*, I, pp.212–13; CWA Antony; CWA Ashburton; CWA Braunton; CWA Camborne; CWA Chagford; CWA Coldridge; CWA Credition; CWA Dartington; CWA Dartmouth; CWA Exeter HT; CWA Exeter SJB; CWA Exeter SMS; CWA Exeter SP; CWA Kilmington; CWA Launceston; CWA Molland; CWA Morebath; CWA N. Petherwin; CWA S. Tawton; CWA Woodbury; HCWA Stratton; Hutton 1987, pp.131–2; Whiting 1989, p.42.
14. *Acts and Monuments*, II, pp.2049–52; CCB 855A, fol.311v; *Foxe*, VIII, pp.103,254; HCWA Stratton; PROB 11 39, fol.391; Bruton 1987, tables; Haigh 1975, pp.69–70, 194; Jordan 1959, pp.246, 375; Loades 1991, pp.298–9; Mayhew 1983, p.52; Turnpenney 1992, tables; Whiting 1989, p.32.
15. CWA Dartington; CWA Morebath; PROB 11 49, fol.55v; 50, fol.152v; Haigh 1975, pp.69–70, 194; Jordan 1959, pp.246, 375; Turnpenney 1992, tables; Whiting 1989, pp.32–3. For the suppression of 'ringing the bells for all christian souls', see (for example) *Tudor Parish Documents*, p.219.
16. TRP, II, pp.146–8; *York Records*, VI, pp.26–8; MacCulloch 1986, pp.182–4.

11 Prayers, Fasts, Feasts

1. PROB 11 21, fol.18v; 23, fol.71; 24, fol.10; Duffy 1992, pp.19, 117–21; Henderson 1935, pp.75–9.
2. Duffy 1992, pp.41–3, 210–14.
3. EHD, p.195; ER XV, fol.30v; PROB 11 21, fol.19; Clark 1977, p.58; Duffy 1992, pp.234–65; Ellacombe 1872, pp.239–48; Palliser 1979, pp.250–1; Turnpenney 1992, tables; Whiting 1989, p.60.
4. *Leland*, I, pp.187, 189, 192, 196, 228, 230, 232–5, 237; 'Lives of Saints', fols.101v–2, 202v–3, 262; STAC 4 8/47; Whiting 1989, p.59.
5. For medieval saint cults in England, see (for example) Farmer 1978.
6. *Foxe*, IV, pp.177, 226, 584; V, p.42; Finucane 1977, pp.195–8.
7. *Certificates, Devon*, p.xxi; *Original Letters*, pp.14–15; PROB 11 29, fol.201; 31, fol.44; 39, fol.203; 44, fol.159v.
8. CCB 855, fols. 5v, 71–1v; *Foxe*, V, p.32; VI, p.32; VIII, pp.284, 383; Hooker, Commonplace Book, fol.351; LP, XII (1), 746, 755–6; XIII (1),

686, 811, 1199; XIII (2), App.19; XIV (1), 684; XIV (2), 71; Parkyn, 'Narrative', p.296; STAC 2 2/267; Strype, *Annals*, I (2), p.436; Strype, *Memorials*, III (2), pp.389–413; TRP, I, pp.260–1; Elton 1972, pp.22, 90–3, 98–9, 102.

9. LP, XI, 580; XII (1), 201, 1126–7; XII (2), 150, 182, 557, 595; *Reformation in England*, pp.73–4; SP 1 106/134–5; 118/247–8; Fletcher 1973, p.36.
10. ER XV, fol.83v; *Foxe*, V, pp.443, 446; LP, VI, 1077, 1329; Add., 871, 879; X, 365; XI, 514; XII (2), 505, 592; XIII (1), 1150; XIV (1), 295, 839; Titus B 1, fol.176; Duffy 1992, pp.394–7; Elton 1972, pp.20–1, 85–90, 250, 329–31.
11. CWA Morebath; *Grey Friars Chronicle*, pp.59, 62, 66–7, 74, 76.
12. CWA Woodbury; *Grey Friars Chronicle*, p.89; *Harpsfield's Visitation*; 'Lives of Saints', fol.388; LP, XVIII (1), 167; *Original Letters*, pp.14–15; *York Records*, VI, p.17.
13. *Acts and Monuments*, II, pp.2049–52; CCB 855, fol.210v; CWA Ashburton, 1554; 'Description of Exeter', pp.31–2; *Harpsfield's Visitation*, especially p.53; *Original Letters*, pp.14–15; *Tudor Parish Documents*, p.208; Birt 1907, pp.427–30; Elton 1972, pp.375–80.
14. *Acts and Monuments*, II, pp.1037–40, 2049–52; *Foxe*, V, pp.39, 404–9, 443; VIII, pp.254, 300; LP, XI, 1424; XII (1), 1147; XII (2), 571; XIII (1), 615; Nichols, 'Answer', p.23v; STAC 2 2/267–72, 287; 23/273; 29/111; Duffy 1992, pp.408–10; Elton 1972, pp.32, 88, 118–19.
15. PROB 11 30, fol.333; Brigden 1989, pp.381–4, 485–6, 629; Clark 1977, pp.58, 76; Cross 1979; Dickens 1982A, pp.171–2, 215–8, 220–1; Dickens 1989, pp.214–15; Palliser 1979, pp.250–1; Shiels 1979, pp.15–18, 21–4; Turnpenney 1992, tables; Whiting 1989, p.63. For bells, see (for example) Ellacombe 1872, pp.226, 255.
16. For discussion of some of these points, see Dickens 1989, p.215; Duffy 1992, pp.472, 509–13.

12 Images (1)

1. CWA Ashburton; CWA Exeter SJB, 1517; *Melford Church*, p.1; STAC 4 8/47; Whiting 1989, pp.48–50.
2. CCB 854, 28 February 1507/8; CWA Ashburton, especially 1521–30; CWA Chagford; CWA Exeter SJB; CWA Morebath, especially 1529–38; CWA N. Petherwin, fols.36v, 43, 49v; CWA S. Tawton; CWA Winkleigh, 1513–20; PROB 11 21, fol.202v; 23, fols.22, 71; Bond and Camm 1909, especially I, p.82; II, p.384; Haigh 1993, p.34; Hoskins 1954, pp.272, 349, 433; Pevsner 1952A, p.121; Whiting 1989, pp.50–2.
3. CWA Iddesleigh, 1536–7; CWA Morebath, 1529–32; E 117 10/59; E 315 126/16–17; EHD, pp.835–7; ER XV, fol.30v; *Foxe*, VII, p.476; Glastonbury Commonplace Book, fol.86; HCWA Stratton, 1512–30; *Leland*, I, p.208; 'Lives of Saints', fols.314–14v; PROB 11 20, fol.124v;

22, fols.254v, 302; 23, fols.29, 71; 24, fol.19; 28, fols.17v, 126; STAC 2 26/257; *Survey of Cornwall*, p.378; Worcestre, p.99; Chanter 1914, pp.290–308; Finucane 1977, p.199; Henderson 1923–4, pp.76, 195–7, 222–3; Hoskins 1954, pp.364–5; Radford 1949, p.165; Risdon 1811, pp.319–24; Whiting 1989, pp.52–5.

4. C 1 924/9–10; CWA Camborne, 1535; CWA Iddesleigh, 1536–7; *Foxe*, IV, pp.175–7, 216, 221–46, 584; *Gleanings*, pp.17–19; *Melford Church*, pp.10–25; Aston 1989; Finucane 1977, pp.208–9; Haigh 1993, p.69; Turnpenney 1992, tables.
5. C 1 728/23; 819/12; CWA Morebath, 1535; *Foxe*, IV, pp.706–7; V, pp.32–9; LP, X, 346; XI, 1424; *Melford Church*, p.12; *Narratives of the Reformation*, p.350; Elton 1972, pp.29, 44, 88; Haigh 1975, p.83; Haigh 1993, pp.69–70; Whiting 1989, p.62.
6. CWA Camborne, especially 1535; CWA Iddesleigh, especially 1536–7, 1541; *Documents of Church History*, pp.269–74; E 117 10/59; E 315 126/16–17; LP, XII (2), 587.
7. CWA Morebath; ER XV, fols.76v–7; LP, XVI, 1377; *Melford Church*, pp.10–35; *Plymouth Records*, p.110; Cox 1913, pp.139–40; Duffy 1992, pp.418, 431–2, 483; Hutton 1987, pp.116–17.
8. CAB 3552, fol.14v; *Foxe*, VI, p.28; *Gleanings*, pp.17–19; Hooker, Commonplace Book, fol.344; LP, XVIII (2), 546; Nichols, 'Answer', fols.21–2; Chanter 1914, pp.290–308; Duffy 1992, pp.402, 413–4, 434–42; Finucane 1977, pp.204–5; Haigh 1993, p.134; Wall 1905, pp.129–30.
9. *Leland*, I, pp.165, 208; III, pp.91–2; V, p.47.
10. Hooker, Commonplace Book, fols.343–4; LP, XII (2), 587; XVIII (2), 546; SP 1 102/33; Duffy 1992, p.403; Elton 1972, pp.81–2.
11. C 1 924/9–10; *Gleanings*, pp.17–19; LP, XII (1), 818; XIII (2), 596; XIV (1), 777; XVIII (2), 546; Wriothesley, *Chronicle*, I, pp.75–81; Elton 1972, pp.81–2, 105–6.
12. CWA Antony; CWA Ashburton; CWA Camborne; CWA Chagford; CWA Dartmouth; CWA Exeter HT; CWA Exeter SJB; CWA Exeter SMS; CWA Exeter SP; CWA Iddesleigh; CWA Modbury; CWA Morebath; CWA S. Tawton; CWA Winkleigh; CWA Woodbury, especially 1546; HCWA Stratton; PROB 11 29, fol.201; SWA Stratton; Hutton 1987, pp.116–17; Turnpenney 1992, tables; Whiting 1989, p.65.
13. *Blanchminster's Charity*, pp.91–4; C 1 1116/49; CWA Ashburton, especially 1537–9; SWA Stratton, especially 1534–9; Haigh 1993, p.157; Hoskins 1954, p.272; Whiting 1989, p.64.

13 Images (2)

1. HCWA Stratton, 1548–9; Nichols, 'Answer', fol.19v; TRP, I, p.394; Finucane 1977, p.213; Haigh 1993, pp.169–70; Hutton 1987, p.121; Rose-Troup 1913, pp.74–96; Russell 1859, pp.47–56; Whiting 1989,

p.76. For the west Cornwall rising and the south-western rebellion, see below, p.108.

2. *Barnstaple Records*, I, p.198; CCB 855, fol.151v; CWA Ashburton, 1548, 1550–1; CWA Exeter HT, 1548–50; CWA Exeter SJB, 1548, 1550; CWA Exeter SP, 1548, 1550; CWA Morebath, especially 1555; CWA N. Molton, 1549; CWA St Breock, fol.6; CWA Woodbury, especially 1550; *Grey Friars Chronicle*, pp.54–5; HCWA Stratton, 1547–9; *Inventories, Exeter*, p.39; Parkyn, 'Narrative', pp.295–6; Hutton 1987, pp.119, 121–1; Whiting 1989, pp.76–7.
3. CCB 855, fol.151v; CWA Crediton, 1551; CWA Exeter SP, 1550; CWA Morebath, 1548, 1551, 1555; CWA St Breock, fol.6; CWA Woodbury, 1547, 1550–1; HCWA Stratton, 1549, 1551; *Inventories, Exeter*, pp.39, 47; Dickens 1982A, p.182; Haigh 1993, pp.169–70; Hutton 1987, p.127.
4. *Acts and Monuments*, II, p.2051; CCB 855, fol.151v; *Copy of a Letter*, pp.49–51; CWA Ashburton, 1550; CWA Morebath, 1555; CWA S. Tawton, 1556; *Foxe*, VI, pp.26, 37; STAC 4 8/47; Dickens 1982A, p.224.
5. CWA Camborne, 1555–6; CWA Chagford, 1555; CWA Dartmouth, 1554; CWA Dartington, 1554; CWA Exeter SJB, 1554; CWA Exeter SMM, fol.13; CWA Exeter SP, 1557; CWA Woodbury, 1554; *Harpsfield's Visitation*; HCWA Stratton, 1556; Haigh 1993, pp.211–12; Hutton 1987, pp.129, 132.
6. CWA Ashburton, 1558; CWA Braunton, 1557–8; CWA Chagford, 1559; CWA Kilmington, 1558; CWA Morebath, 1555–6; CWA S. Tawton, 1556; *English Church Furniture*, especially p.166; *Harpsfield's Visitation*; Haigh 1993, p.211; Hutton 1987, pp.129, 132.
7. CWA Antony, 1555; CWA Ashburton, 1556; CWA Braunton, 1557; CWA Coldridge, 1554; CWA Crediton, 1554–5; CWA Easingwold; CWA Exeter HT, 1556; CWA Exeter SMS, 1557; CWA Exeter SP, 1556–7; CWA Morebath, especially 1535–8; CWA S. Tawton, 1555; CWA St Breock, fol.6; *Harpsfield's Visitation*; HCWA Stratton, 1559; *Tavistock Records*, p.25; Duffy 1992, pp.137, 556–7; Haigh 1993, pp.210–11; Whiting 1989, pp.68–9.
8. CCB 855A, fol.311v; CWA Braunton, 1556; CWA Camborne, 1557–9, 1561; CWA Coldridge, 1558; CWA Morebath; CWA Woodbury, 1557; HCWA Stratton, 1558; *Melford Church*, pp.53–71; Moger, 5, Humphrey Chapel, 1558; 6, William Clapp, 1555; PROB 11 37, fol.191v; Haigh 1993, p.211; Henderson 1925, p.54; Hutton 1987, p.131; Turnpenney 1992, tables; Whiting 1989, p.69.
9. *Acts and Monuments*, II, pp.2049–52; CCB 855, fols.175, 210v; *Foxe*, VI, pp.558–9, 705; VIII, pp.254, 533; *Harpsfield's Visitation*; SP 11 2/15; Haigh 1993, p.232.
10. *Barnstaple Records*, I, pp.212–13; CWA Ashburton, 1560; CWA Chagford, 1560; CWA Dartington, 1559; CWA Exeter SP, 1560; CWA Winkleigh, 1560; CWA Woodbury, 1559; DRO 1660 A 12; *Royal Visitation*, especially p.xxxv; TRP, II, pp.118–19, 123; Haigh 1993, p.245; Hutton 1987, pp.133–5, 137; Whiting 1989, pp.69–70, 80–1. Empty niches are to be seen at (for example) Tiverton.

11. *Barnstaple Records*, I, pp.212–13; CWA Ashburton, 1560; CWA Exeter SMM, fol.16; CWA Exeter SP, 1563; CWA Woodbury, 1559; DRO 1660 A 12; HCWA Stratton, 1570; Hooker, Commonplace Book, fol.352; Machyn, *Diary*, pp.207–8; Strype, *Annals*, I (2), p.436; Duffy 1992, pp.490–1; Haigh 1993, pp.242–3, 245, 247.
12. *English Church Furniture*, pp.29–171; *Tudor Parish Documents*, pp.30, 144–8, 226–7; Haigh 1993, pp.245–7.
13. CCB 779, 15 May 1562; CCB 855A, fol.215; CWA Ashburton, 1564; CWA Chudleigh, 1562; CWA Coldridge, 1564; CWA Dartington, 1563; CWA Exeter SMS, 1564; CWA Exeter SP, 1562–4; CWA Kilmington, 1565; CWA Morebath, 1562; CWA N. Molton, 1562; CWA St Breock, fols.6v, 13v; CWA S. Tawton, 1563; CWA Woodbury, 1562; *English Church Furniture*, pp.29–171; HCWA Stratton, 1563–5, 1570; SWA Stratton, 1564–5, 1572; *Tavistock Records*, p.26; Bond and Camm 1909, I, p.105; Haigh 1993, pp.244–7; Hutton 1987, pp.135–7; Whiting 1989, pp.81–2. For the completion of loft destruction in 1570–9, see (for example) Whiting 1989, p.82, n.128. See also Bond and Camm 1909, II, p.275.
14. CWA Exeter SP, 1562–4; CWA St Breock, fols.6v, 13v; HCWA Stratton, 1570; *English Church Furniture*, pp.29–171.

14 Wells, Relics, Shrines

1. *Bodmin Register*, pp.38–42; E 117 10/59; Harleian 2252, fols.50v–1v; Holme, 'Fall of Rebellion', p.130; *Leland*, I, pp.188, 200; 'Lives of Saints', fols.109v, 131–1v, 202v–3, 262, 308, 312v, 314–14v, 323v–4; *Melford Church*, p.11; *Survey of Cornwall*, p.378; *Tavistock Records*, p.18; Worcestre, pp.29, 99; Pevsner and Radcliffe 1970, p.89; Whiting 1989, pp.55–6.
2. C 1 305/78; CAB 3551, fol.49v; E 117 10/59; Hooker, Commonplace Book, fol.311v; *Leland*, I, p.180; 'Lives of Saints', fols.101v–2, 202v–3, 322v–3, 357v, 359v–60v, 388; PROB 11 22, fol.254v; *Tavistock Records*, p.18; Worcestre, pp.23, 29, 85, 87, 97, 107, 115, 125; Chanter 1914, pp.290–308; Pevsner 1952A, p.70; Radford 1949, pp.164–8; Westcote 1845, pp.308–9; Whiting 1989, pp.56–7.
3. *Bodmin Register*, pp.38–42; CWA Dartmouth, 1530; E 117 10/59; ER XV, fol.31; Henderson 1923–4, p.37; Pevsner and Radcliffe 1970, p.43; Raine 1828, p.111; Wall 1905, pp.2–19, 28, 160, 191; Whiting 1989, p.57.
4. C 1 305/78; CAB 3551, fols.49v, 57v; CWA Ashburton, 1508; ER XV, fol.30v; Glastonbury Commonplace Book, fol.86; Hooker, Commonplace Book, fol.311v; 'Lives of Saints', fols.111v, 114v, 298v, 304, 314–14v, 323v, 327v–8, 359v–60v, 388; LP, XII (2), 301, 1325; PROB 11 21, fol.32v; 22, fol.254v; *Survey of Cornwall*, pp.289, 378; Worcestre, p.115; Chanter 1914, pp.290–308; Finucane 1977, pp.194–5; Henderson 1923–4, pp.222–3, 318, 401–2; Henderson 1925, p.163;

James 1901–2, pp.230–4; Radford 1949, pp.164–8; Raine 1828, pp.111–12; Wall 1905, pp.129–30; Whiting 1989, pp.57–9.

5. Farmer 1978, pp.xviii, 304, 422; Finucane 1977, pp.193–5; Turnpenney 1992, tables; Wilson 1977, pp.9, 18–21.
6. CAB 3551, fol.49v; Hooker, Commonplace Book, fol.311v; Finucane 1977, pp.181, 193, 205, 209; Radford 1949, pp.164–8; Raine 1828, pp.115–17; Venables 1893, p.54; Woodman 1981, p.221.
7. *Foxe*, IV, p.179; Adair 1978, pp.70–1; Finucane 1977, pp.199–201, 210–11.
8. *Documents of Church History*, pp.269–74; E 117 10/59; EHD, p.782; ER XV, fols.76v–7; 'Examination of Aske', p.561; *Leland*, I, p.190; II, p.93; Bowker 1981, pp.93–5; Duffy 1992, pp.383–5; Finucane 1977, pp.204–5, 207–8; Wall 1905, pp.41–3, 129–30, 138–40, 216.
9. *Bodmin Register*, pp.38–42; CWA Dartmouth, especially 1537; *Inventories, Cornwall*, p.32; *Leland*, I, pp.226–7; 'Lives of Saints', fols.202v–3; *Melford Church*, pp.26, 44–7; *Tavistock Records*, especially p.27; Worcestre, p.113; Chanter 1914, pp.290–308; Cox 1913, pp.139–40; Duffy 1992, p.483; Henderson 1923–4, p.63; Hutton 1987, p.116.
10. *Leland*, I, pp.180, 188; Bowker 1981, p.95; Finucane 1977, pp.204–5; Raine 1828, p.176; Wall 1905, pp.60, 130, 167, 196–7, 238.
11. Finucane 1977, p.207; Wall 1905, especially pp.26, 65–74, 79, 97–102, 124–6, 129–30, 153–4, 168–9, 232; Wilson 1977, p.10.
12. 'Examination of Aske', p.561; LP, VIII, 480; Elton 1972, pp.16, 306; Finucane 1977, p.206.
13. Wall 1905, pp.115, 119–22, 129–30, 167, 196–9.
14. Holme, 'Fall of Rebellion', pp.129–30; *Leland*, I, pp.190, 226–7; Nichols, 'Answer', especially fol.13v; Russell 1859, pp.47–56.
15. 'Lives of Saints', fols.323v, 360v; *Melford Church*, pp.70–1; *Zurich Letters*, p.44; Wall 1905, pp.65–6; Whiting 1989, pp.73–4.
16. CWA Braunton, 1554–9; Finucane 1977, p.213; Henderson 1923–4, p.402; Wall 1905, pp.1–2, 232; Whiting 1989, pp.64, 74; Wilson 1977, p.11.
17. *Foxe*, VIII, pp.296–7; 'Lives of Saints', fol.323v; *Tudor Parish Documents*, p.164; *Zurich Letters*, p.44; Finucane 1977, plate 15; Wall 1905, pp.x, 26, 41–3, 60–3, 66–7, 71–2, 87–9, 97–102, 223, 241; Whiting 1989, p.73; Wilson 1977, pp.12–18, 23, n.13.
18. 'Lives of Saints', fols.109v, 262, 327v–8; *Survey of Cornwall*, p.289; Henderson 1923–4, pp.318–19.

Interlude

1. 'Description of Exeter', p.9; EHD, pp.195, 657; *Survey of Cornwall*, p.289; Duffy 1992, pp.83–5, 87; Haigh 1993, p.28.
2. *Butley Priory*, p.67; *Foxe*, VI, p.570; *Grey Friars Chronicle*, p.77; LP, XIII (1), 1199; XIV (1), 295, 839, 1094; OL, II, p.542; Elton 1972, pp.22, 329–31.

3. CSPV, V, p.556; *Foxe*, VIII, p.407; Parkyn, 'Narrative', p.311; Dickens 1989, p.292; Hughes 1950–4, II, pp.347–8; Loades 1970, pp.256–7; Loades 1991, p.225; Thomas 1973, p.45.
4. 'Description of Exeter', p.9; *Original Letters*, pp.8–9, 59; *Survey of Cornwall*, p.289; *Zurich Letters*, pp.44–5; Cliffe 1969, p.167; Haigh 1987, pp.177–9.
5. *Original Letters*, pp.1–83; Trimble 1964, pp.24–36.
6. Connor 1970; Crabbe 1854; Davis 1969; Dunkin 1882; Kite 1969; Rogers 1877; Stephenson 1970. See also Norris 1977; Rex 1990.
7. Jordan 1959, especially pp.246, 375.
8. *Acts and Monuments*, II, pp.1037–40, 2049–52; *Foxe*, VII, pp.329, 345–7; VIII, pp.379–80; Hooker, Commonplace Book, fol.350; LP, XI, 1246; XII (2), 530, 571; XIII (1), 715; *Narratives of the Reformation*, pp.78, 160; Nichols, 'Answer', fols.12, 22; Elton 1972, pp.130–1; Haigh 1993, pp.231–4; Whiting 1989, pp.168–70.
9. *Acts and Monuments*, II, pp.1037–40; APC, V, pp.154, 316; VI, pp.135, 144, 361, 371; CSPS, XIII, p.138; CSPV, VI, pp.93–4; *Foxe*, V, pp.530–2; Hooker, Commonplace Book, fol.341; *Narratives of the Reformation*, pp.211–12; Hughes 1950–4, II, p.283; Loades 1970, pp.164, 166, 241–2; Loades 1991, pp.383–4.
10. Hooker, Commonplace Book, fol.351; SP 11 2/2; *Tudor Parish Documents*, p.205.
11. APC, V, p.224; CSPS, XIII, pp.138–9, 147; *Foxe*, VI, pp.656–8, 697–700; VII, pp.345–7; VIII, pp.379–80, 392, 790; Strype, *Memorials*, III (2), p.501; Haigh 1993, pp.230–1, 233–4; Loades 1970, pp.161, 241–2; Loades 1991, pp.276, 383–4.
12. CSPV, VI, p.251; *Foxe*, IV, p.612; Graves 1985; Jones 1982; Lehmberg 1970; Loach 1986; Loades 1970, pp.164, 243; Loades 1991, especially pp.214–19.
13. Aveling 1976; Bossy 1975; Cliffe 1969, pp.167, 171; Haigh 1987, pp.188–9; Haigh 1993, pp.258–60; Whiting 1989, p.46.
14. 'Examination of Aske', pp.330–48, 550–73; Holme, 'Fall of Rebellion'; LP, XI, 1246; XII (1), 1319; XII (2), 150, 1181; XIII (1), 107, 743; Bush 1996; Davies 1968, pp.54–76; Dickens 1967, pp.39–64; Dickens 1989, pp.147–50; Dodds and Dodds 1915, I, II; Elton 1972, pp.149, 333–5, 365; Fletcher 1973, pp.21–47; James 1970, pp.3–78.
15. *Grey Friars Chronicle*, pp.38–9; LP, XI, 909, 920; XII (1), 990, 1318; XII (2), 150, 908, 959; XIII (1), 822; XIII (2), 1279; Elton 1972, pp.64, 66, 90, 118–19, 129–30, 149, 155–60, 362–3, 380.
16. LP, XI, 580; XII (1), 1045, 1056, 1063, 1125–7, 1171, 1300; XII (2), 56, 68, 182, 557, 595; SP 1 106/134–5; 118/247–8; Elton 1972, pp.144–9, 350.
17. Elton 1972, especially pp.383–400.
18. For the 1548 riot, see CWA Antony, 1549; CWA Launceston, 1548; E 117 1/52; *Plymouth Records*, pp.16, 115; SWA Stratton, 1548; Rose-Troup 1913, pp.74–96, 425n; Rowse 1941, pp.257–60; Whiting 1989, p.76. For the 1549 rebellion, see especially 'Description of Exeter', pp.25–70; Nichols, 'Answer'; *Prayerbook of 1549*; Cornwall 1977; Fletcher 1973,

pp.48–63; Rose-Troup 1913; Whiting 1989, pp.34–8; Youings 1979. For the Seamer riot in Yorkshire, see (for example) *Foxe*, V, pp.738–41.

19. For the northern rising, see *Rising in the North*, especially pp.35, 42–7, 52–5, 69, 91–2, 94, 162, 184–8, 256, 281; Strype, *Memorials*, III (2), p.562; *Tudor Parish Documents*, pp.143–4; Fletcher 1973, pp.91–106. For Cornwall and Devon, see SP 12 60/27, 39.
20. For the Norfolk rebellion, see especially Cornwall 1977; Fletcher 1973, pp.64–77; Russell 1859. For Wyatt's rebellion, see especially *Foxe*, VI, pp.413–5; Proctor, 'Wyatt's Rebellion'; Clark 1977, pp.87–98; Fletcher 1973, pp.78–90; Loades 1965; Thorp 1978. See also Loades 1970, pp.123–4, 163–4, 256–7; Loades 1991, p.228; Whiting 1989, p.164.
21. For 'mixed' wills, see (for example) Mayhew 1983, especially p.61.
22. LP, XVI, 1377; Parkyn, 'Narrative', pp.297, 301; Jordan 1960A, p.423; Jordan 1960B, p.92; Jordan 1961A, pp.438–40; Jordan 1961B, p.158; Jordan 1962, p.117.
23. *Original Letters*, especially pp.11, 31, 57–9, 70–2; Trimble 1964, pp.24–36.
24. Bowker 1981, pp.173–4; Dickens 1957, I, pp.14–15; Frere 1896, pp.52–3; Frere 1904, pp.107–8; Haigh 1975, p.181; Hill 1969, pp.52–3; Houlbrooke 1979, pp.183, 202–3; Whiting 1989, pp.232, 249.
25. *Harpsfield's Visitation*; *Original Letters*, pp.14–15, 18; Strype, *Memorials*, III (2), pp.389–413; Mayhew 1983, p.47; Turnpenney 1992, tables; Whiting 1989, p.145.
26. Elton 1972, p.6; Kreider 1979, pp.78, 87; Whiting 1989, p.146.
27. Harper 1987, tables; Jordan 1959, pp.385–7; Turnpenney 1992, tables.
28. *Grey Friars Chronicle*, pp.59, 67; Palliser 1987, p.104; Whiting 1989, p.146.
29. *Zurich Letters*, pp.44–5; Elton 1972, pp.398–9; Turnpenney 1992, tables.
30. *Foxe*, VII, App. IX; LP, XII (2), 505; VI, 1077, 1329; Add. 871, 879; X, 365; XIII (1), 1150; Elton 1972, pp.20–1, 85–90; Whiting 1989, p.146, n.2.
31. *Foxe*, VII, pp.192, 345; *Grey Friars Chronicle*, p.57; *Narratives of the Reformation*, pp.78, 348–51; Hughes 1950–4, II, pp.347–8; Loades 1970, p.80; Whiting 1989, p.146.
32. *Acts and Monuments*, II, p.2050; Whiting 1989, pp.146–7.
33. *Acts and Monuments*, II, pp.2049–52; EHD, pp.195, 378; *Foxe*, IV, p.177; *Harpsfield's Visitation*, especially p.53; Hooker, Commonplace Book, fol.343; *Narratives of the Reformation*, p.160; SP 1 102/33; Strype, *Memorials*, III (2), pp.389–413; Birt 1907, pp.427–30; Elton 1972, pp.398–9; Whiting 1989, p.147.

15 Spiritual Convictions (1)

1. 'Examination of Aske', p.561; 'Lives of Saints', fol.296v; STAC 2 17/209; 25/80, 142; Whiting 1989, p.90.
2. CWA Ashburton, 1510; Duffy 1992, pp.279–87; Ellacombe 1872, pp.240, 242.

3. Dickens 1989, p.29.
4. ER XV, fol.33; Rushforth 1927B, p.163; Whiting 1989, pp.90–1.
5. Whiting 1989, p.60.
6. *Lancashire and Cheshire Wills*, p.85; LP, VIII, 480; PROB 11 13, fol.198v; Duffy 1992, pp.190–2; Elton 1972, p.16.
7. For Lollardy, see especially Davis 1983; Hudson 1988; Thomson 1965A. For Protestantism, see (for example) McGrath 1988.
8. *Copy of a Letter*, especially pp.3, 14–27, 42–4, 49–51, 55–6; *Godly New Story*, p.47; Murray, 3, John Bougin, 1548; Nichols, 'Answer', fols.21–6; STAC 2 2/267; Whiting 1989, pp.151–3.
9. *Acts and Monuments*, II, pp.1037–40, 2049–52; Nichols, 'Answer', fols.11–17v, 22–6; Whiting 1989, pp.153–4.
10. EHD, pp.656, 663, 828; LP, IV (3), 6385; TRP, I, pp.193–7; Elton 1972, p.219.
11. *Acts and Monuments*, II, pp.1037–40; APC, I, pp.97, 150–1; *Copy of a Letter*, p.5; 'Description of Exeter', pp.41, 55; *Foxe*, VII, App.IX; LP, IX, 1115; XII (2), 557; XIII (1), 865; *Narratives of the Reformation*, p.77; Cross 1976, p.95; Dickens 1989, pp.283–4; Elton 1972, pp.36, 41, 152; Loades 1970, p.84; Price 1938, p.112.
12. *Acts and Monuments*, II, p.2051; CSPS, XI, p.307; *Foxe*, VI, p.708; VIII, p.383; Hooker, Commonplace Book, fols.350–1, 353, 357; Ramsey, 'Epistle', especially fols.8v–9, 26v–8; SP 11 2/15; Strype, *Memorials*, III (2), p.446; Cross 1969, pp.95–6; Loades 1970, p.110; Loades 1991, pp.118, 160, 275; Prince 1701, pp.75, 387–8.
13. LP, IV (3), 6385; Thomas More, p.235; Haigh 1987, p.179; Hughes 1950–4, III, p.50.
14. *Acts and Monuments*, II, pp.1038–9; ER XV, fols.121–1v; *Foxe*, VII, p.573; Collinson 1967, p.26; Fletcher 1973, p.147; Hughes 1950–4, III, p.58.
15. *Foxe*, especially IV, pp.173, 217; Dickens 1989, pp.46–60; Thomson 1965A.
16. *Foxe*, VIII, pp.598–600; Brigden 1989, pp.320–2; Dickens 1982A, pp.16–52, 221–35.
17. Strype, *Memorials*, III (2), pp.389–413; *Harpsfield's Visitation*, especially p.217; Whiting 1989, pp.154–5.
18. CSPS, XIII, p.138; *Foxe*, V, pp.530–2; VI, pp.611, 650, 670, 672, 697–700, 777; VII, pp.115, 326; VIII, pp.103, 307, 392, 559; *Narratives of the Reformation*, p.75; Strype, *Memorials*, III (2), p.498.

16 Spiritual Convictions (2)

1. PROB 11 44, fol.274; 45, fol.60v; 46, fol.258v; Mayhew 1983, especially p.60; Whiting 1989, pp.155–7.
2. Brigden 1989, pp.381–4, 485–6, 629; Clark 1977, pp.58, 76; Cross 1979; Palliser 1979, pp.250–1; Shiels 1979, pp.15–18, 21–4; Turnpenney 1992, tables.

3. Murray, 3, John Bougin, 1548; PROB 11 27, fol.4v; 44, fol.274.
4. *Wills and Inventories*, p.213; Brigden 1989, pp.381–4, 485–6, 629; Clark 1977, pp.58, 76; Cross 1979; Palliser 1979, pp.250–1; Shiels 1979, pp.15–18, 21–4; Turnpenney 1992, tables; Whiting 1989, p.157.
5. CWA Ashburton, 1549, 1553, 1560; Hutton 1987, pp.125, 137; Whiting 1989, pp.157–9. For the 1552 prayerbook, see also CWA Antony, 1553; CWA Camborne, 1552; CWA Coldridge, 1553; CWA Crediton 1552; CWA Dartmouth, 1552; CWA Exeter HT, 1552; CWA Exeter SJB, 1552; CWA Exeter SMM, fol.12; CWA Exeter SMS, 1552; CWA Morebath, 1553; CWA Woodbury, 1552; HCWA Stratton, 1553; *Tavistock Records*, p.23.

   For the 1559 prayerbook, see also *Barnstaple Records*, I, pp.212–13; CWA Antony, 1559; CWA Braunton, 1559; CWA Camborne, 1560; CWA Chagford, 1560; CWA Coldridge, 1560; CWA Credition, 1559; CWA Dartington, 1559; CWA Exeter SJB, 1559; CWA Exeter SMM, fol.16; CWA Exeter SMS, 1559; CWA Exeter SP, 1560; CWA Kilmington, 1559; CWA Molland, 1559; CWA Morebath, 1559; CWA S. Tawton, 1559; CWA Winkleigh, 1560; CWA Woodbury 1559; HCWA Stratton, 1559.

   For psalters, see (for example) CWA Woodbury, 1550, 1559. For bread and wine, CWA Kilmington, 1560; CWA Woodbury, 1552–3. For Edwardian tables, CWA Ashburton 1551; CWA Chagford, 1551; CWA Exeter HT, 1550; CWA Woodbury, 1550; ER XV, fols. 119v–20; *Inventories, Exeter*; Parkyn, 'Narrative', p.301. For Elizabethan tables, *Barnstaple Records*, I, p.213; CWA Chagford, 1560; CWA Coldridge, 1560; CWA Exeter SMS, 1559; CWA Molland, 1559; CWA S. Tawton, 1559; CWA Winkleigh, 1560; CWA Woodbury, 1559; DRO 1660 A 12; HCWA Stratton, 1559.

   For cloths, CWA Coldridge, 1551; CWA St Breock, fol.16. For benches, CWA Crediton, 1552; CWA Exeter SP, 1569. For kneeling mats, CWA Exeter SJB, 1568; CWA Woodbury, 1553. For desks, CWA Ashburton, 1567; CWA Chagford, 1564; CWA Chudleigh, 1562; CWA Coldridge, 1560; CWA Dartington, 1565; CWA Molland, 1560; CWA S. Tawton, 1565; CWA Winkleigh, 1563; CWA Woodbury, 1570; Cox 1915, pp.197–9. For surplices, CWA Crediton, 1566; CWA Morebath, 1567; HCWA Stratton, 1563.

   For preaching, see below, pp.169, 171, 173.
6. *Barnstaple Records*, I, p.213; CWA Ashburton, 1551; CWA Coldridge, 1560; CWA Crediton, 1566; CWA Exeter HT, 1550; CWA Morebath, 1567; CWA Woodbury, 1550, 1559; DRO 1660 A 12; HCWA Stratton, 1559, 1563; Cox and Harvey 1973, pp.12–13.
7. CWA Crediton, 1568; CWA Woodbury, 1567; *Inventories, Exeter*, p.75; Cox and Harvey 1973, pp.34–7; Pevsner 1952B, p.31; Whiting 1989, pp.159–60 and n.28.
8. CWA Dartmouth, 1555; CWA St Breock, fol.3v; *Harpsfield's Visitation*; Strype, *Memorials*, III (2), pp.389–413; TRP, II, pp.57–60; Hutton 1987, p.128.

9. *Foxe*, VI, p.579; VIII, pp.383, 458–60, 464, 556–9, 562; LP, VIII, 87, 676; X, 52, 462; XI, 166; XII (1), 152–3; XII (2), 480; XIX (2), 340; *Narratives of the Reformation*, p.178; Dickens 1989, pp.302–6; Elton 1972, p.36.
10. CAB 3552, fols.140, 145–8; Hooker, Commonplace Book, fols.352–3; Machyn, *Diary*, p.193; *Puritanism in Tudor England*, pp.78–9.
11. *Documents of Church History*, pp.369–72; ER XV, fols.121–1v; *Grey Friars Chronicle*, pp.67, 76; Hooker, Commonplace Book, fols.352–3; SP 12 6/17; *York Records*, V, p.77; Russell 1859, pp.37–8.
12. CCB 856, fols.15–16, 202–3v, 311–11v, 319v, 321, 370–3v; *Exeter Records*, pp.24, 315; *York Records*, VI, p.7; Aveling 1970, pp.165–8; Collinson 1982, p.203; Guy 1990, pp.295–6; Houlbrooke 1979, pp.278–81; Peter and Peter 1885, pp.203–4; Whiting 1989, pp.166–7.
13. CCB 855B, 7 February 1566/7; CCB 856, fols.15v–16, 297–7v.
14. Haigh 1993, pp.190–1; Hughes 1950–4, II, pp.259–64, 291; Loades 1970, p.12.
15. Garrett 1966, especially pp.32, 41–2, 67–349; Whiting 1989, pp.164–5.
16. *Foxe*, VIII, p.465.
17. *Foxe*, VIII, pp.598–600; Alexander 1987, p.167. For Tracey, see above, p.6.
18. Dickens 1989, pp.325–9; Fines 1981; Haigh 1993, pp.197–8; Hughes 1950–4, III, p.50; Mayhew 1983, pp.47–8.
19. LP, XII (1), 1147; Elton 1972, pp.26, 118–19; Haigh 1993, pp.197–8; Harper 1987, tables; Hughes 1950–4, III, p.50; Mayhew 1983, p.47; Whiting 1989, p.260.
20. *Copy of a Letter*, p.5; Dickens 1989, pp.331–2; Fines 1981; Haigh 1993, pp.195–6; Hughes 1950–4, III, p.50; Loades 1991, p.118; Whiting 1989, p.260.
21. *Foxe*, V, pp.537–550; VIII, p.182; Haigh 1993, pp.196–7; Prince 1701, p.75; Whiting 1989, p.260.
22. *Acts and Monuments*, II, p.2052; CCB 855B, 7 February 1566/7; *Copy of a Letter*, p.36; *Foxe*, VIII, p.254; LP, XIII (1), 1509; XIII (2), 194; Machyn, *Diary*, p.228; Brigden 1982; Garrett 1966, especially pp.92–4, 183, 318; Loades 1991, p.111; Whiting 1989, p.260.

17 Emotional Loyalties

1. LP, VIII, 386; X, 950; Nichols, 'Answer', fols. 7v, 25; *Rising in the North*, p.42; Elton 1972, pp.25–6.
2. CCB 779, 15 May 1562; *Foxe*, IV, p.217; VII, App.IX; LP, VIII, 20; Nichols, 'Answer', fols. 23–3v; Elton 1972, pp.43, 115.
3. *Copy of a Letter*, pp.19–21, 58–9; Hooker, Commonplace Book, fol.342; LP, VII, 146; IX, 1059; Elton 1972, pp.33–4, 352–4.
4. Palliser 1987, p.104.
5. For inscriptions and coats of arms, see (for example) Whiting 1989, p.220.

6. CCB 779, 15 May 1562; CWA Dartington, 1563; CWA Kilmington, 1562, 1565; CWA S. Tawton, 1563; HCWA Stratton, 1563–5; SWA Stratton, 1564–5; Hill 1969, pp.343–69.
7. Elton 1972, p.65. For regional sentiment in (for example) the 1536 rebellion, see 'Examination of Aske', p.561; LP, XI, 1246, especially articles 15 and 23.
8. EHD, pp.194–6.
9. *Copy of a Letter*, p.13; LP, IX, 740; Nichols, 'Answer', fol. 22; Rowse 1941, pp.22–3.
10. Loades 1970, pp.25–30.
11. APC, V, pp.265, 290; VI, pp.179, 303; CSPS, XIII, p.351; EHD, p.866; SP 11 2/2, 5, 15; Loades 1970, especially pp.142, 158, 162, 236, 238, 252–6; Loades 1991, especially pp.61, 69–70, 159, 161, 176, 227–8, 304–9, 315, 325, 376.
12. LP, VIII, 457; IX, 791; X, 346, 594; Elton 1972, pp.18, 28, 358, 418.
13. *Foxe*, VI, p.413; Nichols, 'Answer', especially fols.3–5, 35, 37v; Hughes 1950–4, II, pp.347–8; Loades 1970, p.75; Morris 1953, p.70.
14. *Foxe*, VI, pp.387, 394–5; Loades 1970, pp.91, 116, 123–4.
15. *Grey Friars Chronicle*, pp.40–1; LP, VII, 449; Elton 1972, pp.14–15; Loades 1970, p.57.
16. LP, VI, 503; X, 14; Dickens 1989, pp.187–8; Elton 1972, pp.120–1, 230, 242, 370.
17. 'Description of Exeter', especially pp.37–8, 42, 52; *Foxe*, VII, p.573; *Rising in the North*, p.54.
18. LP, XII (1), 567, 1127; *Original Letters*, p.57; SP 1 106/134; 12 60/27, 39; Stowe 141, fol. 67; Elton 1972, pp.9–12, 24, 100.

18 Material Interests

1. EHD, p.782; Holme, 'Fall of Rebellion', p.129; LP, XIII (1), 1199; Duffy 1992, pp.200–5, 279–87, 383–5; Elton 1972, p.22; Thomas 1973, p.72.
2. 'Examination of Aske', pp.330–48, 561–2; Fletcher 1973, p.34.
3. 'Examination of Aske', p.561; Davies 1968, pp.70–1.
4. LP, VIII, 799; XII (2), 1181; XIII (1), 107, 743, 1257; *Original Letters*, p.49; Elton 1972, pp.95–6, 333–4; Haigh 1993, p.68; Hughes 1950–4, II, pp.347–8; Loades 1991, p.42.
5. LP, IX, 404; Davies 1968, p.69; Elton 1972, pp.348–9.
6. Latimer, pp.393–5, 403; LP, X, 346; Elton 1972, p.29; Finucane 1977, p.204; Whiting 1989, pp.52, 54, 64, 66–7, 183.
7. Davies 1968, pp.73–4; Loades 1991, p.56; above, pp.107–8.
8. *Rising in the North*, especially pp.52–3; Whiting 1989, pp.164–5
9. Collinson 1988, p.52.
10. Hughes 1950–4, II, pp.347–8; Loades 1970, pp.94, 97–8, 111.

11. EHD, pp.654, 670; LP, XIV (1), 295, 839, 1094; Clark 1977, p.28; Elton 1972, pp.329–31; Haigh 1993, p.48; Platt 1981, pp.85–7.
12. C 1 728/23; 781/26; 1061/30; 1138/88; CCB 855, fols. 375, 376v; STAC 3 2/20; Haigh 1993, pp.73, 86–7.
13. E 117 1/48–52B; 2/7, especially fols.2v, 4v, 10–11; Hooker, Commonplace Book, fol.347; SP 15 3/29; Dickens 1989, pp.171, 235; Duffy 1992, pp.42–3.
14. Hooker, Commonplace Book, fol.344; LP, XII (2), App. 14; Elton 1972, p.354.
15. 'Description of Exeter', pp.53–5, 65; *Rising in the North*, p.232; Dickens 1989, p.181; Rose-Troup 1913, pp.380–1, 505, 507; Rowse 1941, pp.231, 290, 296–8.
16. CWA Ashburton, 1560; Wall 1905, pp.115, 198–9.
17. Nichols, 'Answer', fol.33v; Kitching 1977, pp.128–36; Rose-Troup 1913, pp.491–2.
18. EHD, p.867; Dickens 1989, p.183; Hughes 1950–4, II, pp.347–8; Whiting 1989, p.177.
19. 'Description of Exeter', pp.30–1; Elton 1972, p.320.
20. Dickens 1989, pp.30, 64–8; Haigh 1993, pp.243–4.
21. 'Description of Exeter', p.65; *Documents of Church History*, pp.458–67; Rose-Troup 1913, pp.381–3.
22. LP, X, 5, 6; XII (2), 800; SP 1 106/134; 132/3–4; Davies 1968, p.70; Elton 1972, p.63; Fletcher 1973, p.21.
23. ER XV, fol.115v; Harleian 352, fols.65v–6v; LP, XII (2), 357; STAC 3 2/20; Duffy 1992, p.554; Elton 1972, p.70.
24. LP, VIII, 518; XII (1), 456, 808, 1316; XIII (1), 1508; Elton 1972, pp.47, 70–1.
25. CWA Woodbury, 1546; PROB 11 32, fol.15v; STAC 3 2/20; Cook 1954, pp.261–2; Duffy 1992, pp.553–4; Woodward 1966, pp.171–2.
26. C 1 924/9–10; Loades 1970, p.250.
27. C 1 1138/93–4; CWA Ashburton, 1544; CWA Braunton, 1558, 1563, 1569; CWA Camborne, 1543, 1546; CWA Chagford, 1545–6; CWA Dartmouth, 1545, 1547; CWA Modbury, 1545; E 117 2/7, fols. 4v–5, 11; *Plymouth Records*, p.113; SWA Stratton, 1544, 1546; Whiting 1989, pp.180–1. See also (for example) CWA Antony, 1559; CWA Camborne, 1557; CWA Dartington, 1557; CWA Exeter SP, 1570; CWA Molland, 1557; SWA Stratton, 1558.
28. PROB 11 24, fol.10; 48, fol.491v; Bowker 1981, p.177; Bruton 1987, tables; Mayhew 1983, pp.52, 55–7; Turnpenney 1992, tables; Whiting 1989, p.181.
29. CCB 856, fols. 15–15v, 26, 311v, 351v–2, 392; CWA Antony, 1546, 1549, 1551, 1553, 1559; CWA Ashburton, 1544, 1551, 1554; CWA Camborne, 1557; CWA Chagford, 1551, 1558; CWA Dartmouth, 1547; CWA Exeter SMS, 1552; CWA Modbury, 1548; CWA Molland, 1559; CWA Morebath, 1549; CWA St Breock, fol.16; CWA S. Tawton, 1558; CWA Woodbury, 1548; HCWA Stratton, 1547; *Plymouth Records*, pp.232–3; SWA Stratton, 1558; *York Records*, IV, pp.168–9; MacCaffrey 1958, p.111; Rose-Troup 1913, pp.503–7; Whiting 1989, pp.181–2.

30. CCB 855, fols.63,214v; Hooker, Commonplace Book, fol.351; Duffy 1992, pp.390–1; Haigh 1993, p.182; above, pp.21, 24–6, 42.
31. Kreider 1979, pp.90–1, 157–9.

19 Physical Drives

1. EHD, pp.835–7; Duffy 1992, pp.100–1; Thomas 1973, pp.32–3, 36–9.
2. E 117 10/59; Holme, 'Fall of Rebellion', p.130; Hooker, Commonplace Book, fol.311v; 'Lives of Saints', fols.111v, 298v, 327v–8, 393v; *Survey of Cornwall*, p.289; Worcestre, pp.29, 31; Duffy 1992, pp.195–7, 383–5; Henderson 1923–4, p.318; Radford 1949, pp.164–8; Raine 1828, pp.111–12; Risdon 1811, pp.319–24; Westcote 1845, p.287; Whiting 1989, pp.60–1.
3. Finucane 1977, pp.214–6; Thomas 1973, especially pp.13,133–4, 215, 316, 764.
4. CCB 855, fols.115v–16, 150v–1v; CCB 856, fols.15v–16; LP, VI, 1077, 1329; Add., 871, 879; X, 365; XII (2), 505; XIII (1), 1150, 1509; XIII (2), 194; *York Records*, V, p.77; Duffy 1992, pp.42–3; Elton 1972, pp.20–1, 31–2, 85–90; Price 1938, pp.89, 143.
5. Duffy 1992, p.529; Hughes 1950–4, II, pp.347–8; Loades 1970, pp.69, 94–6.
6. CCB 855, fols.186, 369; Parkyn, 'Narrative', p.311.
7. EHD, p.672; Nichols, 'Answer', fols.9v–10.
8. *Rising in the North*, pp.53–4, 57, 258; Davies 1968, pp.68–9; Rose–Troup 1913, pp.307, 346, 489.
9. *Acts and Monuments*, II, pp.1037–40; *Documents of Church History*, pp.303–19; Hooker, Commonplace Book, fols. 350–1; Nichols, 'Answer', fol.10v.
10. *Grey Friars Chronicle*, p.90; *Foxe*, IV, p.179; VII, p.252; Haigh 1993, p.229; Hughes 1950–4, II, pp.347–8; Loades 1991, pp.285, 382; Palliser 1987, p.105.
11. CSPV, VI, p.31; *Foxe*, VIII, pp.205–6; Loades 1970, pp.151, 154, 155–7, 160, 220–1, 235–6.
12. *Grey Friars Chronicle*, pp.37–8, 40–1, 44, 46; LP, XII (1), 479, 685, 1127; XIII (1), 371, 416, 453, 580; SP 1 80/193; Elton 1972, especially pp.263–92, 294, 384–5, 388–95.
13. 'Description of Exeter', pp.55–70; *Grey Friars Chronicle*, pp.65, 69; *Rising in the North*, especially pp.121, 133–5, 187–8; Rose–Troup 1913, pp.89–92, 306–12; Rowse 1941, pp.285–6.
14. EHD, p.784; *Foxe*, VIII, p.110; LP, X, 346; XII (1), 479; *Prayerbook of 1549*, p.54; Stowe 142, fol.14; Titus B 1, fols.172–9; Elton 1972, p.29.
15. Hooker, Commonplace Book, fols.343–4; LP, VIII, 643; XII (1), 825; Elton 1972, pp.348–50, 370–5; Farmer 1978, p.341.
16. CCB 855B, 2 April 1565; *Rising in the North*, p.163; Whiting 1989, p.186.
17. LP, VIII, 1000; Elton 1972, p.24; Hutton 1987, pp.137–8.

20 Families, Employers, Neighbours, Strangers, Foreigners

1. 'Description of Exeter', p.42; Haigh 1993, pp.26–7, 142–3; Rose–Troup 1913, pp.85, 90–1.
2. C 1 976/32–3; 1042/7–9; *Certificates, Devon,* p.xxi; CWA Exeter SP, 1556–7; 'Description of Exeter', pp.42–6; *Foxe,* VI, p.732; LP, XII (2), 571; PROB 11 26, fol.76; 37, fol.144; Loades 1970, p.80; Prince 1701, pp.387–8.
3. LP, VII, 146; XIII (1), 1241; XIII (2), App. 43; *Narratives of the Reformation,* pp.60–1; Elton 1972, pp.340–1, 352–4.
4. *Acts and Monuments,* II, pp.1038, 2050–1; *Foxe,* VI, pp.677, 722; VII, pp.749–50; VIII, pp.598–600; *Harpsfield's Visitation,* pp.191–2; Strype, *Memorials,* III (2), p.498; Garrett 1966, pp.92–4, 183, 236–7; Prince 1701, p.75.
5. CCB 856, fols.143v–6; PROB 11 24, fol.10; 27, fol.226v; Aveling 1970, pp.165, 167–8.
6. *Acts and Monuments,* II, p.2050; *Foxe,* VIII, pp.392, 598–600; *Harpsfield's Visitation,* especially p.189; SP 1 102/33; Aveling 1970, p.166.
7. *Acts and Monuments,* II, pp.1039–40; CCB 855, fols.111v, 174v–5; *Foxe,* VIII, pp.598–600; *Harpsfield's Visitation*; Dickens 1982A, pp.226–7; Garrett 1966, especially pp.92–4; Prince 1701, p.75.
8. CCB 855, fol.63; LP, XIII (1), 1304; *Foxe,* VI, p.677; VIII, pp.598–600; *Narratives of the Reformation,* p.349; PROB 11 39, fol.203; Garrett 1966, especially pp.72, 92–4, 318; Haigh 1993, pp.26–7.
9. 'Description of Exeter', pp.26–7; *Foxe,* IV, p.218; VIII, p.464; LP, IX, 230; XII (2), 594, 624; XIV (2), 42; *Narratives of the Reformation,* p.171; Ramsey, 'Epistle', fol.11; STAC 2 2/272; 29/111; *Tudor Treatises,* pp.123–6; Elton 1972, pp.162–4.
10. *Foxe,* IV, pp.208–14, 584; *Rising in the North*; SP 1 118/247–8; Dickens 1989, pp.55–6; Dodds and Dodds 1915; Rose–Troup 1913.
11. CAB 3552, fols.140, 145–8; *Copy of a Letter*; 'Description of Exeter', p.55; *Foxe,* VII, pp.192–3; *Godly New Story*; Hooker, Commonplace Book, fol. 352; LP, X, 462; *Tudor Parish Documents,* p.206; Dickens 1989, pp.54, 56; Garrett 1966, pp.92–4, 240; MacCaffrey 1958, pp.80, 253; Powell 1972.
12. *Blanchminster's Charity,* pp.91–4; CWA N. Petherwin, fols. 36v, 43, 49v; 'Description of Exeter', p.33; HCWA Stratton, 1539; *Leland,* I, p.179; LP, XII (2), 301, 1325; XIV (1), 1126; PROB 11 41, fol. 253v; Cornwall 1977, pp.79, 104; Elton 1972, p.237; Rose–Troup 1913, p.85.
13. LP, VII, 261, 930; XII (1), 537; XIII (2), 156, 1146; Elton 1972, pp.33, 339, 367.
14. 'Description of Exeter', p.64; *Foxe,* V, pp.448–51; VIII, pp.443–4; Hooker, Commonplace Book, fol.343; LP, XIV (1), 184, 1095; PROB 11 39, fol.415v; SP 1 102/33; Dickens 1989, pp.260–1; Elton 1972, pp.100–7.
15. *Acts and Monuments,* II, p.2051; *Foxe,* V, pp.32, 37, 44, 417; VI, pp.429–30; LP, XIII (1), 811; XIII (2), App.19; XIV (1), 684; XIV (2), 71; OL, II, p.560; TRP, I, pp.227–8, 272–3; Dickens 1989, p.92; Elton

1972, pp.98–9, 221; Loades 1970, p.84, n.45; Loades 1991, p.100; Pettegree 1986.
16. *Foxe*, IV, p.584; *Narratives of the Reformation*, p.84; Dickens 1989, pp.57–8; Garrett 1966, especially pp.32, 41–2, 67–349.

21 Lay Authorities

1. *Blanchminster's Charity*, pp.91–4; HCWA Stratton, 1518; LP, XIII (2), 21; STAC 2 21/158; 30/115; Pevsner 1952A, pp.75, 157; Pevsner 1952B, pp.40, 121, 203, 221, 255; Pevsner and Radcliffe 1970, pp.74, 97.
2. 'Description of Exeter', p.37; 'Life of Carew', p.lxxxvi; *Prayerbook of 1549*, p.49; *Rising in the North*, especially p.10; Dickens 1989, p.148; Dodds and Dodds 1915; Rose–Troup 1913, especially p.355; Youings 1979.
3. *Original Letters*, pp.9–11, 19–20, 57; SP 12 60/27, 39; Duffy 1992, p.420; Elton 1972, pp.306–7.
4. APC, V, p.63; E 315 126/16–17; LP, VI, 503; XII (1), 1000, 1127; XIII (1), 416; Add., 1241; SP 1 80/193; 102/33; Elton 1972, p.369; Loades 1970, p.138.
5. 'Examination of Aske', pp.330–48; LP, XIII (1), 533, 705; Titus B 1, fols.172–9; Elton 1972, pp.21–2; Rowse 1941, p.241.
6. CWA Ashburton, 1548–51; E 117 1/48–52B; 2/7; SP 15 3/29–46; STAC 3 2/14; Hutton 1987, pp.120, 122.
7. 'Description of Exeter', especially pp.27–34, 55–7, 66; Harleian 352, fol.65v; *Plymouth Records*, pp.16, 115; *Prayerbook of 1549*, p.65; *Survey of Cornwall*, pp.265, 292, 380; Garrett 1966, pp.118–19; Rose–Troup 1913, especially p.488.
8. CAB 3552, fol.137; *Rising in the North*, especially pp.30, 55; Hutton 1987, p.134.
9. C 1 959/35–7; 1482/97; CWA Braunton, 1555; CWA Woodbury, 1554; HCWA Stratton, 1540; Parkyn, 'Narrative', p.308; Loades 1970, pp.112–13.
10. *Acts and Monuments*, II, pp.1040, 2051; EHD, p.867; Elton 1972, pp.375–80.
11. *Barnstaple Records*, I, pp.198–9; C 1 601/1; 631/4; 1228/63; 1378/39; C 3 202/65; CCB 855, fols.5v, 127v–8v; *Certificates, Cornwall*, pp.28, 53–4; *Certificates, Devon*, pp.xxi–xxii, 25; SP 11 2/15; STAC 2 21/94, 96; 29/55; Henderson 1923–4, p.389; Rose–Troup 1913, pp.505–7; Rowse 1941, p.176.
12. C 1 1325/35; 1341/77–9; 1378/19–21; 1381/68; 1386/17; CAB 3551, fol.147, etc.; CAB 3552, fols.50v–1, 118v; STAC 2 30/4; Rowse 1941, pp.143–4, 292–5.
13. C 1 1369/11–20; 1389/68–71; 1467/41; CCB 855, fols.36v, 50v–1v, 53; STAC 2 21/163; 30/104; 32/4; Prince 1701, pp.181–2.
14. *Acts and Monuments*, II, p.2051; *Copy of a Letter*, dedication, pp.1–2; 'Description of Exeter', pp.31–3, 66–7; 'Life of Carew', p.cxiv; *Original*

Letters, pp.9–10, 70–2; Ramsey, 'Epistle', fols.26v–7v; STAC 2 29/111; Garrett 1966, pp.104–8, 337; Roberts 1962–4, pp.295–6.
15. 'Description of Exeter', pp.26, 28; *Original Letters*, pp.64, 69; Price 1938, p.112.
16. APC, V, pp.112–13; C 1 1020/4–9; CWA S. Tawton, 1559; 'Description of Exeter', p.42; E 315 122/15–28; *Grey Friars Chronicle*, p.66; Hooker, Commonplace Book, fols.343–4, 349–51; LP, XIII (1), 453; XIII (2), 354, 381, 389; *Original Letters*, pp.11, 14–15, 66; *Plymouth Records*, p.110; SP 1 102/33; 11 2/15; *Tudor Parish Documents*, p.203.
17. Hooker, Commonplace Book, fol.343; *Original Letters*, p.11; above, pp.120–1, 127.
18. LP, XII (1), 389, 1212; *Prayerbook of 1549*, p.42; *Rising in the North*, p.121; SP 15 3/31; STAC 2 29/111; 31/11, 178; STAC 3 2/20; *York Records*, VI, p.7; Elton 1972, pp.120–1, 142, 336; Rowse 1941, p.98.

22 Clerics (1)

1. *Certificates, Cornwall*, pp.11–12, 29–31, 38–40, 46, 50–3; *Certificates, Devon*, pp.xiii, 64, 68–9; 'Life of Carew', p.lxviii; *Survey of Cornwall*, p.282; Dickens 1989, p.238; Duffy 1992, pp.58–61; Finberg 1951, pp.274–5; Orme 1973; Pevsner and Radcliffe 1970, p.239; Rowse 1941, pp.168–9; Whiting 1989, pp.232–3, 235–7.
2. *Acts and Monuments*, II, p.1038; CAB 3551, fol.51; CR Dartmouth, Mayoral Accounts, 1528; ER XV, fols. 3, 4v, 14–14v; Hooker, Commonplace Book, fol. 342; 'Lives of Saints', fols. 323v, 358v; LP, IV, 771; PROB 11 21, fol. 128; Cox 1915; Cox 1916; Cox and Harvey 1973, pp.147–50; Dickens 1989, p.72; Pevsner 1952B, p.181; Platt 1981, p.147; Whiting 1989, pp.237–40. For bedes bidding from pulpits, see (for example) PROB 11 23, fol. 29.
3. *Acts and Monuments*, II, pp.1037–40; *Certificates, Cornwall*, p.52; *Foxe*, IV, p.620; V, pp.414–5; VI, pp.676–7; VII, pp.438–9; *Godly New Story*, pp.61–2; 'Lives of Saints', fols. 323v, 358v; Haigh 1993, pp.59, 61–3, 67–8; Whiting 1989, pp.240–1.
4. CWA Exeter SP, 1562; TRP, I, p.401; Cox and Harvey 1973, pp.150–1; Whiting 1989, pp.241–2. For pulpits, see also (for example) CWA Camborne, 1550; CWA Exeter SMS, 1552; HCWA Stratton, 1544, 1547; Hooker, Commonplace Book, fol.353; *Inventories, Exeter*, p.62. For bench-ends, see below, pp.190–1.
5. 'Examination of Aske', p.561; LP, VI, 1664; VII, 449, 595, 694, 807, 939; VIII, 624, 667; IX, 315, 632; X, 346, 594; XI, 1216; XII (1), 508, 1147; XII (2), 65, 557; XIII (2), 596, 709, 935; *Plymouth Records*, p.109; SP 1 80/193; Elton 1972, pp.14–20, 117–18, 139–41.
6. LP, VII, 260, 869; VIII, 407; IX, 740, 846; XI, 954, 1393; XII (2), 557; XIII (1), 921, 1199; XIII (2), 361; XIV (1), 525, 1338; Elton 1972, pp.22–3, 26–7, 41–2. For the institution of former monks in parochial benefices, see (for example) Rowse 1941, p.209.

7. *Certificates, Cornwall*, p.52; EDCL 3498/88; ER XV, fols. 74v–5; *Foxe*, VIII, p.31; Hooker, Commonplace Book, fols. 342, 346, 349; LP, VII, 449; VIII, 292, 869, 922, 963; XI, 211; XIII (1), 75, 105; *Survey of Cornwall*, pp.282–3; Elton 1972, pp.211–6, 232–5.
8. APC, I, pp.97, 150–1; *Foxe*, V, pp.428–38; VII, pp.454, 459–63; *Grey Friars Chronicle*, pp.43–4, 50–1; Hooker, Commonplace Book, fols.342, 349; 'Life of Carew', p.cxiv; LP, V, 246–7; VI, 411–12, 433, 596, 799, 1192; VII, 411, 420; VIII, 20, 625, 1001; XI, 138; XII (1), 40, 308, 701, 757; XII (2), 215, 302–3, 496, App.13; XIII (1), 715; XIII (2), 1279; XV, 183; XVI, 578; SP 1 154/181–2; Elton 1972, pp.30, 36–8, 40–1, 43–4, 112–17, 121–3, 139–41, 211–16, 375–80; Haigh 1993, pp.188–9; Thompson 1934–5, pp.352–5.
9. *Acts and Monuments*, II, p.1305; C 1 1341/77–9; 1369/11–20; *Copy of a Letter*, pp.5–6, 33–4, 51; *Certificates, Cornwall*, pp.32, 39, 46; *Certificates, Devon*, p.69; CPR, I, pp.43–5; *Cranmer*, II, pp.502–3, 547; 'Description of Exeter', pp.65–8; *Grey Friars Chronicle*, p.56; Nichols, 'Answer', fols.3, 29, 37–7v; *Prayerbook of 1549*, pp.15–19; Cornwall 1977, p.202; Dickens 1989, p.238; Henderson 1923–4, p.458; Hoskins 1954, p.247; Rose-Troup 1913, pp.91–2, 337, 497–502; Rowse 1941, pp.253, 283–4.
10. *Exeter Records*, p.365; *Grey Friars Chronicle*, pp.57,63; Nichols, 'Answer', fol.29; TRP, I, p.396; Price 1938, pp.123–4.
11. *Foxe*, VI, pp.639, 677; VII, pp.335, 463; *Grey Friars Chronicle*, pp.55–76; *Narratives of the Reformation*, pp.72–3, 77–8; Haigh 1993, pp.189–90; Loades 1991, p.271.
12. APC, II, p.220; CWA Ashburton, 1549; 'Description of Exeter', p.58; ER XVII, fols. 18–18v; *Foxe*, VI, pp.639, 644; VII, pp.143–4, 204–5; VIII, p.444; Hooker, Commonplace Book, fol. 348; *Prayerbook of 1549*, pp.6–8; Haigh 1993, pp.189–90.
13. *Acts and Monuments*, II, p.2051; *Barnstaple Records*, II, p.99; CCB 855, fol.48v; CWA Crediton, 1551–2; CWA Exeter SMM, fol.13; Hooker, Commonplace Book, fol.349; 'Life of Carew', p.cxiv; Murray, 3, John Bougin, 1548; *Plymouth Records*, pp.114, 117; PROB 11 44, fol.274; 'Synopsis Chorographical', p.107.
14. *Certificates, Cornwall*, pp.11, 16, 25–7, 29–32, 36, 38, 46, 50–1; 'Description of Exeter', p.26; *Godly New Story*, pp.72–3; TRP, I, pp.402, 432–3; Hutton 1987, p.124; Price 1938, p.112. For the purchase of homilies, see (for example) CWA Crediton, 1551; CWA Exeter SJB, 1547; CWA St Breock, fol. 3v; CWA Woodbury, 1547, 1550.
15. CAB 3552, fol.82; CWA Credition; CWA Dartmouth, 1555; CWA S. Tawton, 1557; *Foxe*, VI, p.612; VII, p.372; VIII, pp.383–4; *Grey Friars Chronicle*, pp.83, 90; Hooker, Commonplace Book, fols. 349–50; 'Lives of Saints', fol.323v; Ramsey, 'Epistle', fol.10; TRP, II, pp.6–7, 38; *York Records*, V, p.105; Haigh 1993, pp.216–17, 224–5; Loades 1991, p.271; Whiting 1989, pp.243–4. For exile and deprivation, see (for example) C 1 1325/35; Hooker, Commonplace Book, fol.350; Garrett 1966, pp.132–4, 270–1. For outward conformity, see (for example) *Acts and Monuments*, II, p.2051; Hooker, Commonplace Book, fol.350.

16. CAB 3552, fol. 138v; *Exeter Records*, p.39; Machyn, *Diary*, p.216; *Original Letters*, pp.3, 19, 34; *Rising in the North*, pp.280–1; *Zurich Letters*, pp.44–5; Field 1973; Haigh 1993, pp.243–4, 248–9, 253–6; Whiting 1989, p.231.
17. CCB 41, pp.17, 25–7, 29, 38, 42; CCB 855A, fol.215v; CCB 856, fol.202; *Original Letters*, p.35; *Tudor Parish Documents*, p.20; TRP, II, pp.119, 126–7; Aveling 1970, pp.166–7; Haigh 1993, pp.270–1. For Protestant schools at Exeter and Plymouth in the 1560s, see Hooker, Commonplace Book, fol.354; *Plymouth Records*, pp.50–1.
18. Alley Report (references under place names); APC, VII, pp.65–6; Hooker, Commonplace Book, fol.353; 'Lives of Saints', fol.323v; *Original Letters*, p.49; *Rising in the North*, pp.256, 259; TRP, II, pp.102, 120.
19. Alley Report; CCB 41, pp.9, 21, 27, 44; 'Description of Exeter', p.190; Hooker, Commonplace Book, fol.352; 'Synopsis Chorographical', p.161; TRP, II, pp.118–19, 123; Frere 1904, pp.107–8; Garrett 1966, pp.311–12; Hill 1969, pp.52–3; Houlbrooke 1979, pp.183, 202–3; Shiels 1979, p.92; Whiting 1989, p.249.
20. *Barnstaple Records*, II, pp.99, 126; CR Dartmouth, Receivers' Accounts, 1570; CWA Crediton, 1561, 1565, 1567–70; *Exeter Records*, pp.41–2; Ramsey, 'Epistle', fol.27; Cross 1969, pp.95–6.
21. CAB 3552, fol.138; CCB 855B, 19 January 1565/6; CCB 856, fol.319; CWA S. Tawton, 1565; CWA Woodbury, 1565; Hooker, Commonplace Book, fols.352, 356; Machyn, *Diary*, pp.189, 193, 199, 207–8, 212, 216, 225, 228, 247, 271, 279; *Original Letters*, p.66; *Tudor Parish Documents*, p.216; Cross 1969, pp.95–6.
22. Alley Report; *Barnstaple Records*, I, p.213; CCB 855A, loose sheet, charges v. unnamed cleric; CCB 855B, 19 January 1565/6, 17 December 1566; CCB 856, fols.319–20; CWA Antony, 1559; CWA Coldridge, 1559–60, 1570; CWA Crediton, 1559; CWA Dartington, 1559; CWA Exeter SJB, 1559–60; CWA Exeter SMM, fol.16; CWA Exeter SMS, 1571; CWA Kilmington, 1560; CWA Morebath, 1559; CWA St Breock, fols.3v, 16; CWA S. Tawton, 1559; CWA Woodbury, 1563; *Exeter Records*, pp.41–2; HCWA Stratton, 1559; SP 12 6/17; TRP, II, pp.118–19, 123, 132–3; *Tudor Parish Documents*, pp.16–17, 20–1; Haigh 1993, p.250; Hutton 1987, p.137; Rose-Troup 1913, p.106n.

23 Clerics (2)

1. LP, XIII (2), 561; Elton 1972, pp.25–6, 96–8; Haigh 1993, pp.224–5; Whiting 1989, p.256.
2. 'Description of Exeter', pp.26–7; Parkyn, 'Narrative', especially p.308; Dickens 1989, p.73; MacCaffrey 1958, p.191; Rowse 1941, pp.155, 187–93; Whiting 1989, p.256.

3. *Copy of a Letter*, pp.1–4; 'Life of Carew', p.cxiv; Porter 1958; Price 1938; Whiting 1989, p.257.
4. *Acts and Monuments*, II, p.2051; C 1 1347/16–18; *Original Letters*, p.9.
5. This analysis of the bishops is based primarily on Frere 1896, App.I; Smith 1953. For Longland, see also Bowker 1981.
6. *Acts and Monuments*, II, p.1038; Alley Report; *Godly New Story*, pp.72–3; LP, XII (2), 557; Dickens 1989, pp.68, 72; Price 1938, p.101; RBM 1928–9, I, pp.38–41; Rowse 1941, p.160.
7. LP, XII (1), 479; *Original Letters*, pp.20–1, 67; *Prayerbook of 1549*, pp.15–19; Wall 1905, pp.129–30; Whiting 1989, p.230.
8. *Acts and Monuments*, II, p.1039; *Copy of a Letter*, pp.11, 31; *Foxe*, VII, App.IX; *Prayerbook of 1549*, p.18; Elton 1972, pp.112–17; Rose-Troup 1913, p.337; Whiting 1989, p.235.
9. 'Synopsis Chorographical', pp.105–6; Prince 1701, pp.383f, 387–8, 418f; above, p.168.
10. *Foxe*, V, p.535; LP, VII, 406, 595, 694; VIII, 667; IX, 740,1059; XII (1), 588; XIII (2), 361; XIV (1), 526, 531, 721; Elton 1972, pp.112–17.
11. *Acts and Monuments*, II, p.2051; *Copy of a Letter*, p.5; *Foxe*, VIII, p.790; *Grey Friars Chronicle*, pp.57, 83, 90; Loades 1991, pp.384–5.
12. *Acts and Monuments*, II, pp.1037–40; *Foxe*, VII, p.731; *Grey Friars Chronicle*, p.74; *Survey of Cornwall*, pp.282–3, 293; Craig 1955, pp.357–60; Loades 1970, p.80.
13. *Foxe*, V, pp.39, 444–6, 756; VI, p.639; VII, pp.407, 485, 716–17; LP, X, 346; Machyn, *Diary*, p.228; *Narratives of the Reformation*, p.158; Elton 1972, pp.27–30.
14. APC, V, p.30; *Foxe*, VI, pp.676–8; VII, p.297; VIII, pp.31, 581–4; LP, IX, 230, 1059; Elton 1972, pp.33–4; Loades 1970, p.138; Russell 1859, pp.38–9, 49.
15. *Foxe*, VI, p.613; VII, p.473, App.IX; VIII, pp.247–50; LP, VII, 1192; X, 804, 850; XII (2), 215, 302–3, 496; XIII (2), 1279; *Narratives of the Reformation*, p.75; Cross 1969, pp.95–6; Elton 1972, pp.30, 112–17, 212–13, 375–80.
16. *Acts and Monuments*, II, p.2050; APC, I, pp.97, 150–1; Hooker, Commonplace Book, fols.342, 348–9; 'Life of Carew', p.cxiv; Ramsey, 'Epistle', fols. 9v–10v.
17. Strype, *Memorials*, III (2), p.562; Aveling 1970, p.168.
18. *Certificates, Cornwall*, pp.11, 16, 25–7, 29–32, 36, 38, 46, 50–1; 'Description of Exeter', pp.26–7; LP, XVI, 1377; Nichols, 'Answer', fol.21; Strype, *Annals*, I (2), p.436; Strype, *Memorials*, III (2), p.562; TRP, I, p.402.
19. *Foxe*, VII, pp.288–9; Hooker, Commonplace Book, fol.342; 'Life of Carew', p.cxiv; LP, XII (2), 215, 302–3, 496; XIII (1), 1509; XIII (2), 194, 1279; Machyn, *Diary*, p.271; *Narratives of the Reformation*, pp.73–4, 78, 159–60; SP 1 154/181–2; *Tudor Parish Documents*, p.216; Elton 1972, pp.112–17, 375–80.
20. *Grey Friars Chronicle*, p.76; Hooker, Commonplace Book, fols.342, 349; PROB 11 26, fol. 76; Loades 1970, p.90.

24 Playwrights, Players

1. *Ancient Cornish Drama*; *Beunans Meriasek*; Craig 1955, pp.155–8, 320–4, 341–53; Whiting 1989, p.199.
2. Craig 1955, pp.132, 153–4, 298–9, 304, 324, 330–2; Whiting 1989, p.200.
3. *Bodmin Register*, pp.38–42; CWA Ashburton, especially 1529, 1535, 1537–8; *Survey of Cornwall*, p.192; Craig 1955, pp.114–27, 166–7, 203.
4. *Beunans Meriasek*, especially 844–58, 874–90, 1317–20; Duffy 1992, pp.66–8.
5. *Ancient Cornish Drama*: Resurrexio; *Beunans Meriasek*; Craig 1955, pp.155–8.
6. *Ancient Cornish Drama*: Passio Domini Nostri, especially 3223–34; *Beunans Meriasek*, especially 1000–8, 4302–9, 4553–6.
7. Craig 1955, pp.360–1; Rushforth 1927B, pp.154–9; Whiting 1989, p.107.
8. Craig 1955, pp.92, 129–30, 163, 285–6, 298–9, 355; Fowler 1961.
9. CWA Ashburton, especially 1543, 1546, 1548; *York Records*, IV, p.176; Craig 1955, pp.355–7; Finucane 1977, pp.194, 211.
10. CWA Ashburton, especially 1554, 1556, 1559–60; *York Records*, V, p.100; Craig 1955, pp.141–3, 209–10, 295, 355–7, 362–3; Finucane 1977, p.213.
11. *Survey of Cornwall*, p.192; *York Records*, VI, pp.8, 135; Craig 1955, pp.141, 299–300, 356–61.
12. CWA Ashburton; *York Records*, VI, p.134; Craig 1955, pp.334–7, 355, 357–63.
13. *Inventories, Cornwall*, p.32; Craig 1955, pp.143, 152–3, 301–2, 320–4, 376–7; Finucane 1977, p.214.
14. Palliser 1979, pp.250–1.
15. *King John*; Craig 1955, pp.369–71; Elton 1972, pp.185–6; White 1993.
16. APC, VI, pp.102, 110, 118–19, 148, 168–9; *Foxe*, V, p.446; Strype, *Memorials*, III (2), pp.413–4; Craig 1955, pp.362–3; Loades 1970, pp.80–1; Loades 1991, pp.379–80.

25 Artists, Craftsmen

1. Whiting 1989, p.203. For particular types of religious art, see n.3 to Introduction.
2. BA Bodmin, Receivers' Accounts, 1508; CWA N. Petherwin, fol.43v; Bond and Camm 1909, I, pp.139–40; II, p.280; Cave 1948, p.20; Rushforth 1927A, pp.29–31; Rushforth 1927B, pp.150–90.
3. For example, much of the extant stained glass is datable by style, inscription or arms to the fourteenth and fifteenth centuries. Fifteenth-century examples include the east windows at Doddiscombsleigh and Holy Trinity, Goodramgate, York.

4. Rushforth 1927B, pp.150–90. The well remains. For the horn, see above, p.96.
5. *Foxe*, IV, p.240; VI, p.27; Duffy 1992, p.360; Whiting 1989, p.205.
6. TRP, I, pp.275–6, 401; II, p.123.
7. CWA Ashburton, 1558; CWA Dartington, 1554; CWA Exeter SMS, 1559; CWA Exeter SP, 1551; CWA S. Tawton, 1557; DRO 1660 A 12; *English Church Furniture*, especially p.110; HCWA Stratton, 1548; *Inventories, Exeter*, p.38; SWA Stratton, 1549; *Tudor Parish Documents*, pp.31–4.
8. For 'sacrament' fonts, see Duffy 1992, p.65.
9. Bond and Camm 1909, II, p.287; Cox 1915, pp.51, 56, 60–1; Cox 1916, pp.67, 78; Pevsner 1952A, pp.81, 129; Pevsner 1952B, pp.27–8, 125.
10. Bond and Camm 1909, II, pp.228, 330, 353, 388, 392; Duffy 1992, p.160; Pevsner 1952A, pp.121, 147–9; Pevsner 1952B, p.125.
11. Bond and Camm 1909, I, p.92; II, p.347; Duffy 1992, pp.33, 55, 58–9, 141; Pevsner 1952A, plate 19; Pevsner 1952B, pp.78, 125, 267.
12. CWA Dartmouth, 1542; *Tavistock Records*, p.29; Rushforth 1927B, pp.150–90.
13. CWA Easingwold; HCWA Stratton, 1567; STAC 4 8/47; *Tudor Parish Documents*, p.34; *Harpsfield's Visitation*, especially p.109; Hutton 1987, p.121; Whiting 1989, p.209.
14. For Fairford, see Cook 1954, p.202n.
15. CWA Antony, 1549; CWA Ashburton, 1550–1; CWA Exeter HT, 1548, 1550; CWA Exeter SJB, 1548; CWA Exeter SP, 1549; *Grey Friars Chronicle*, p.54; HCWA Stratton, 1548, 1551; *Melford Church*, p.40; Hutton 1987, p.121.
16. *Barnstaple Records*, I, p.211; CWA Ashburton, 1560; CWA Chagford, 1567; CWA Dartington, 1559; CWA Kilmington, 1562; CWA S. Tawton, 1566; CWA Woodbury, 1565; *Melford Church*, p.73; *Tudor Parish Documents*, p.34. For Marian failure to repaint obliterated murals, see (for example) CWA Exeter SP; HCWA Stratton; SWA Stratton.
17. For St Mawes, see *Leland*, I, p.200. For recovery in the nineteenth and twentieth centuries, see (for example) Peter and Peter 1885, p.359; Pevsner and Radcliffe 1970, p.103.
18. CWA Woodbury, 1570; MacCulloch 1990, p.167; Watt 1991.

26 Writers, Translators, Printers

1. APC, II, pp.538–9; Hooker, Commonplace Book, fols.344, 354; *Narratives of the Reformation*, p.158; SP 1 102/33; Elton 1972, p.200.
2. Bennett 1970; Dickens 1989, pp.31–2; Duffy 1992, pp.77–87, 210–14; Elton 1972, pp.171, 175, 256; Haigh 1993, pp.25–6, 165.
3. Baskerville 1979; Haigh 1993, pp.216–17, 223–4, 254; Loach 1975; Loades 1970, pp.136, 240; Loades 1991, pp.282, 285–7.
4. CCB 856, fols.143v–6; EHD, p.835; *Original Letters*, p.67; *Tudor Parish Documents*, p.149.

5. *Acts and Monuments*, II, pp.1037–40; *Foxe*, IV, pp.176–7, 216, 239–40; V, pp.565–8; *Narratives of the Reformation*, p.158; Dickens 1989, pp.52–3; Haigh 1993, pp.57–67; Loades 1991, p.283.
6. *Acts and Monuments*, II, pp.1037–40; EHD, p.828; *Foxe*, V, pp.38, 452–3; *Grey Friars Chronicle*, pp.48, 52; LP, IV (3), 6385; XIV (1), 897; *Narratives of the Reformation*, p.350; Elton 1972, p.25.
7. Duffy 1992, pp.382–3; Elton 1972, pp.171–211.
8. 'Description of Exeter', p.46; *Narratives of the Reformation*, p.172; Dickens 1989, p.247; Garrett 1966; Whiting 1989, p.189.
9. C 1 1347/16–18; CCB 856, fol.146; CWA S. Tawton, 1561; *Foxe*, VI, p.561; VIII, pp.393–4, 539, 598–600; Baskerville 1979; Loades 1970, pp.238–40, 250; Loades 1991, pp.116, 286.
10. EHD, p.828; *Foxe*, VIII, p.384; LP, XI, 1246; XII (1), 1147; *Readings in Church History*, p.665; TRP, II, p.90; Elton 1972, p.26.
11. *Acts and Monuments*, II, p.2050; CCB 856, fols.143v–6; *Foxe*, IV, pp.240, 688–94; VIII, p.205; LP, VII, 140, 145–6, 454; Elton 1972, pp.208–10; Loades 1991, p.284n.
12. *Foxe*, IV, pp.617–19; V, pp.410–12; Dickens 1989, pp.32, 151–6; Haigh 1993, pp.59–60.
13. CCB 855B, 28 February 1566/7; *Foxe*, IV, pp.177–8, 184, 216, 218, 234; V, p.37; HCWA Stratton, 1570; *Narratives of the Reformation*, p.349; STAC 2 29/111; Haigh 1993, pp.59–60, 67.
14. *Bodmin Register*, pp.38–42; CWA Antony; CWA Ashburton, 1541; CWA Camborne, 1543; CWA Chagford, 1540, 1542; CWA Dartmouth, 1539; CWA Exeter SJB; CWA Exeter SMS; CWA Exeter SP, 1540; CWA Iddesleigh, 1539, 1542; CWA Morebath, 1538, 1542–3; CWA S. Tawton; CWA Woodbury, 1539, 1542; ER XV, fol.76; HCWA Stratton, 1541–2; LP, XVI, 803; SWA Stratton, 1540; *Tavistock Records*, pp.16–19; TRP, I, p.296; Hutton 1987, pp.116, 118; MacCaffrey 1958, p.271.
15. CWA Antony, 1549, 1553; CWA Ashburton, 1549, 1551, 1554; CWA Dartmouth, 1553–5; CWA Exeter HT, 1548–9; CWA Exeter SJB, 1548–50; CWA Exeter SMM, fol.11; CWA Exeter SP, 1549; CWA Kilmington, 1559; CWA Morebath, 1549, 1555; CWA St Breock, fol.3v; CWA S. Tawton, 1560; CWA Woodbury, 1547–8; *Foxe*, VI, pp.565–6; *Grey Friars Chronicle*, p.54; *Harpsfield's Visitation*, especially p.53; HCWA Stratton, 1560; *Inventories, Exeter*, p.62; *Melford Church*, pp.41, 60; SWA Stratton, 1548; TRP, I, pp.395–6; Bond and Camm 1909, I, p.101; Hutton 1987, pp.124–5, 137.
16. For bibles and paraphrases, see (for example) *Barnstaple Records*, I, p.213; CAB 3552, fol.138; CWA Antony, 1559–60; CWA Ashburton, 1569; CWA Braunton, 1559; CWA Coldridge, 1560; CWA Crediton, 1559; CWA Dartington, 1559; CWA Exeter SJB, 1559, 1565; CWA Exeter SMM, fol.16; CWA Exeter SP, 1560, 1563; CWA Molland, 1559; CWA Morebath, 1559; SWA Stratton, 1564; TRP, II, p.119; Hutton 1987, p.137.

    For commandments, see CWA Ashburton, 1562, 1568; CWA Braunton, 1568; CWA Chudleigh, 1579; CWA Coldridge, 1570; CWA Crediton, 1561, 1563, 1565; CWA Dartington, 1563, 1568; CWA Exeter

SJB, 1561; CWA Exeter SMS, 1561, 1570; CWA Exeter SP, 1561, 1563; CWA Kilmington, 1562; CWA Molland, 1561, 1569; CWA Morebath, 1568; CWA S. Tawton, 1561, 1566; CWA Winkleigh, 1563, 1569; CWA Woodbury, 1561, 1570; *Documents of Church History*, p.471; HCWA Stratton, 1561; *Tavistock Records*, p.26; Hutton 1987, p.137.

17. *Acts and Monuments*, II, p.1037; CCB 855B, 28 February 1566/7; *Foxe*, IV, p.584; V, pp.451–2; VI, pp.676–7; *Narratives of the Reformation*, p.349.
18. *Foxe*, V, p.535; LP, X, 1140; XIV (1), 525; *Reformation in England*, p.115; Elton 1972, p.24; Haigh 1993, pp.151, 161.
19. *Acts and Monuments*, II, p.1037; *Foxe*, VIII, pp.247–50; *Narratives of the Reformation*, pp.158, 349–50; Nichols, 'Answer', fols.27, 28; Strype, *Memorials*, III (2), p.503.
20. CCB 855B, 28 February 1566/7; *Copy of Letter*, pp.44–5, 49–50; *Godly New Story*, pp.57–8; *Narratives of the Reformation*, p.349; Nichols, 'Answer', fols.27, 28–8v; STAC 2 29/111; *Tudor Parish Documents*, pp.30, 33–4; Haigh 1993, p.159.
21. *Godly New Story*, pp.66–7; Nichols, 'Answer', fol.28.
22. *Acts and Monuments*, II, pp.1037–40; PROB 11 26, fol.91v; 37, fol.73v; Cressy 1980; Dickens 1989, pp.235–6; Orme 1973; Whiting 1989, pp.197, 235–6.
23. 'Description of Exeter', p.46; *Foxe*, III, p.718; IV, pp.252–3; Dickens 1989, p.57; Duffy 1992, p.212; MacCulloch 1990, pp.163–4.
24. CCB 855B, 28 February 1566/7; *Copy of Letter*, pp.44–5, 49–50; *Godly New Story*, pp.65–7; LP, X, 1140; XIV (1), 796; TRP, I, pp.181–6, 193–7, 235–7; II, pp.53–4, 128–9; Elton 1972, pp.24–7.
25. C 1 1347/16–18; CWA Crediton, 1559; Nichols, 'Answer', fol.20; Cressy 1980; Whiting 1989, pp.197–9, 236.

BIBLIOGRAPHY AND ABBREVIATIONS

Unless otherwise indicated, the place of publication for books is London.

Depositories

BL	British Library
CRO	Cornwall Record Office, Truro
CUL	Cambridge University Library
DCRSL	Devon and Cornwall Record Society Library, Exeter
DRO	Devon Record Office, Exeter
EDCL	Exeter Dean and Chapter Library
PRO	Public Record Office
TCCL	Trinity College, Cambridge, Library

Primary Sources

Acts and Monuments	J. Foxe, *Acts and Monuments* ..., 2 vols, 1583
Alley Report	DRO, Transcript 009/9, Bishop Alley, Report on Clergy
Ancient Cornish Drama	*The Ancient Cornish Drama*, ed. E. Norris, 2 vols, Oxford, 1859
APC	*Acts of the Privy Council of England*, ed. J.R. Dasent, 32 vols, 1890–1907
BA Bodmin	CRO, Borough Accounts, Bodmin
Barnstaple Records	*Reprint of the Barnstaple Records*, ed. J.R. Chanter and T. Wainwright, 2 vols, Barnstaple, 1900
Beunans Meriasek	*Beunans Meriasek: The Life of St Meriasek*, ed. W. Stokes, 1872
Blanchminster's Charity	*Records of ... Blanchminster's Charity*, ed. R.W. Goulding, Louth, 1898

Bodmin Register	*The Bodmin Register*, 1827–38
Butley Priory	*The Register or Chronicle of Butley Priory*, ed. A.G. Dickens, 1951
C 1	PRO, Chancery, Early Chancery Proceedings
C 3	PRO, Chancery, Chancery Proceedings, Series II
C 82	PRO, Chancery, Warrants for the Great Seal, Series II
CAB	EDCL, Chapter Act Books, 3551, 3552
CCB	DRO, Consistory Court Books, 41, 775, 776, 777, 778, 779, 854 (I, II), 854A (I, II), 855, 855A, 855B, 856
Certificates, Cornwall	*The Chantry Certificates for Cornwall*, ed. L.S. Snell, Exeter 1953
Certificates, Devon	*The Chantry Certificates for Devon and the City of Exeter*, ed. L.S. Snell, Exeter, 1961
Certificates, Yorkshire	*The Certificates of the Commissioners ... in the County of York*, ed. W. Page, Surtees Society, 91–2, 1894–5
Copy of a Letter	BL, Reading Room 3932 A 28, P. Nichols, *The Copy of a Letter*, 1547
CPR	*Calendar of the Patent Rolls, Edward VI*, 6 vols, 1924–9
CR Dartmouth	DRO, Corporation Records, Dartmouth
Cranmer	*Memorials of Archbishop Cranmer*, ed. J. Strype, 3 vols, Oxford, 1848–54
CSPD	*Calendar of State Papers, Domestic, Edward VI-James I*, ed. R. Lemon and M.A.E. Green, 12 vols, 1856–72
CSPS	*Calendar of State Papers, Spanish*, ed. R. Tyler et al., 1862–1964
CSPV	*Calendar of State Papers, Venetian*, ed. R. Brown et al., 1864–98
CWA Antony	Churchwardens' Accounts, Antony (transcript loaned by Mr F.L. Harris)
CWA Ashburton	*Churchwardens' Accounts of Ashburton, 1479–1580*, ed. A. Hanham, Devon and Cornwall Record Society, Torquay, 1970
CWA Bodmin	CRO, Churchwardens' Accounts, Bodmin
CWA Braunton	DRO, Churchwardens' Accounts, Braunton
CWA Broadhempston	DRO, Churchwardens' Accounts, Broadhempston (transcript)

CWA Camborne — CRO, Churchwardens' Accounts, Camborne

CWA Chagford — DRO, Churchwardens' Accounts, Chagford

CWA Chudleigh — DRO, Churchwardens' Accounts, Chudleigh

CWA Coldridge — DRO, Churchwardens' Accounts, Coldridge

CWA Crediton — DRO, Churchwardens' Accounts, Crediton

CWA Dartington — DCRSL, Churchwardens' Accounts, Dartington (transcript)

CWA Dartmouth — DRO, Churchwardens' Accounts, Dartmouth

CWA Easingwold — Churchwardens' Account, Easingwold, 1556 (photocopy loaned by Dr W.J. Shiels)

CWA Exeter HT — DRO, Churchwardens' Accounts, Exeter Holy Trinity

CWA Exeter SJB — DRO, Churchwardens' Accounts, Exeter St John's Bow

CWA Exeter SMM — DRO, Churchwardens' Accounts, Exeter St Mary Major

CWA Exeter SMS — DRO, Churchwardens' Accounts, Exeter St Mary Steps

CWA Exeter SP — DRO, Churchwardens' Accounts, Exeter St Petrock

CWA Iddesleigh — DRO, Churchwardens' Accounts, Iddesleigh

CWA Kilmington — *The Churchwardens' Accounts of Kilmington, 1555–1608*, ed. R. Cornish, Exeter, 1901

CWA Launceston — CRO, Churchwardens' Accounts, St Thomas-by-Launceston

CWA Modbury — DRO, Churchwardens' Accounts, Modbury

CWA Molland — 'Molland Accounts', ed. J. Phear, *Transactions of the Devonshire Association*, 35, 1903

CWA Morebath — *The Accounts of the Wardens of the Parish of Morebath, 1520–73*, ed. J.E. Binney, Exeter, 1904

CWA N. Molton — DRO, Churchwardens' Accounts, North Molton (transcript)

CWA N. Petherwin — CRO, Churchwardens' Accounts, North Petherwin

CWA St Breock — CRO, Churchwardens' Accounts, St Breock

CWA S. Tawton	DCRSL, Churchwardens' Accounts, South Tawton (transcript)
CWA Winkleigh	DCRSL, Churchwardens' Accounts, Winkleigh (transcript)
CWA Woodbury	DRO, Churchwardens' Accounts, Woodbury
CWA Woodland	DRO, Churchwardens' Accounts, Woodland (transcript)
Dartmouth	*Dartmouth*, I, ed. H.R. Watkin, Torquay, 1935
'Description of Exeter'	DRO, Book 52, J. Hooker, 'The Description of the City of Exeter'
Documents of Church History	*Documents Illustrative of English Church History*, ed. H. Gee and W.J. Hardy, 1896
Documents of Reformation	*Documents of the English Reformation*, ed. G. Bray, Cambridge, 1994
DRO 1660 A 12	DRO, 1660 A 12, Church Inventory, Crediton
E 117	PRO, Exchequer, King's Remembrancer, Church Goods
E 134	PRO, Exchequer, King's Remembrancer, Depositions
E 135	PRO, Exchequer, King's Remembrancer, Ecclesiastical Documents
E 178	PRO, Exchequer, King's Remembrancer, Special Commissions of Inquiry
E 315	PRO, Exchequer, Augmentations, Miscellaneous Books
EDCL 2864, 2920, 3498, 3508	EDCL, Miscellaneous Documents
EHD	*English Historical Documents*, 5, ed. C.H. Williams, 1967
English Church Furniture	*English Church Furniture, Ornaments and Decorations at the Period of the Reformation*, ed. E. Peacock, 1866
ER	DRO, Episcopal Registers 13–19, Bishops Oldham, Veysey, Coverdale, Turberville, Alley
'Examination of Aske'	'The Pilgrimage of Grace and Aske's Examination', ed. M. Bateson, *English Historical Review*, 5, 1890
Exeter Records	*Report on the Records of the City of Exeter*, Historical Manuscripts Commission, 1916
Foxe	*The Acts and Monuments of John Foxe*, ed. J. Pratt, 8 vols, 1853–70

Glastonbury Commonplace Book	TCCL, 0/9/38, Monk of Glastonbury, Commonplace Book
Gleanings	*Gleanings ... A.D. 1533–88*, ed. G. Gorham, 1857
Godly New Story	BL, Reading Room 4404 B 61, P. Nichols, *A Godly New Story*, 1548
Grey Friars Chronicle	*The Chronicle of the Grey Friars of London*, ed. J. Nichols, Camden Society, 53, 1852
Harleian 352	BL, Harleian MS 352, Privy Council Letter Book
Harleian 2252	BL, Harleian MS 2252, J. Colyn, Miscellaneous Collections
Harpsfield's Visitation	*Archdeacon Harpsfield's Visitation, 1557*, ed. L.E. Whatmore, Catholic Record Society, 45–6, 1950–1
HCWA Stratton	BL, Additional MS 32243, Stratton High Cross Wardens' Accounts
Holme, 'Fall of Rebellion'	Wilfrid Holme, 'The Fall and Evil Success of Rebellion', in A.G. Dickens, 'Wilfrid Holme of Huntington ...', *Yorkshire Archaeological Journal*, 39, 1956–8
Hooker, Commonplace Book	DRO, Book 51, J. Hooker, Commonplace Book
In God's Name	*In God's Name: Examples of Preaching in England ... 1534–1662*, ed. J. Chandos, 1971
Inventories, Cornwall,	*The Edwardian Inventories of Church Goods for Cornwall*, ed. L.S. Snell, Exeter, 1956
Inventories, Exeter	*The Edwardian Inventories for the City and County of Exeter*, ed. B.F. Cresswell, 1916
Kentish Visitations	*Kentish Visitations of Archbishop William Warham and his Deputies, 1511–1512*, ed. K. Wood-Legh, Kent Archaeological Society, 24, 1984
King John	John Bale, *King John: a Play in Two Parts*, ed. J.P. Collier, Camden Society, 2, 1838
Lancashire and Cheshire Wills	*Lancashire and Cheshire Wills and Inventories*, ed. G.J. Piccope, Chetham Society, 33, 1857
Latimer	Hugh Latimer, *Works*, ed. G.E. Corrie, 2 vols, Parker Society, 1844–5
Leland	*The Itinerary of John Leland in or about the years 1535–1543*, ed. L. Toulmin Smith, 5 vols, 1964

Letters to Cromwell	*Letters to Cromwell and others on the Suppression of the Monasteries*, ed. G.H. Cook, 1965
'Life of Carew'	J. Hooker, 'Life of Sir Peter Carew', in *Calendar of the Carew Manuscripts preserved in the Archiepiscopal Library at Lambeth, 1515–1574*, ed. J.S. Brewer and W. Bullen, 1867
'Lives of Saints'	CUL, Additional MS 3041, N. Roscarrock, 'Lives of the Saints'
London Wills	*London Consistory Court Wills, 1492–1547*, ed. I. Darlington, London Record Society, 3, 1967
LP	*Letters and Papers, Foreign and Domestic, of the Reign of Henry VIII*, ed. J.S. Brewer, J. Gairdner and R.H. Brodie, 23 vols in 38, 1862–1932
Machyn, *Diary*	*The Diary of Henry Machyn … 1550–1563*, ed. J. Nichols, Camden Society, 42, 1848
Melford Church	*The Spoil of Melford Church: The Reformation in a Suffolk Parish*, ed. D. Dymond and C. Paine, Ipswich, 1989
Moger	DRO, Moger Abstracts of Wills, 47 vols
Murray	DCRSL, Oswyn Murray Abstracts of Wills, 39 vols
Narratives of the Reformation	*Narratives of the Days of the Reformation*, ed. J. Nichols, Camden Society, 77, 1859
Nichols, 'Answer'	BL, Royal MS 18 B XI, [P. Nichols], 'An Answer to the Articles'
OL	*Original Letters relative to the English Reformation*, ed. H. Robinson, 2 vols, Parker Society, 1846–7
Original Letters	*A Collection of Original Letters from the Bishops to the Privy Council, 1564*, ed. M. Bateson, Camden Society, NS 53, 1895
Parkyn, 'Narrative'	'Robert Parkyn's Narrative', in A.G. Dickens, *Reformation Studies*, 1982, pp.293–312
Plymouth Records	*Calendar of Plymouth Municipal Records*, ed. R.N. Worth, Plymouth, 1893
Prayerbook of 1549	*Troubles connected with the Prayerbook of 1549*, ed. N. Pocock, Camden Society, NS 37, 1884
PPC	*Proceedings and Ordinances of the Privy Council of England, 1368–1542*, ed. H. Nicolas, 7 vols, 1834–7

PROB 11	PRO, Prerogative Court of Canterbury, Registered Copy Wills
Proctor, 'Wyatt's Rebellion'	J.Proctor, 'The History of Wyatt's Rebellion', in *An English Garner*, ed. E. Arber, 8, 1877–96
Puritanism in Tudor England	*Puritanism in Tudor England*, ed. H.C. Porter, 1970
Ramsey, 'Epistle'	BL, Landsowne MS 377, W. Ramsey, 'Epistle to the Moltonians'
Readings in Church History	*Readings in Church History*, ed. C.J. Barry, Westminster, Maryland, 1985
Reformation in England	*The Reformation in England*, ed. A.G. Dickens and D. Carr, 1967
REQ 2	PRO, Court of Requests, Proceedings
Rising in the North	*The Rising in the North: the 1569 Rebellion*, ed. C. Sharp, Durham, 1975
Royal Visitation	*The Royal Visitation of 1559*, ed. C.J. Kitching, Surtees Society, 187, 1975
SP 1, 10, 11, 12, 15	PRO, State Papers, Henry VIII, General Series; State Papers Domestic, Edward VI, Philip and Mary, Elizabeth I, Addenda Edward VI–James I
STAC 1, 2, 3, 4	PRO, Star Chamber, Proceedings, Henry VII, Henry VIII, Edward VI, Philip and Mary
Stowe 141, 142	BL, Stowe MSS 141, 142, State Letters
Strype, *Annals*	J. Strype, *Annals of the Reformation*, Oxford, 1824
Strype, *Memorials*	J. Strype, *Ecclesiastical Memorials*, Oxford, 1822
Survey of Cornwall	R. Carew, *Survey of Cornwall*, 1811
SWA Stratton	BL, Additional MS 32244, Stratton Stockwardens' Accounts
'Synopsis Chorographical'	DRO, H783, J. Hooker, 'Synopsis Chorographical'
Tavistock Records	*Calendar of Tavistock Parish Records*, ed. R.N. Worth, Tavistock, 1887
Testamenta Eboracensia	*Testamenta Eboracensia*, 6, ed. J.W. Clay, Surtees Society, 106, 1902
Thomas More	*The Essential Thomas More*, ed. J.J. Greene and J.P. Dolan, New York, 1967
Titus B 1	BL, Cotton MS Titus B 1, Instructions to the Council in the West Parts
TRP	*Tudor Royal Proclamations*, ed. P.L. Hughes and J.F. Larkin, 2 vols, New Haven, Conn., 1964–9
Tudor Parish Documents	*Tudor Parish Documents of the Diocese of York*, ed. J. Purvis, Cambridge, 1948

Tudor Treatises — *Tudor Treatises*, ed. A.G. Dickens, Yorkshire Archeological Society, 125, 1959

Wills and Inventories — *Wills and Inventories*, ed. J. Raine, Surtees Society, 2, 1835

Worcestre — *William Worcestre, Itineraries*, ed. J.H. Harvey, Oxford, 1969

Wriothesley, *Chronicle* — C. Wriothesley, *A Chronicle of England*, ed. W.D. Hamilton, Camden Society, NS 11, 20, 1875–7

York Records — *York Civic Records*, ed. A. Raine, 8 vols, Yorkshire Archaeological Society, 1939–53

Zurich Letters — *The Zurich Letters, 1558–1579*, ed. H. Robinson, 2 vols, Cambridge, 1842–5

Secondary Sources

Adair 1978 — J. Adair, *The Pilgrims' Way: Shrines and Saints in Britain and Ireland*

Alexander 1987 — G. Alexander, 'Bonner and the Marian Persecutions', in C. Haigh, ed., *The English Reformation Revised*, Cambridge

Anderson 1955 — M.D. Anderson, *The Imagery of British Churches*

Aston 1984 — M. Aston, *Lollards and Reformers: Images and Literacy in Late Medieval Religion*

Aston 1989 — –, 'Iconoclasm at Rickmansworth, 1522', *Journal of Ecclesiastical History*, 40

Aveling 1970 — J.H.C. Aveling, *Catholic Recusancy in the City of York, 1558–1791*

Aveling 1976 — –, *The Handle and the Axe: the Catholic Recusants in England from Reformation to Emancipation*

Baskerville 1979 — E.J. Baskerville, *A Chronological Bibliography of Propaganda and Polemic published in English between 1553 and 1558*, American Philosophical Society

Bennett 1970 — H.S. Bennett, *English Books and Readers, 1475–1557*, 2nd edn, Cambridge

Bernard 1992 — G.W. Bernard, 'The Dating of Church Towers: Huntingdonshire Re-examined', *Archaeological Journal*, 149

Birt 1907 — H.N. Birt, *The Elizabethan Religious Settlement*

Boggis 1922 R.J.E. Boggis, *History of the Diocese of Exeter*, Exeter

Bond 1908 F. Bond, *Fonts and Font Covers*

Bond 1910 –, *Wood Carvings in English Churches*, 2 vols, Oxford

Bond and Camm 1909 – and B. Camm, *Roodscreens and Roodlofts*, 2 vols

Bossy 1975 J.A. Bossy, *The English Catholic Community, 1570–1850*

Bowker 1981 M. Bowker, *The Henrician Reformation: The Diocese of Lincoln under John Longland, 1521–1547*, Cambridge

Bowker 1987 –, 'The Henrician Reformation and the Parish Clergy', in C. Haigh, ed., *The English Reformation Revised*, Cambridge

Brigden 1982 S. Brigden, 'Youth and the English Reformation', *Past and Present*, 95

Brigden 1989 –, *London and the Reformation*, Oxford

Bruton 1987 J. Bruton, 'The Reformation in Bristol and Somerset: The Evidence of Wills', University College of Ripon and York St John [UCRYSJ], Special Study

Bush 1996 M. Bush, *The Pilgrimage of Grace: A Study of the Rebel Armies of October 1536*, Manchester

Caiger-Smith 1963 A. Caiger-Smith, *English Medieval Mural Paintings*, Oxford

Cave 1948 C. Cave, *Roof Bosses in Medieval Churches*, Cambridge

Chanter 1914 J.F. Chanter, 'St Urith of Chittlehampton', *Transactions of the Devonshire Association*, 46

Clark 1977 P. Clark, *English Provincial Society from the Reformation to the Revolution: Religion, Politics and Society in Kent, 1500–1640*, Hassocks

Cliffe 1969 J.T. Cliffe, *The Yorkshire Gentry from the Reformation to the Civil War*

Collinson 1967 P. Collinson, *The Elizabethan Puritan Movement*

Collinson 1982 –, *The Religion of Protestants: the Church in English Society, 1559–1625*, Oxford

Collinson 1988 –, *The Birthpangs of Protestant England: Religious and Cultural Change in the Sixteenth and Seventeenth Centuries*

Connor 1970 A.B. Connor, *Monumental Brasses in Somerset*, Bath

Cook 1954 G. Cook, *The English Medieval Parish Church*

Cornwall 1977	J. Cornwall, *Revolt of the Peasantry, 1549*
Cox 1913	J.C. Cox, *Churchwardens' Accounts*
Cox 1915	–, *Pulpits, Lecterns and Organs in English Churches*, Oxford
Cox 1916	–, *Bench-ends in English Churches*, Oxford
Cox and Ford 1943–4	– and C.B. Ford, *The Parish Churches of England*
Cox and Harvey 1973	–, and A. Harvey, *English Church Furniture*, Wakefield
Crabbe 1854	W.R. Crabbe, *Some Account of the Monumental Brasses of Devon*, Exeter
Craig 1955	H. Craig, *English Religious Drama of the Middle Ages*, Oxford
Cressy 1980	D. Cressy, *Literacy and the Social Order: Reading and Writing in Tudor and Stuart England*, Cambridge
Cross 1969	C. Cross, *The Royal Supremacy in the Elizabethan Church*
Cross 1976	–, *Church and People, 1450–1660*, Hassocks
Cross 1979	–, 'Parochial Structure and the Dissemination of Protestantism in Sixteenth Century England', in D. Baker, ed., *Studies in Church History*, 16, Oxford
Cross 1982	–, 'The Development of Protestantism in Leeds and Hull, 1520–1640', *Northern History*, 18
Davies 1968	C.S.L. Davies, 'The Pilgrimage of Grace Reconsidered', *Past and Present*, 41
Davis 1969	C. T. Davis, *The Monumental Brasses of Gloucestershire*, Bath
Davis 1983	J.F. Davis, *Heresy and Reformation in the South-East of England, 1520–1559*
Dickens 1941	A.G. Dickens, 'The First Stages of Romanist Recusancy in Yorkshire', *Yorkshire Archaeological Journal*, 35
Dickens 1957	–, *The Marian Reaction in the Diocese of York*, York
Dickens 1967	–, 'Secular and Religious Motivation in the Pilgrimage of Grace', in G.J. Cuming, ed., *Studies in Church History*, 4, Leiden
Dickens 1982A	–, *Lollards and Protestants in the Diocese of York, 1509–1558*, 2nd edn
Dickens 1982B	–, *Reformation Studies*
Dickens 1989	–, *The English Reformation*, 2nd edn

Dodds and Dodds 1915 — M.H. Dodds and R. Dodds, *The Pilgrimage of Grace and the Exeter Conspiracy*, 2 vols, Cambridge

Duffy 1992 — E. Duffy, *The Stripping of the Altars: Traditional Religion in England, c.1400-c.1580,* New Haven and London

Dunkin 1882 — E.H.W. Dunkin, *The Monumental Brasses of Cornwall*

Ellacombe 1872 — H.T. Ellacombe, *The Church Bells of Devon*, Exeter

Elton 1958 — G.R. Elton, *Star Chamber Stories*, 1958

Elton 1972 — –, *Policy and Police: The Enforcement of the Reformation in the Age of Thomas Cromwell*, Cambridge

Farmer 1978 — D.H. Farmer, *The Oxford Dictionary of Saints*, Oxford

Field 1973 — C.W. Field, 'The Province of Canterbury and the Elizabethan Settlement of Religion', unpublished typescript, York Minister Library

Finberg 1951 — H.P.R. Finberg, *Tavistock Abbey*, Cambridge

Fines 1981 — J. Fines, *A Biographical Register of Early English Protestants, c.1525–1558*, I, Sutton Courtenay

Finucane 1977 — R.C. Finucane, *Miracles and Pilgrims: Popular Beliefs in Medieval England*

Fletcher 1973 — A.J. Fletcher, *Tudor Rebellions*, 2nd edn

Fowler 1961 — D. Fowler, 'The Date of the Cornish Ordinalia', *Medieval Studies*, 23

Frere 1896 — W.H. Frere, *The Marian Reaction in its Relation to the English Clergy*

Frere 1904 — –, *The English Church in the Reigns of Elizabeth and James I*

Garrett 1966 — C.H. Garrett, *The Marian Exiles*, 2nd edn, Cambridge

Gilyard-Beer 1976 — R. Gilyard-Beer, *Abbeys: An Illustrated Guide to the Abbeys of England and Wales*

Graves 1985 — M. Graves, *The Tudor Parliaments: Crown, Lords and Commons, 1485–1603*

Guy 1990 — J. Guy, *Tudor England*, Oxford

Haigh 1975 — C. Haigh, *Reformation and Resistance in Tudor Lancashire*, Cambridge

Haigh 1987 — –, ed., *The English Reformation Revised*, Cambridge

Haigh 1993 — –, *English Reformations: Religion, Politics and Society under the Tudors*, Oxford

Harper 1987 — R. Harper, 'The Reformation in the Midlands, 1530–60: the Evidence of Wills', UCRYSJ Special Study

Heath 1969 — P. Heath, *The English Parish Clergy on the Eve of the Reformation*

Henderson 1923–4 — C. Henderson, *Ecclesiastical History of the 109 Western Parishes of Cornwall*, Truro

Henderson 1925 — –, *Cornish Church Guide*, Truro

Henderson 1935 — –, *Essays in Cornish History*, Oxford

Hill 1969 — C. Hill, *Society and Puritanism in Pre-Revolutionary England*

Hoskins 1954 — W.G. Hoskins, *Devon*

Houlbrooke 1979 — R. Houlbrooke, *Church Courts and the People during the English Reformation, 1520–1570*, Oxford

Hudson 1988 — A. Hudson, *The Premature Reformation: Wycliffite Texts and Lollard History*, Oxford

Hughes 1950–4 — P. Hughes, *The Reformation in England*, 3 vols

Hutton 1987 — R. Hutton, 'The Local Impact of the Tudor Reformations', in C. Haigh, ed., *The English Reformation Revised*, Cambridge

Hutton 1994 — –, *The Rise and Fall of Merry England: The Ritual Year, 1400–1700*, Oxford

James 1901–2 — M.R. James, 'St Urith of Chittlehampton', *Cambridge Antiquarian Society Proceedings*, 10

James 1970 — M.E. James, 'Obedience and Dissent in Henrician England', *Past and Present*, 48

James 1973 — –, 'The Concept of Order and the Northern Rising, 1569', *Past and Present*, 60

Jones 1982 — N.L. Jones, *Faith by Statute: Parliament and the Settlement of Religion, 1559*

Jordan 1959 — W.K. Jordan, *Philanthropy in England, 1480–1660*

Jordan 1960A — –, *The Charities of London, 1480–1660*

Jordan 1960B — –, *The Forming of the Charitable Institutions of the West of England*, American Philosophical Society, NS 50

Jordan 1961A — –, *The Charities of Rural England, 1480–1660*

Jordan 1961B — –, *Social Institutions in Kent, 1480–1660*, Archaeologia Cantiana, 75

Jordan 1962 — –, *The Social Institutions of Lancashire*, Chetham Society

Kitching 1977 C. Kitching, 'The Disposal of Monastic and Chantry Lands', in F. Heal and R. O'Day, eds, *Church and Society in England: Henry VIII to James I*

Kite 1969 E. Kite, *The Monumental Brasses of Wiltshire*, Bath

Knowles 1948–59 D. Knowles, *The Religious Orders in England*, 3 vols, Cambridge

Knowles and Hadcock 1971 – and R.N. Hadcock, *Medieval Religious Houses: England and Wales*

Kreider 1979 A. Kreider, *English Chantries: The Road to Dissolution*, Cambridge, Mass.

Kümin 1996 B. Kümin, *The Shaping of a Community: The Rise and Reformation of the English Parish, c.1400–1560*, Aldershot

Lander 1987 S. Lander, 'Church Courts and the Reformation in the Diocese of Chichester, 1500–58', in C. Haigh, ed., *The English Reformation Revised*, Cambridge

Lehmberg 1970 S.E. Lehmberg, *The Reformation Parliament, 1529–36*, Cambridge

Loach 1975 J. Loach, 'Pamphlets and Politics, 1553–8', *Bulletin of the Institute of Historical Research*, 48

Loach 1986 –, *Parliament and the Crown in the Reign of Mary Tudor*, Oxford

Loades 1965 D.M. Loades, *Two Tudor Conspiracies*, Cambridge

Loades 1970 –, *The Oxford Martyrs*

Loades 1991 –, *The Reign of Mary Tudor: Politics, Government and Religion in England, 1553–58*, 2nd edn

MacCaffrey 1958 W. MacCaffrey, *Exeter, 1540–1640*, Cambridge, Mass.

MacCulloch 1986 D. MacCulloch, *Suffolk and the Tudors: Politics and Religion in an English County*, Oxford

MacCulloch 1990 –, *The Later Reformation in England, 1547–1603*

McGrath 1988 A.E. McGrath, *Reformation Thought: an Introduction*, Oxford

Manning 1969 R.B. Manning, *Religion and Society in Elizabethan Sussex*, Leicester

Mayhew 1983 G.J. Mayhew, 'The Progress of the Reformation in East Sussex, 1530–1559: The Evidence from Wills', *Southern History*, 5

Moran 1983 — J.H. Moran, 'Clerical Recruitment in the Diocese of York, 1340–1530: Data and Commentary', *Journal of Ecclesiastical History*, 34

Morris 1953 — C. Morris, *Political Thought in England: Tyndale to Hooker*, Oxford

Morris 1979 — R. Morris, *Cathedrals and Abbeys of England and Wales: The Building Church, 600–1540*

Morris 1989 — –, *Churches in the Landscape*

Mozley 1940 — J. Mozley, *John Foxe and his Book*

Nelson 1913 — P. Nelson, *Ancient Painted Glass in England, 1170–1500*

Norris 1977 — M. Norris, *Monumental Brasses*

O'Day 1986 — R. O'Day, *The Debate on the English Reformation*

Orme 1973 — N. Orme, *English Schools in the Middle Ages*

Oxley 1965 — J.E. Oxley, *The Reformation in Essex*, Manchester

Palliser 1979 — D.M. Palliser, *Tudor York*, Oxford

Palliser 1987 — –, 'Popular Reactions to the Reformation during the Years of Uncertainty, 1530–70', in C. Haigh, ed., *The English Reformation Revised*

Peter and Peter 1885 — R. and O. Peter, *The Histories of Launceston and Dunheved*, Plymouth

Pettegree 1986 — A. Pettegree, *Foreign Protestant Communities in Sixteenth Century London*, Oxford

Pettegree 1996 — *Marian Protestantism: Six Studies*, Aldershot

Pevsner 1952A — N. Pevsner, *The Buildings of England: North Devon*, Harmondsworth

Pevsner 1952B — –, *The Buildings of England: South Devon*, Harmondsworth

Pevsner and Hubbard 1971 — – and E. Hubbard, *The Buildings of England: Cheshire*, Harmondsworth

Pevsner and Radcliffe 1970 — – and E. Radcliffe, *The Buildings of England: Cornwall*, Harmondsworth

Pevsner and Radcliffe 1974 — – and E. Radcliffe, *The Buildings of England: Suffolk*, Harmondsworth

Phelps Brown and Hopkins 1956 — E.H. Phelps Brown and S.V. Hopkins, 'Seven Centuries of the Prices of Consumables', *Economica*, NS 23

Phillips 1973 — J. Phillips, *The Reformation of Images*, Berkeley, Calif.

Pill 1963 D.H. Pill, 'The Diocese of Exeter under Bishop Veysey', Exeter University MA dissertation

Pill 1968 –, 'Exeter Diocesan Courts in the Early Sixteenth Century', *Transactions of the Devonshire Association*, 100

Platt 1981 C. Platt, *The Parish Churches of Medieval England*

Pogson 1987 R.H. Pogson, 'Revival and Reform in Mary Tudor's Church: a Question of Money', in C. Haigh, ed., *The English Reformation Revised*

Porter 1958 H. Porter, *Reformation and Reaction in Tudor Cambridge*, Cambridge

Powell 1969 K.G. Powell, 'The Beginnings of Protestantism in Gloucestershire', *Transactions of the Bristol and Gloucestershire Archaeological Society*, 90

Powell 1972 –, *The Marian Martyrs and the Reformation in Bristol*, Bristol

Price 1938 F.D. Price, 'Gloucester Diocese under Bishop Hooper, 1551–3', *Transactions of the Bristol and Gloucestershire Archaeological Society*, 60

Prince 1701 J. Prince, *Worthies of Devon*, Exeter

Radford 1949 U.M. Radford, 'The Wax Images Found in Exeter Cathedral', *The Antiquaries' Journal*, 29

Raine 1828 J. Raine, *St Cuthbert*

RBM 1928–9 R.B.M., 'Devon Clergy in 1561', *Devon and Cornwall Notes and Queries*, 15

Reid 1906 R. Reid, 'The Rebellion of the Earls, 1569', *Transactions of the Royal Historical Society*, 20

Rex 1990 R. Rex, 'Monumental Brasses and the Reformation', *Transactions of the Monumental Brass Society*, 14

Risdon 1811 T. Risdon, *The Chorographical Description or Survey of the County of Devon*

Roberts 1962–4 J. Roberts, 'A Group of Elizabethan Puritans', *Devon and Cornwall Notes and Queries*, 29

Rogers 1877 W. Rogers, *The Ancient Sepulchral Effigies ... of Devon*, Exeter

Rose-Troup 1913 F. Rose-Troup, *The Western Rebellion of 1549*

Rowse 1941 A.L. Rowse, *Tudor Cornwall*

Rushforth 1927A — G.M. Rushforth, 'The Kirkham Monument in Paignton Church', *Exeter Diocesan Architectural and Archaeological Society Transactions*, 15

Rushforth 1927B — –, 'The Windows of the Church of St Neot, Cornwall', *Exeter Diocesan Architectural and Archaeological Society Transactions*, 15

Russell 1859 — F.W. Russell, *Kett's Rebellion in Norfolk*

Scarisbrick 1984 — J.J. Scarisbrick, *The Reformation and the English People*, Oxford

Shiels 1979 — W.J. Shiels, *The Puritans in the Diocese of Peterborough, 1558–1610*, Northamptonshire Record Society, 30

Slader 1968 — J. Slader, *The Churches of Devon*, Newton Abbot

Smith 1953 — L.B. Smith, *Tudor Prelates and Politics, 1536–1558*, Princeton, N.J.

Stephenson 1970 — M. Stephenson, *A List of Monumental Brasses in Surrey*, Bath

Storey 1989 — R.L. Storey, 'Ordinations of Secular Priests in Early Tudor London', *Nottingham Medieval Studies*, 33

Swanson 1989 — R.N. Swanson, *Church and Society in Late Medieval England*, Oxford

Tanner 1984 — N.P. Tanner, *The Church in Late Medieval Norwich, 1370–1532*, Toronto

Thomas 1973 — K. Thomas, *Religion and the Decline of Magic*, Harmondsworth

Thompson 1934–5 — C.H. Thompson, 'Chantry Priests at Plymouth', *Devon and Cornwall Notes and Queries*, 18

Thomson 1965A — J.A.F. Thomson, *The Later Lollards, 1414–1520*, Oxford

Thomson 1965B — 'Piety and Charity in Late Medieval London', *Journal of Ecclesiastical History*, 16

Thorp 1978 — M.R. Thorp, 'Religion and the Wyatt Rebellion of 1554', *Church History*, 47

Trimble 1964 — W.R. Trimble, *The Catholic Laity in Elizabethan England, 1558–1603*, Cambridge, Mass.

Turnpenney 1992 — G. Turnpenney, 'Wills as a Source for the Reformation Historian', UCRYSJ Special Study

Venables 1893 — E. Venables, 'The Shrine and Head of St Hugh of Lincoln', *Archaeological Journal*, 50

Wall 1905 J.C. Wall, *Shrines of British Saints*

Watt 1991 T. Watt, *Cheap Print and Popular Piety, 1550–1640*, Cambridge

Westcote 1845 T. Westcote, *A View of Devonshire in 1630*, Exeter

White 1993 P. White, *Theatre and Reformation: Protestantism, Patronage and Playing in Tudor England*, Cambridge

Whiting 1982 R. Whiting, 'Abominable Idols: Images and Image Breaking under Henry VIII', *Journal of Ecclesiastical History*, 33

Whiting 1983 –, 'For the Health of my Soul: Prayers for the Dead in the Tudor South-West', *Southern History*, 5

Whiting 1989 –, *The Blind Devotion of the People: Popular Religion and the English Reformation*, Cambridge

Whiting 1995 –, 'Local Responses to the Henrician Reformation', in D. MacCulloch, ed., *The Reign of Henry VIII: Politics, Policy and Piety*, Basingstoke

Wilson 1977 C. Wilson, *The Shrines of St William of York*, York

Woodman 1981 F. Woodman, *The Architectural History of Canterbury Cathedral*

Woodward 1966 G.W.O. Woodward, *The Dissolution of the Monasteries*

Youings 1971 J.A. Youings, *The Dissolution of the Monasteries*

Youings 1979 –, 'The South-Western Rebellion of 1549', *Southern History*, 1

Zell 1977 M. Zell, 'The Use of Religious Preambles as a Measure of Religious Belief in the Sixteenth Century', *Bulletin of the Institute of Historical Research*, 50

Index

Abbreviations
Bd (Bedfordshire); Br (Berkshire); Bu (Buckinghamshire); Ca (Cambridgeshire); Ch (Cheshire); Co (Cornwall); Cu (Cumberland); Db (Derbyshire); Do (Dorset); Du (Durham); Dv (Devon); Es (Essex); Gl (Gloucestershire); Ha (Hampshire); Hf (Herefordshire); Ht (Hertfordshire); Hu (Huntingdonshire); Ke (Kent); La (Lancashire); Le (Leicestershire); Li (Lincolnshire); Mi (Middlesex); Nb (Northumberland); Nf (Norfolk); Np (Northamptonshire); Nt (Nottinghamshire); Ox (Oxfordshire); Ru (Rutland); Sf (Suffolk); Sh (Shropshire); So (Somerset); Sr (Surrey); Ss (Sussex); St (Staffordshire); Wa (Warwickshire); We (Westmorland); Wi (Wiltshire); Wo (Worcestershire); Yo (Yorkshire).